The Self as Mind

The Self as Mind

Vision and Identity in
Wordsworth, Coleridge,
and Keats

Charles J. Rzepka

Harvard University Press
Cambridge, Massachusetts
and London, England   1986

Publication of this book has been aided by a grant from the
Andrew W. Mellon Foundation.

This book is printed on acid-free paper, and its binding materials
have been chosen for strength and durability.

Library of Congress Cataloging in Publication Data

Rzepka, Charles J.
  The self as mind.

  Bibliography: p.
  Includes index.
  1. English poetry—19th century—History and
criticism.   2. Self in literature.   3. Identity
(Psychology) in literature.   4. Romanticism—England.
5. Wordsworth, William, 1770–1850—Criticism and
interpretation.   6. Coleridge, Samuel Taylor, 1772–1824—
Criticism and interpretation.   7. Keats, John, 1795–1821
—Criticism and interpretation.   I. Title.
PR585.S44R97   1986   821'.7'09   85-8632
ISBN 0-674-80085-0   (alk. paper)

For Adam and Toby,
and for Jane—always

Acknowledgments

Many people helped with the preparation of this book, and some were indispensable in the constructive criticism and encouragement they offered. My thanks go, first of all, to Andrew Griffin, of the University of California at Berkeley, for the pains he took in helping me to articulate the ideas that form the core of this work, and to Hubert Dreyfus, of the Philosophy Department at UCB, for helping me to give those articulations philosophical consistency. Thanks, also, are due to the patient readers who agreed to examine and offer advice on all or part of the work-in-progress since then: Patricia Craddock, Frances Ferguson, Peter Manning, and David Wagenknecht. I thank Paul Magnuson especially for his close reading and sound advice on Coleridge.

Two colleagues in particular have provided me with a great deal of encouragement, as well as painstaking criticism. To Norman Fruman, who took the time not only to read scrupulously and to comment with care on my Coleridge chapter, but to correspond at length on the issues he had initially raised and to offer moral support at a crucial moment in the development of this manuscript, I offer special thanks. To Helen Vendler, my "companion never lost through many a league," for her constant encouragement and support, her wisdom and sensitivity, her exemplary devotion to the word, and not least of all, her sound advice on Keats, I am indebted much more than a simple acknowledgment can convey.

I also wish to thank the English Department and the College of Letters and Arts of Boston University for granting me the leave necessary for the completion of this work.

Much of the section on *Otho the Great* previously appeared as "*Theatrum Mundi* and Keats's *Otho the Great:* The Self in 'Saciety,' " in *Romanticism Past and Present,* 8 (1984):34–50; I thank the journal for permission to make use of the material. I am also grateful to the following publishers for granting permission to quote material from their editions of the major poets treated in this book: Oxford University Press, for *The Complete Poems of Thomas Gray, English, Latin and Greek,* ed. H. W. Starr and J. R. Hendrickson (1966); *The Poetical Works of William Wordsworth,* ed. Ernest de Selincourt and Helen Darbishire (1940); and *Coleridge: Poetical Works,* ed. Ernest Hartley Coleridge (1912; rpt. 1967); Harvard University Press, for *The Poems of John Keats,* ed. Jack Stillinger (1978); and W. W. Norton and Company, for *The Prelude: 1799, 1805, 1850,* ed. Jonathan Wordsworth, M. H. Abrams, and Stephen Gill (1979).

Contents

The waking have one common world, but sleepers turn aside each into a world of his own.

—Heraclitus

1 The Idea of the Self as Mind

I refute it *thus!*
—Samuel Johnson

I HAVE always admired Dr. Johnson for his impulsive attempt to refute idealism: he kicked a rock. This showed him to be an indifferent philosopher, but an excellent phenomenologist. Obviously, kicking the rock "proved" nothing. The pain in Dr. Johnson's toe remained an idea, as securely enclosed by his private sphere of perception as the visual image of the rock in question. But Johnson clearly understood how we distinguish what seems real from what seems a dream, or a mere image of reality: the world's reality begins where the "I" leaves off, at the surface of the body. When Johnson kicked the rock, he marked something he could not establish as easily by sight alone—the corporeal boundary between "I" and "it," the "inside" and the "outside" of the self: mind and world.

From the suddenness of his outburst, I assume Dr. Johnson would have liked to have kicked Boswell for bringing up the subject of idealism, but settled for a rock instead, leaving Boswell free to witness and record the event. I wonder whether, in fact, Johnson didn't kick the rock primarily to demonstrate to his young admirer the real, embodied existence of a person called "Johnson." Would he have kicked the rock without a Boswell looking on? I think not. The gesture seems histrionic, self-conscious. Johnson is playing himself; he is becoming what Boswell expects him to be.

Why *did* Dr. Johnson kick the rock? It is unlikely that he ever really doubted the rock's existence, or his own. And if Boswell made him self-conscious, that could only have heightened his awareness of his embodied existence, and of the boundary between "I" and "it." But though he may have been certain *that* he was, Johnson may not have been completely certain of *who* he was. Perhaps playing himself in front of Boswell made him feel more secure in his own identity.

Embodiment, the sense of possessing a body that others can perceive and recognize, is a prerequisite of self-consciousness and a sense of the real. The reason we commonly mistake our dreams for reality, but rarely mistake reality for a dream, is that it is easier to imagine one's embodiment in a world one dreams than to doubt one's embodiment in a world one shares with others. And yet, such doubts were voiced repeatedly in the philosophy and poetry of the seventeenth and eighteenth centuries, and well into the next, with both exhilarating and disturbing effects on the poet's perceptions of world, self, and others. Since those effects first appear as a constellated whole sometime during the Age of Sensibility, it is there that I will begin.

The Body Vanishes: Solipsism and Vision in Gray's "Elegy"

The age of Sterne and Cowper had, as Northrop Frye has pointed out, its own internal coherence, and to search for harbingers of Romanticism in Thomas Gray's "Elegy Written in a Country Church Yard" may seem, for this reason, rather out of date.[1] Indeed, since the appearance, some fifty years ago, of Amy Louise Reed's *The Background of Gray's "Elegy"*, critics generally have held to the view that the poem represents less the inauguration of a new sensibility in the history of English letters than the culmination of a genre. It was a typical product of its time.[2]

But precisely because of its summary qualities, the "Elegy" is also, in its modest way, a benchmark in the history of English poetry. The principal features of the poem that I will discuss—bodily disidentification, the experience of a waking-dream state, a feeling of oneness with a transcendent mind or consciousness, trust in an imaginative, introspective empathy with other minds—have a certain urgency and structural coherence that is new. They may have appeared as fragmentary symptoms in verse immediately preceding Gray's, but in his poem they crystalize into a syndrome that recurs repeatedly in English Romantic poetry. Certainly, it was no accident that the peak of the poem's popularity came not in Gray's lifetime but between 1790 and 1810, when it was reprinted some sixty-seven times.[3]

In Gray's "Elegy" the self becomes identified largely with mind and dissociated from the body. This intense identification with consciousness is reinforced by encroaching night, and its immediate effects appear in the poem's opening lines. Darkness, whatever else it may do to suggest the somber mood typical of eighteenth-century elegy, also suspends the poet's sense of embodiment, erasing the boundary between the mind and what it perceives:

The Curfew tolls the knell of parting day,
The lowing herd wind slowly o'er the lea,
The plowman homeward plods his weary way,
And leaves the world to darkness and to me.

Now fades the glimmering landscape on the sight.[4]

The phrasing of line 5 bears emphasis: not the light, but the very
"landscape" is extinguished. It is almost as though the herd, the lea,
the plowman no longer remained "out there," in the dark; rather, the
"glimmering" world itself "fades," like a dimming picture on a mental screen. "Glimmer" and "fade" become indices not simply of dusk
but of a world being reduced to its image in the mind, becoming
gradually insubstantial, and finally nonexistent. Gray's "Elegy"
opens with an experience quite close to solipsism, to making the
world one's dream.

Fredric Bogel has observed that doubts about the substantiality
of the self and its world, "an incapacity to experience one's world
and oneself as the robust presences we normally require them to be,"
became a central feature of late eighteenth-century poetry.[5] Moments like this also recur frequently, and with greater intensity, in
Romantic poetry, in high transports of imaginative revelation or visionary experience. The phenomenal world, perceived in darkness,
isolation, or at a distance, becomes dreamlike or, in fact, gives way to
a dream of the world. Keats's "Ode to a Nightingale"—a "waking
dream" that ends with the words "Do I wake or sleep?"—grows in
imaginative intensity as the darkness deepens around the poet.[6] For
the solitary speaker of Coleridge's "Frost at Midnight," watching the
low, fluttering flame on his grate while the inmates of his house sleep,
"sea, and hill, and wood, / With all the numberless goings-on of life"
become "Inaudible as dreams" (11–13).[7] Wordsworth, on numerous
occasions but especially when alone, feels overcome by similar experiences of the world's unreality, when all appears "like something in
myself, a dream, / A prospect in the mind" (*Prelude*, II, 351–352).[8]

In English poetry this prospect opens up for the first time in Gray's
"Elegy." The transformation of something outside the mind into
something inside is facilitated by the poet's having momentarily lost,
in the darkness surrounding him, the tenuous conviction of his embodied being that delimits outside and inside: as the world fades out,
the body vanishes. The phrase, "leaves the world to darkness and to
me," suggests both that the poet is akin to darkness—something

shapeless, obscure, indefinable, the very negation of embodiment— and that the world has in some way been appropriated *by* him, as a part of his own spiritual being.

The world flickers and fades, moreover, at precisely the moment that the plowman *leaves* it *to* the poet. His departure, likened to a bequest or the relinquishment of a claim, reinforces the feeling that the landscape is possessed solely by this mind and no other, that its existence outside this mind can no longer be independently confirmed. The departure also reinforces the reader's impression that the self has lost that sense of its finitude and outwardness, not only as a body extended in space, but as a body *others can perceive*, which would delimit, locate, and thus make relative rather than absolute its point of view. In phenomenological terms, the plowman represents "the Other," that conscious presence, real or conceived, through which we become self-conscious by considering ourselves as another would.[9] I shall return to the idea of the Other later in this chapter, but for now, I wish simply to point out that the plodding plowman is not merely a picturesque detail in the scene. His leaving—and *leaving to*—so nearly precedes the onset of the poet's experience of solipsism as to seem its proximate cause. As the plowman departs, the world of others disappears, and with it, the sense of being an object and participant in their world.

Quite as much as the incursion of darkness, it is this felt absence of the Other, and the withdrawal of his implicit claims on the embodied self, that enables the self to float free of embodiment: the physical boundaries of the person become vague, the power of the Other potentially to fix consciousness within those boundaries is weakened, and mere sight, which ordinarily establishes a reciprocally determinative relation between self and world, gives way to imaginative insight, a vision that oversteps the ordinary boundaries of the finite self. "The light of sense / Goes out," Wordsworth later wrote of such visitings of the Imagination, "but with a flash that has revealed / The invisible world" (*Prelude*, VI, 600–602). For Gray's amorphous poet, too, an "invisible world" opens up *within* the mind as the "light of sense," which is understood to radiate from a world beyond the self, "goes out." It is an imagined world of invisible lives, of hidden hopes and fears (45–76):

Perhaps in this neglected spot is laid
Some heart once pregnant with celestial fire,
Hands, that the rod of empire might have sway'd,
Or wak'd to extasy the living lyre . . .

Some village-Hampden, that with dauntless breast
The little Tyrant of his fields withstood;
Some mute inglorious Milton here may rest,
Some Cromwell guiltless of his country's blood.

Th' applause of list'ning senates to command,
The threats of pain and ruin to despise,
To scatter plenty o'er a smiling land,
And read their hist'ry in a nation's eyes,

Their lot forbad . . .
.   .   .   .   .

Far from the madding crowd's ignoble strife,
Their sober wishes never learn'd to stray;
Along the cool sequester'd vale of life
They kept the noiseless tenor of their way.

Freed of his sense of embodiment, the poet enjoys the speculative fiction of seeing into the souls of others, in the manner of a deity who is omniscient yet obscure, spiritually intimate yet physically indistinct. Solipsism becomes visionary, opening to the mind vistas inaccessible to ordinary sight. Losing awareness of the limitations placed on its identity from without, the narrator's mind, like the mind of Keats's self-annihilated "camelion Poet," can expand and fasten on the presumed characters of other souls.[10]

Disembodied lives, then, are the disembodied poet's concern: the abstract self, the self as mind. Gray's speaker is not greatly interested in facts about the dead. He is fascinated above all by what is unknown, inaccessible to the elegiac memory, which feeds only on the surface of life. He mourns not what has been lost to death but what was, "perhaps," lost to the everyday course of false living. In the "Elegy" this "perhaps" is soon lost sight of, and human potential, here speculative to begin with, eventually seems as real as, if not more real than, human accomplishments.

From this dreamlike state of self-diffusion and empathic projection, the poet comes to himself at line 93. But his identity as something distinct appears only when he imagines it as a self for others: for the "kindred Spirit" who inquires his fate and for the "hoary-headed Swain" who tries to answer these inquiries (93–108):

For thee, who mindful of th' unhonor'd Dead
Dost in these lines their artless tale relate;

If chance, by lonely contemplation led,
Some kindred Spirit shall inquire thy fate,

Haply some hoary-headed Swain may say,
"Oft have we seen him at the peep of dawn
. . . . .

"Hard by yon wood, now smiling as in scorn,
"Mutt'ring his wayward fancies he wou'd rove,
"Now drooping, woeful wan, like one forlorn,
"Or craz'd with care, or cross'd in hopeless love.

"One morn I miss'd him on the custom'd hill," continues the old
man (113–116),

"The next with dirges due in sad array
"Slow thro' the church-way path we saw him born[e].
"Approach and read (for thou can'st read) the lay,
"Grav'd on the stone beneath yon aged thorn."

Here, the Other, who in the person of the plowman "left the world to
darkness" and the poet in the first stanza, reenters in the person of
the hypothetical Swain. As he contemplates his own fate, the poet
apprehends himself as a daylight shape *another* has seen "at the peep
of dawn." The poet comes to; the world of others reappears; the body
comes to light.

Self-consciousness requires the presence, real or imagined, explicit
or implied, of another. The Swain appears almost immediately following the poet's sudden self-awareness, when, as Cleanth Brooks
first observed, he begins to address himself at line 93 in the second
person: "For thee . . ."[11] In this explicit self-address, the poet becomes
estranged from his true self, the very "thee" he addresses, transforming the monological, entirely interior being he has assumed up to this
point into something "other" to him, and trying to picture that former self the way another—the Swain—would, from without. At one
point the poet is even pictured as "mutt'ring . . . wayward fancies"
under his breath, a partial allusion to his own soliloquy up to this
line.[12]

But the self merely as an object of consciousness is, like any other
object, "dead, fixed, incapable in itself of any action, and necessarily
finite," as Coleridge, plagiarizing Schelling, was to observe in the
Biographia Literaria.[13] That the poet's self-for-another should finally

take the form of one who has died is, then, appropriate. The anxiety of being an object for another is intimately connected with anxiety about death, the ultimate loss of subjectivity. Death is the fate of the self as something in the world, an object for others to judge and interpret as they will and, finally, make theirs.

Much of the poignancy of the "Elegy," in fact, derives from the contrast between the Swain's recollections of the young man he observed from afar, and what we have just heard the poet tell us of the secret lives of the "rude Forefathers of the hamlet" (16). Both tales are elegies and thus might be taken as attempts to sum up a person's life. But the poet dwells on the impossibility of such a finite summing up and on the infinite, indeterminable potential of quiet, hidden human souls. The Swain, by contrast, is content to describe what has appeared in the world as a self, what he has *seen* of the poet, and with trying to draw conclusions from a distance. "Oft have we *seen* him . . . smiling *as* in scorn . . . Now drooping . . . *like* one forlorn, / Or craz'd . . . *or* cross'd." The Swain's conjectures demonstrate what the poet has been at pains to remark in his reflections on the rural dead: our insurmountable opacity to each other's gaze.

The poet remains a mystery, except in part to the reader, his true "kindred Spirit," who has, as it were, "overheard" the poet's most intimate self in its private meditations. Not ingenuously, Gray has the Swain remind the kindred Spirit that he or she *can* read, and thus has access to a side of the speaker beyond the reach of the illiterate. The kindred Spirit and the Swain, in fact, seem to represent contrasting kinds of audiences, one empathic and intimate, the other dyspathic and distant: the first is a projected, "kindred" version of the poet himself, whose disembodied voice, in the soliloquy comprising the first half of the poem, has made his true self accessible to the imagination of the eavesdropping reader without the apparent mediation of embodiment; the second kind of audience beholds only the self without, the estranged, public self.

But the poet is not, after all, content merely with being "overheard" in his isolated meditations, nor with assuming his reader's speculative empathy. If he were, the poem could have ended at line 92. Instead, he pictures the kindred Spirit stepping forward to "inquire" of the Swain the speaker's "fate" as a being in the world, a being *others* have seen. Now the kindred Spirit must try to piece together, from what he or she knows of the true self within, the meaning of the poet's otherwise baffling behavior. *Do* the poet's muttered "wayward fancies" concern only his reflections on the dead, and nothing more? Or might he indeed be "cross'd by hopeless love," or vexed by other anxieties? "Inquiring" is the task set the kindred Spirit—not merely to understand the disembodied self but to interpret the phenomenal self according to this preestablished understanding. We as readers are to bring to light the mystery of the true self in its otherwise incomprehensible acts of embodiment. We are to reunite inner and outer, and thus heal the poet's divided self.

In the end the kindred Spirit is asked to read the narrator's epitaph, a "lay" or verse composed, like the "Elegy" in which it appears, by the narrator himself. It eulogizes *"a youth to fortune and to fame unknown"* (118), large of bounty and sincere of soul, and ends (125–128),

> *No farther seek his merits to disclose,*
> *Or draw his frailties from their dread abode,*
> *(There they alike in trembling hope repose)*
> *The bosom of his Father and his God.*

On the simplest level "The Epitaph" asserts the poet's final inaccessibility—it defeats our efforts fully to "disclose" the self within, and at the same time seals in stone the "fate" of the self without: the embodied person is merely a corpse, the husk of a being that, as consciousness, "abides" elsewhere, in the "bosom" of the all-knowing Mind. Not surprisingly, this Mind is much like that with which the poet himself identified as he sought, in turn, to share imaginatively in the secret, unexpressed lives of anonymous villagers. Ultimately, it seems, the withdrawal from embodiment leads to an identification with the ineffable so complete that reuniting inner and outer becomes impossible.

But the ineffable is also amorphous, indistinct, impersonal, abstract—in the end, frighteningly so. Sounding through the poignant injunctions of the poem's final stanzas is an urgent counter-theme, a desperate plea for definitive self-recognition. For if "The Epitaph" tells us how ignorant we remain of the true self within, it also climaxes a fantasized interrogation into the fate of an embodied person whom others may perceive but do not comprehend. "Approach and *read*": the kindred Spirit is being asked, knowing what he knows from his reading, to *read into these lines* and into this entire poetic performance—just as he is to "read into" the Swain's matter-of-fact observations from afar—the true self that is there adverted to but that cannot be fully embodied for others, either in person or poem, in actions or in artifact.

Writing a poem, publishing it, gives the self up irrevocably to the eyes of the world. It has the finality of death, and the poem itself is always a kind of epitaph for the momentary being who wrote it. Gray worked on the "Elegy" for many years, reluctant to finish, reluctant to publish. He was a shy man, fearful of being misunderstood, and lacking confidence in his talent. The second half, particularly, was much revised. Indeed, as we near line 92, the "applause of list'ning senates" and the gratulatory history to be read in "a nation's eyes" give way in the speaker's imagination to "a madding crowd," and then to a single, uncomprehending stranger. From *his* unknown audience, a madding crowd of strangers that threatens to expropriate this poem as the embodied expression of the poet's true self, Gray asks for the kind of empathic, intimate understanding that will make of the man writing—as much as of the man "smiling," "mutt'ring," "drooping"—something consonant with the self within: the poet in his silent meditations, his love for the humble and obscure, his good intentions.

As the century nears its end, the fears expressed by Gray's poet— fear of being misunderstood and a consequent fear of self-loss in the presence of others—will give rise to two contradictory reactions among the English Romantics, reactions foreshadowed by the "Elegy" itself: on the one hand, a solipsistic self-diffusion and mental appropriation of the perceived world as part of the self within, and on the other, a search for right recognition that will give this indefinite, inner self outward form and definition. The poet's audience, as represented in various encounters and confrontations in the poetry, takes on exaggerated importance as a vehicle by which the poet can reunite inner and outer, being and doing, mind and body. Complementing the radical withdrawal of self which eventuates in what I will hereafter call visionary solipsism is the poet's anxious need for self-assurance, and his strategies for securing it.

The Persistence of the Embodied Self

It is only in recent years that scholars have begun to probe the historical significance of the empirical skepticism informing much of late eighteenth-century literature. Bogel astutely notes that this pervasive feeling of insubstantiality "approximates in historical terms the state of experiential disrepair to which the psychiatrist R. D. Laing has given the label 'ontological insecurity,'" a state in which "the line between self and other may be indistinct or shifting, and other persons, things, or natural processes may seem as unreliable or insubstantial as the self."[14] Though Bogel does not go on to draw conclusions for Romanticism, this "ontological insecurity" with respect to the reality of the self and of the world it perceives becomes more pronounced by the end of the century.

Informing eighteenth- and nineteenth-century doubts over self-embodiment was the fundamental belief that the self is divided into the living subject and the dead object of perception, the "true" and the "false." Gray's poet is anxious about the inadequacy of physical appearances to convey what was in former times called the soul because he identifies the true self exclusively with consciousness.[15] In this respect the "Elegy" demonstrates the profound influence of Cartesian dualism on modern thought, an influence, particularly as adapted and transformed by English empiricism, that is still with us. Rarely, since Descartes, have we questioned our deep-rooted conviction that self, soul, and consciousness are identical and only tenuously connected with (if not in fact belied by) the body.

The effects of Cartesian and empirical thought on eighteenth-century and Romantic literature have been amply documented.[16] We recognize now that Romantic poetic theory, particularly in the writings of Wordsworth and Coleridge, derives ultimately from Locke's theories of perception and from the empiricist model of the mind as a camera obscura. Into this "dark room," argued the empiricists, "ideas" of the outside world enter through the "windows" of the senses, there to be organized into more complex and abstract ideas. We know, too, that by the time Wordsworth published his "Preface" to the 1800 edition of *Lyrical Ballads,* the focus of "empirical" attention had shifted from the world as an object of knowledge, with its universally accepted constant laws and "primary qualities," to the thinking subject's point of view on the world, and the ways in which the mind (according to the theory Wordsworth borrowed, via Coleridge, from Locke's follower, David Hartley) "associates ideas in a state of excitement."[17]

By 1816, when Coleridge's *Biographia Literaria* appeared, English poetics was well on the way to a revolution that, some thirty years ago, F. G. Steiner identified as paralleling Kant's "Copernican revolution" in the philosophy of mind.[18] The hero of both revolutions was the Imagination, no longer a mimetic stepchild of memory but, in Coleridge's words, "The living Power and prime Agent of all human Perception."[19] The Imagination organized the chaos of Locke's atomistic "qualities" of perception into what Kant called a coherent "intuition," or idea. For the Romantics order is no longer assumed to inhere in a physical universe of objects (the advance of the natural sciences notwithstanding); rather, it inheres in the organized mental universe of percepts. Bishop Berkeley's dictum, *esse est percipi,* "to be is to be perceived," becomes the appropriate motto for Romantic epistemology.

But if "to be is to be perceived," what are we to make of the self as perceiver, the Cartesian *"ego cogito"?* Hume, in his *Enquiry concerning the Human Understanding,* dismissed the notion that the "self" as a mental, "immaterial substance" could be perceived at all, or conceived, as Descartes and Locke had maintained, as the object of its own thought. For, said Hume, we can have no real idea of an entity unless we derive that idea from some impression on the mind. Thus, unless the self was somehow embodied as a clear impression on the mind, it could not be said to give rise to any idea of itself. Consciousness, affirmed by however rigorous and ruthless a method of doubt, such as Descartes's, could never find its "self," for the mind is explicitly aware only of its perceptions: "For my part, when I enter most intimately into what I call *myself,* I always stumble on some particular perception or other, of heat or cold, light or shade, love or hatred, pain or pleasure. I never can catch *myself* at any time without a perception, and never can observe any thing but the perception."[20] Hume's cool skepticism anticipates Coleridge's nightmarish fears in the fragment "Self-Knowledge" (6–8):

> What is there in thee, Man, that can be known?—
>   Dark fluxion, all unfixable by thought,
>   A phantom dim of past and future wrought.

If *esse est percipi,* then the self which is imperceptible must not exist.[21] Coleridge's poem, like Hume's philosophy, points up the ephemeral nature of this "who" of consciousness, its tendency, when looked at closely, to fall apart into a contingent series of isolated sensations without an inner logic or necessary principle of coherence.

The attempt by Coleridge's great hero, Kant, to formulate that principle of internal coherence marked the beginning of a modern European metaphysics of personal identity. The self was to be identified as the power, not the object, of perception. This was a stunning metaphysical advance. However, positing the "ego" as the agent of mental syntheses meant that in both the *Prolegomena* and the *Critique of Pure Reason* Kant, like his philosophical forebears, continued to look for the self within, as a form of consciousness and not of bodily existence.[22] Kant, in these pioneering treatises, does not even approach the question of embodiment. Self-consciousness, he says, is consciousness identifying itself as the ground of all its contents over time, and is *logically* presupposed by, though not necessarily *experienced* in, consciousness of anything whatsoever. The self for Kant is something of which we must assume the existence. It is "apparent" only in its epistemological effects.

For the most part, philosophers and critics since Kant have allowed the self to languish in a metaphysical limbo, an entity to be inferred but not directly experienced. Those of us who labor to trace the effects of the Romantic imagination on the world it perceives still tend to take those effects for the locus of identity. In his classic study *The Poetry of Experience,* for instance, Robert Langbaum argued that the Romantic self appears as a consciousness enriched or qualified by perception, its contents and subjective history: "The process of experience is for the romanticist a process of self realization, of a constantly expanding discovery of the self through the discovery of its imprint on the external world . . . Since the romanticist finds in the object [of experience] the values he puts there, he finds also the objectification of at least one aspect of the values compatible with his own fullest existence . . . values he has known potentially all along in himself."[23] Of course, the Romantics themselves subscribed to this view and thus set the terms for later criticism. Only very recently have critics begun to pay attention to the cost of such voyages of self-discovery and to what is left out of the equation of self with perception: in the experiential "process of self-realization" they have found the germ of a suffocating self-enclosure, alienation, estrangement, and isolation.[24]

Like Kant, the Romantics advanced beyond the Cartesian and Lockean position—obviously, there is no self that can appear introspectively except the self that, as consciousness, has experienced a world that it has made somehow meaningful and coherent. The Romantic self, however, like the Kantian self and the Cartesian and Lockean self, was still exclusively identified with mind. As in Gray's poem and in much of the poetry of Wordsworth, Coleridge, and Keats, this identification creates problems with respect to one's history as an "object," as a public person, a historical and social being, and especially as a poet, "a man speaking to men," as Wordsworth defined him in the 1800 Preface to *Lyrical Ballads.*[25] For having a sense of one's identity depends on the ability not only to introspect in a Kantian fashion but also to accept completely the possibility of one's becoming conscious of oneself as embodied in the eyes of another. A real sense of personal identity depends, at the most primitive level, on the assumption of embodiment.

Ironically, while this fundamental truth was ignored by both empiricists and idealists from Descartes to Kant, it infected nearly all their attempts to explain the nature of the self as mind. A corporeal bias informs even the most metaphysical philosophies of personal identity. Descartes and Locke, for instance, both tend to "materialize" the soul when imagining it in relation to its body, as though it were impossible to conceive the self in any other way. Descartes, for all his caveats against our natural tendency to think of the "substance" of soul as "material," cannot avoid envisioning the immaterial self as somehow situated physically within the body. At one point in the *Meditationes*, "ego" even becomes a "pilot" in the corporeal "vessel."[26]

Locke, too, feels constrained in certain parts of his argument to find a home for the *mens*, to locate it and give it space, a "dark room," for example, from which to view the world:

> External and internal sensations are the only passages that I can find of knowledge to the understanding. These alone, as far as I can discover are the windows by which light is let into this dark room. For methinks the understanding is not much unlike a closet wholly shut from light, with only some little openings left to let in external visible resemblances, or ideas of things without: would the pictures coming into such a dark room but stay there, and lie so orderly as to be found upon occasion, it would very much resemble the understanding of a man in reference to all objects of sight and the ideas of them.[27]

Though Locke feels comfortable likening the mind to a "tabula rasa" upon which simple images or "ideas" of the outside world (or of the body itself) impinge, this conception only begs the question of where to place the viewer of these images. Elsewhere, Locke again searches for a "room" in which to house the mind: "And if these organs, or the nerves, which are the conduits to convey [ideas] from without to their audience in the brain, the mind's presence room (as I may so call it), are any of them so disordered, as not to perform their functions, they have no postern to be admitted by; no other way to bring themselves into view, and be perceived by the understanding."[28] But who or what is present in this "presence room"? Who is there to view these ideas, many of which are, in any case, auditory or olfactory or tactile to begin with? The self or ego as mind always verges, absurdly, on becoming another body inside the body. The "I" as a self disembodied is, practically speaking, inconceivable, as Hume demonstrated.

Locke, of course, makes it clear that he is reverting to illustration. He is not to be taken literally. All the same, he obviously feels the urge to reify this abstraction, the self. Why? One reason may be that at a time when, more and more, only the physical world with its mathematically calculable qualities was taken to be real, the self as mind could only assume a convincing degree of reality when conceived physically. Locke's dependence on the buried metaphor of the "little man in a big man" reveals the deeper, ineradicably materialistic biases of Lockean and Cartesian dualism. In short, the self as mind, though felt to be "true," was not felt to be "real." The mind was "in here"; reality was "out there." This is the crux of the problem for a poet like Gray: the true self cannot always be "realized," and what can be realized will not necessarily be recognized as corresponding to the true self. In an age that assumed that what is real *must* correspond to what is true, the felt discrepancy was disturbing.

To assume a real presence *in* and *for* the physical world, and thus with respect to other people, the self must, it seems, be conceived as taking up space and being located in space as an extended, material thing. But if such is the case, then once again, it requires only the slightest effort to assume that the self or "ego" as mind is indeed not "present" at all. Descartes turns his attention to "human beings passing on the street below": "When looking from a window and saying I see men who pass in the street, I really do not see them, but infer that what I see is men . . . And yet what do I see from the window but hats and coats which may cover automatic machines? Yet I judge these to be men . . . solely by the faculty of judgment which rests in my mind."[29]

It is easy to see how Descartes's heuristic scepticism could have inspired La Mettrie's *L'homme machine,* a work in which mind and volition are dismissed as a fiction, and persons are reduced to automatons.[30] With ego encased in the opaque carapace of a biological engine, other minds and selves can be known only by an inferential act of faith. Descartes makes the reality of others, like the reality of the world itself, a matter of judgment, not of immediate certainty, and all judgments about appearances, as he asserts, are subject to doubt.

We are on the verge of a fiction that intrigued the creators of the

Ancient Mariner and Frankenstein's "wretch," obsessed E. T. A. Hoffman, and shaped the philosophy of Carlyle's Teufelsdröckh: the reduction of others to unsouled clockworks, walking corpses, dancing dolls, or clotheshorses. Though confident in his faith that, when all is said, the Supreme Being (being supremely good) could no more deceive his creatures with respect to the reality of other minds than he could with respect to the reality of the world, Descartes presages a more modern and skeptical fascination with the possibility of such a deception, the suspicion that the true self is not real, and that the real self cannot be true.

As inhabitants of Eliot's "Unreal City," we too are accustomed to thinking of the true self much as Descartes and Kant did, as immaterial, indeterminable, hidden. We identify the self solely with mental events; it is the implied perceiver of all objects of our inner sense. We feel that "self" is vaguely interchangeable with "soul" and "mind," and that these entities stand opposed, conventionally, to the notion of "body," which by comparison seems to us a machinelike excrescence: a "false Body," Blake calls it, "an Incrustation over my Immortal Spirit."[31] "My body," I might argue, *"that* is not my true self."

Blake goes on to call this "false body" "a Selfhood" which "must be put off and annihilated alway."[32] By "Selfhood" Blake means what he calls elsewhere "the Spectre," "Satan," or "the limit of opacity." This is the person reduced to the phenomenal level, or in Sartre's words, the "object" and not "the owner of consciousness."[33] Blake understood that, protestations of the spirituality of the self notwithstanding, we, like Descartes and Locke, naturally tend to take as an individual "selfhood" an embodied being. For Blake the principle of human individuation—which keeps the "Sublime Body" of the Poetic Genius, Albion, broken into millions of helpless, frightened, self-acquisitive fragments—is inextricably linked to physical definition, to being a finite thing in a material universe. The Romantic enterprise, if Blake is any indication, is to free the true self, the unindividuated "Immortal Spirit" or "Sublime Body," from all such extrinsic, imposed definitions and make it once more "the owner of consciousness." Blake seeks to reunite the "Spirit" with the "Body" on a level that subsumes individual self-consciousness in the collective, social embodiment of human desire that is the ideal city of art: the New Jerusalem.

Blake understood what Locke and Descartes did not: that the assumption of embodiment is the necessary precondition of "Selfhood."[34] For it is not, after all, enough to say that we are individuated in the way Henry James, prefacing *The Portrait of a Lady*, pictures the community of writers to be—all inhabiting the same "house of fiction" (in our case, life) but possessing different views of the world outside.[35] Having a self is not simply a matter of perspective, of peering out of our separate windows; it is not simply a matter of having "my form of the world." The "my" can have no meaning unless "I" (an otherwise undifferentiated consciousness) occupy some place in the world that can be pointed out and attended to from some other place in the world. To have a form of the "world for me" the "I" must already be understood to be engaged in some spatial, mutually determining relationship with the world of things and others. It must understand itself to be a "thing" among other things, defined from without by others or, like Gray's elegist, by itself assuming the position of "another."

Descartes argued the wrong way around: I do not infer the presence of other minds "in" others' bodies by extrapolating from the apparent union of myself and my body. Rather, I feel, immediately, my "self" embodied, made an object of and individuated by the minds of others, whose consciousness of me and of the world we all inhabit is fundamental and axiomatic to my self-definition. As Gray and Hume show, the more we search for the self within, the more it shrinks to a ghost haunting the fringes of experience.

Hume himself provides an object lesson for resolving the very doubts he raised. Alone at his studies, he takes his identity, like the evidence of his senses, like the soundness of his reason, like knowledge itself, to be fantastic:

> I am first affrighted and confounded with that forlorn solitude, in which I am plac'd in my philosophy, and fancy myself some strange uncouth monster, who not being able to mingle and unite in society, has been expell'd all human converse, and left utterly abandon'd and disconsolate ... when I turn my eye inward, I find nothing but doubt and ignorance. All the world conspires to oppose and contradict me; tho' such is my weakness, that I feel all opinions loosen and fall of themselves, when unsupported by the approbation of others.[36]

"Where am I, or what?" asks the isolated skeptic. "What beings surround me?" He begins to imagine himself "in the most deplorable condition imaginable, inviron'd with the deepest darkness and utterly depriv'd of the use of every member and faculty."

What is the cure for "this philosophical melancholy and delirium," this radical self-doubt? "I dine, I play a game of backgammon, I converse, and am merry with my friends; and when after three or four hours amusement, I wou'd return to these speculations, they appear so cold, and strain'd, and ridiculous, that I cannot find in my heart to enter into them any further."[37] We "find" the self, as we find a world of real objects, in the presence of others who, we understand, recognize it and confirm its being out there as well as in here. The self is located neither inside the mind nor outside; it is not re-presented by our behavior in the world, but present and apprehended therein. The inner self is but the virtual focus of intentions, passions, values, motivations which we enact, or can imagine enacting, in a world of others, where they come to possess a shared meaning.[38]

This fundamental dependence of the sense of self on the sense of a meaningful embodiment for others becomes more evident in studies of the growth of self-awareness in children. Maurice Merleau-Ponty observes that the development of other-awareness in the child seems to coincide with, even precede, the psychogenesis of solitary or introspective self-awareness. In an essay entitled "The Child's Relations with Others," he makes the following observations with respect to the child's ability to recognize self and others in the mirror: "One notices, in effect, that [the child] distinguishes more quickly between the other's specular image and the reality of the other's body than he does in the case of his own body. Thus it is possible that the experience he has of the other's specular image helps him arrive at an understanding of his own."[39]

Only when this understanding is achieved, at about the age of three years, can the child recognize the difference between his or her own consciousness of the world and that of others. Up to that time, the child will confuse dreams and reality as well as attribute to others feelings and points of view that only he or she could be aware of. This lack of a sense of individuation is also evidenced in the child's inability to understand perspective in drawing, which depends on "the idea that he sees [things] from a single point of view instead of living in them."[40] Merleau-Ponty cites the French psychologist Henri Wallon, who in his book *Les origines du caractère chez l'enfant*, "shows the change in the child's reactions to the look of the other" that occurs at about the same time the child gains a sense of perspective, a sense of distance between himself and "the spectacle of others and the world": "Up to the age of three years, in general, except in pathological cases, the other's look encourages the child or helps him. Beginning at three years . . . the other's look becomes an annoyance for the child and everything happens as though, when he is looked at, his attention is displaced from the task he is carrying out to a representation of himself in the process of carrying it out."[41]

Thus, the perspectival sense of a particular view of the world as "mine" emerges only with the ability to recognize others *as* others and to see oneself according to others. In short, "the ego cannot emerge at the age of three years without doubling itself *as an ego in the eyes of the other.*"[42]

We should not be misled by this relationship between self-consciousness and embodiment for another into supposing that the self can somehow be reduced to a physical thing—an automaton, for instance, as Descartes fantasized. What others view when they encounter me is not a body, but my self as an explicit object of consciousness. The body merely as a material substance has no social significance, while the self as an explicit object of consciousness is always already posture, pose, act, or potency, displayed in a world of signs—defined objects, poses, speech-acts, actions—and "actors." As a self, one always assumes an intentional presence, a public meaning that challenges recognition, even when one is just "minding one's own business." A self, then, is a body that "means" something because *it* is conscious, has immediate ends and an ultimate destiny, and is assumed to be responsible in a literal sense: it is able to respond to another's address, another's expectations or judgments, and thus engage in relations mutually determinative of identity.

If having a self depends on being defined as an object in a world that is given over to a cultural system of signs, preeminently language, then it is quite possible that we may not always be who we think we are. The self we present to the "madding crowd" may not always be recognized in the way we wish, and we may even fool ourselves as to how we wish to be recognized by the world. Thus R. D. Laing, who coined the term "ontological insecurity" precisely to define the extreme consequences of such disidentifications, traces the clinical attribution of psychoses to what is essentially a failure of mutual self-recognition between two persons, one of whom, the doctor, is sane "by common consent."[43] Laing sees the clinical postulation of an unconscious as the mistaken result of a disjunction between the symbolic significance of the patient's speech or behavior patterns and the doctor's inability to respond coherently, from the patient's point of view, to the self represented in that behavior. Finding no satisfactory response to its representations in the surrounding society, the self cannot recognize, and thus consciously acknowledge for others, itself therein. As a result, the patient begins to doubt the very reality of his or her self as an embodied being and, by extrapolation, the reality of others in their embodiment. With the reality of other presences denied, even the reality of the world of objects, which are assumed to *be* objects precisely to the extent that their reality for others can be counted on, is made tenuous.

French psychoanalysis has taken a similar turn toward explaining the unconscious in terms of "intersubjective relativity." Paul Ricoeur, like Laing, believes the unconscious depends upon the meaning attributed to self-representations, but he maintains that the patient in psychoanalysis remains unaware of the responses he or she seeks. For Ricoeur, the unconscious is not a fiction, but he sees the "hermeneutical situation"—the context of reciprocal self-interpretation—as necessary to any attempt at understanding it. In his view, " 'Psychology' grasps only a shadow or outline, which is present in all men, of what it means to be esteemed, approved, and recognized as a person. My existence for my self depends utterly on this self-constitution in the opinion of others. My Self—if I dare say so—is received from the opinion of others, who consecrate it."[44] Ricoeur contends that what is most important in psychoanalysis is "that the facts which the analysis attributes to the unconscious are *meaningful for another,*" for a "witness-consciousness," and that "it is only for someone other that I even possess an unconscious."[45] For Ricoeur's contemporary, Jacques Lacan, "the unconscious *is* the discourse of the other"; it appears only in what others can help articulate *for* the subject, but this articulation is always anticipated by the behavior of the subject. The Other is that implied being "through whom and for whom the subject poses *his question,*" that is, the question of his identity.[46]

The discrepancy between the self-for-itself and the self-for-another causes anxiety. The fact that I do not always appear to be who I think I am introduces an element of ambiguity into my complacent, everyday self-certainty. Others' expectations or reactions may cast doubt on my idea of myself, my intentions, values, innocence. But such is the risk that must be run if consciousness is ultimately to assure itself of its identity. In the last analysis we are no more sure of our "selves" than we are sure of any object of awareness that cannot be called to another's attention and subjected to shared methods of analysis and interpretation. The real self, like the real world, is always presumed to be communally accessible, and its certainty, like that of any proposition, is finally assured only by means of its articulation—by its being put into words, symbols, or even gestures (such as pointing)—and thus made available to interpretation by others. The way we dress, talk, and eat, our choice of books, cars, careers, and dwellings, all convey an image of the self that we intend, sometimes without knowing it, to be validated in this manner.

If the self cannot exist for long without the assurance of recognition, certainly it cannot grow. The attainment of psychological maturity and the acquisition of self-certainty are, as Erik Erikson has observed, one process involving the gradual integration and coherence of self-presentations in public roles. The "ego" (consciousness) strives to synthesize the "self" by gaining recognition from family, friends, and society: "What the I reflects on when it sees or contemplates the body, the personality, the role to which it is attached for life . . . are the various selves which make up our composite Self. There are constant and often shock-like transitions between these selves."[47] Self-identity as it evolves through life is the result of successive reintegrations of "temporarily confused selves . . . in an ensemble of roles which also receive social recognition."[48]

But this reintegration cannot take place without the establishment of a strong, central power of internal self-reflection and synthesis. In order for the ego, which performs these functions, to become independent of those everyday, phenomenal self-images that it seeks to manipulate and reconcile, it must recapitulate the processes of "introjection" by which, as a child, it first came to establish an interiorized power of reflection and self-consciousness.[49] In the scenarios of Merleau-Ponty and Wallon the child must internalize the authoritative reflective presence of the parental Other in order to establish its sense of individuality and independence from others within the context of the family. So also must the adolescent or young adult interiorize a succession of adult role models, idealized or even spiritualized parent substitutes, in order to establish a sense of individuality and independence from others in the wider context of society (especially from his or her former, idealized authority figures, the parents) and to arrive at a sense of his or her destiny within the impersonal unfolding of history.

Of the three poets I have chosen for this study, only Wordsworth and Keats can be said to have negotiated with some success the difficult transition to a mature sense of self-certainty in their vocation as poets. Their final acceptance of their roles was helped in part by the search for parent substitutes, at first human, later of divine or semi-divine origins. For Wordsworth, revolutionaries like Michel Beaupuy and political philosophers like William Godwin provided early and, as it soon appeared, dangerous role models of the committed self. Though retaining his admiration for men like Beaupuy in the years of crisis following his involvement in the Revolution, Wordsworth rejected the revolutionary model. He turned, instead, to the indispensable source of comfort and acceptance that he had habitually located in nature following his mother's death, and eventually came to personify that power in a mother substitute chosen from within his own family: his sister, Dorothy. It was she who encouraged him, not only in his passive and solitary love of nature but in his public expression of that love, his true vocation, his "office upon earth" as poet. Eventually the source of Wordsworth's poetic self-assurance came to reside in a spiritual entity called "the People," whose authority was understood to derive from God. It is the "Vox Populi which the Deity inspires," he writes, as distinct from "the Public," a clamorous and factitiously influenced readership.[50] For Keats, Leigh Hunt and Benjamin Haydon provided early role models of the committed artist, though Keats eventually rejected the influence of Hunt. Later, the parental mirror of self-certainty was interiorized and imaginatively embodied as the goddess, Moneta, in *The Fall of Hyperion.*

To cite such developments is not to say that all qualms about the phenomenal self disappeared for Wordsworth and Keats, nor that absolute independence had been achieved. The very need to affirm, repeatedly, their indifference to public opinion suggests how sensitive to it they remained. Coleridge, however, was apparently incapable of interiorizing these authoritative yet accepting presences: authoritative figures abound in his poetry, but they are not accepting or approving. Though his poetry shows a desperate need to create scenarios of poetic power and dominance over imagined audiences, it does not progress beyond this stage of preoccupation with others' judgments of him. In fact, he abandoned his poetic career, for all practical purposes, after 1802.

On the one hand, then, and despite solipsistic tendencies, these Romantic poets discovered that the self could not be exclusively identified with consciousness, not even when it found itself "embodied" in a style of perception or feeling. The identity of the self could not be separated from one's habitual appearance for others or from the responses to one's presence that one habitually came to expect from others. But on the other hand, the poet could not depend exclusively on these responses without losing his sense of authenticity. This dialectic appears quite clearly in the work of Wordsworth, Coleridge, and Keats, where the tendency towards visionary solipsism can sometimes lead to such extreme feelings of isolation and self-diffusion, a state verging so closely on nothingness, that they are counter-pointed throughout the most prolific and creative periods of the poet's life by a struggle to test the reality of the finite self in the eyes of others. Confrontation provides a counter-moment to solipsistic withdrawal, but it also threatens the independence of the self embodied for others. To keep from falling back into self-dispersion, the poet must make his own place and determine his own function in the world, by means of a confirming presence he can count on to recognize him as the poet he is. It is through the encounters depicted in their poetry that these three poets seek to test, reintegrate, and come to terms with their disparate and often temporarily confused selves and affirm the historical and social reality of the true self that persists behind the masks and throughout the vicissitudes of the search of recognition.

"Visionary Solipsism" and Its Discontents

To say that the sense of self depends on the sense of embodiment is not to say that the self cannot subsist in isolation; it is only to say that the self cannot subsist without at least the implied or tacit understanding of an audience for which it can assume embodiment. Nor does this argument require taking the absurd position that there is no inner life—no emotions, thoughts, attitudes, cognition. It implies only that the self cannot subsist if it is exclusively identified with these mental events. For the feeling of being an individual in possession of these events depends necessarily on understanding oneself to be embodied in a world inhabited and perceivable by others. Without the assumption of embodiment, there may be consciousness, but no self.

Ordinarily, we learn to live with the duality between what Erikson calls the "composite Self" and our many "selves," unless we fail to overcome the trauma of individuation described by Merleau-Ponty and Wallon. We come to see little that is incompatible between the notion of "self" as a corporeal object of consciousness, a self-for-others, and the idea of "Self" as an allusive, implicit subject of consciousness. I may be right in saying, "No one *really* knows me," thus retaining my private sphere of knowing and believing and willing, "my form of the world" as the most intimate realization of my Self, and this statement will not logically contradict my wife's saying, "I know him better than he knows himself," that is, "Whatever his secret intentions, desires, or image of the world, I know what he does or will do in such and such a situation; I know how he behaves."

This does not make my wife a "behaviorist"—just the opposite. She does not, like a behaviorist, dismiss the intentionality apparent in my actions; she assumes that my behavior is meaningful and that it does reveal some sort of awareness of what I am about, though that "awareness" might for the moment escape even me. Descartes's hypothetical reduction of persons to clockworks, or Hoffman's fascination with the likeness of automata to real persons, or Carlyle's facetious clothes-philosophy would not mislead or confuse her. Such views of the self are as incomplete as Locke's concept of a cranial homunculus.

My wife's good faith notwithstanding, such notions as those of Hoffman or Carlyle still have as much imaginative impact on us as they did on their originators, a power of suggestion that, I suspect, generations of writers previous to the Romantics could not have felt as keenly. Gray's "madding crowd," after all, was just beginning to proliferate by the end of the century, uprooted from villages and ancestral homes by enclosures and the urban lure of work or sudden fortunes. Greater social mobility, mass urbanization, the disappearance of sumptuary laws, all had the general effect of making England an island of strangers. It became increasingly difficult for the self to find a recognizable place in English society, harder to tell if what others saw was the true self, or if the self was being compromised, made false, taken away from its "owner" by more fluid and less dependable categories of public identification.

"The dualism of the inner self is peculiar to the nineteenth century," writes J. H. van den Berg in *The Changing Nature of Man*. It grew out of the replacement of small groups—in which the individual found a single place, a name, and a role with which he or she could closely identify—by large, vague groups which, being "autonomous and therefore more compelling," "forced a self onto the individual."[51] This dualism has evolved into our twentieth-century "pluralism" of identities, only a few of which manage to remain in close enough communication with each other to form a single, coherent personality. "We are not ourselves; actually there is nothing we can call a 'self' anymore; we are manyfold; we have as many selves as there are groups to which we belong. 'A neurosis is the conflict between the different social egos.' The neurotic has overtly a disease from which everybody is suffering: the disease not to be able to be one's self, which means not to be able to be identical with one's self in different contexts and in different situations."[52] Today the person is one body playing too many different and incompatible, or simply unrelated, parts.

Whatever the social origins of our modern anomie and self-alienation, the loss of faith in the ability of embodiment to represent the whole person had complex repercussions in the writings of the Romantics.[53] If Blake is any indication, they seem to have been anxious and despondent at the thought of a self that is embodied and exposed, not least, perhaps, because they understood that the embodied self, however subject it may be to a conflict of interpretations, is more real than the self within. The Cartesian assumption that the self is identical to mind provided, ultimately, the condition of the possibility of Romanticism.[54] Beginning with that assumption, and tracing the contradictions it gives rise to, we can arrive at an understanding of what I have called visionary solipsism, that state of waking dream which many of the Romantic poets considered the profoundest source not only of poetic insight but of their very identities as poets, and which arose as a consequence of the poet's attempt to come to terms with his embodied being, the existence of others, and the facticity of the world in an age when the self as mind was taken to be true, but not real.

By the phrase "visionary solipsism" I do not mean to imply anything pejorative or, necessarily, delusory. Nor do I wish to deny the value or validity of such experiences as revelatory of a transcendent power of imaginative synthesis or, in the adumbration of symbols, of the finite mind's desires or ideals. Visionary solipsism refers simply to a state of mind where attention is focused so exclusively on the "sole self" (from the Latin of which, *solus + ipse*, we derive solipsism) and its sphere of perception that objects of perception no longer appear as objects of bodily sight, whatever their degree of correspondence to the world which is assumed to exist outside the mind. They become, instead, objects of "vision" in the oldest English sense of the word— things "seen otherwise than by ordinary sight,"[55] and often possessing an extraordinary, otherworldly significance. I wish also to emphasize that I use "solipsism" in its widest sense to mean not only the process of *making* reality a dream but also instances of *mistaking* or substituting a dream for reality, as in the case of Gray's elegist, where what is imagined concerning the forefathers of the hamlet takes on the unquestioned appearance of having been so. Visionary solipsism, furthermore, should be conceived as an extreme limit or boundary condition—rarely reached—of that withdrawal of the true self, that subjectivity, which characterizes Romanticism generally: it is the point at which the self begins to evanesce and incorporate the world outside as part of its own consciousness. This contemplation of all objects of thought—ideas, people, and things—as the contents of a magisterially isolated mind makes them, for the Romantic, visionary rather than merely objects of sight; they become meaningful reflections of the appropriative mind's own fears and desires, and establish an almost mystical sense of continuity between self and Nature, self and others, self and God. Once disembodied, mind becomes Mind, the formative and figurative ground of being.

Freed of its sense of embodiment, the Romantic self can, in Coleridge's words, "shoot" its "being through earth, sea, and air, / Possessing all things with intensest love" ("France: An Ode," 103–104). Repeated instances of empathic self-projection or impersonation (which not long after the Romantic period will eventuate, as Langbaum observes, in Browning's monologues)[56] complement the volatility of the Romantic self as mind. Coleridge pictured the ideal poet, like Shakespeare, to be possessed of a "Protean" flexibility, the power to transcend all particular self-embodiments while realizing the self as a pan-optic consciousness informing each of his characters or personae. The great poet is an intelligence embracing his fictive world, and all the individual minds within it, while withholding itself from commitment to any particular worldly form. Keats, of course, is the epitome of the prehensile poet susceptible to "filling some other Body" than his own. And even Wordsworth, Keats's "egotistical sublime," reveals in the numerous voices and masks of *Lyrical Ballads* an intelligence restlessly assuming fictional embodiment in "dramatic" situations. In *The Excursion* the poet practically ventriloquizes the characters of the Wanderer and the Recluse in what amounts to an extended, but hardly suspenseful, psychomachy.[57]

It is the poet's tendency to identify the self wholly with consciousness, with something abstract and not concrete, that allows him such versatility in impersonation and empathic characterization. But embracing the notion of the self as mind also engenders feelings of emptiness and dissociation from the poet's own embodied self as it is experienced and recognized in daily life. The world held suspended in the poet's mind can offer nothing apart from that mind to reflect for him his own real presence as something definite *in* that world, rather than as an unanchored perception or series of perceptions *of* the world. The champion of the protean poet comes finally to ask, "What is there in thee, man, that can be known?"

Furthermore, the unreality of a universe that is merely dreamed becomes horrifying as others lose psychological depth. Life in general appears "theatrical," a "death-in-life," and embodied selves become mere actors or caricatures, or in more severe cases, insensate things altogether, like automata or walking corpses. For Keats, drawing-room "Society" was apt to turn into "an acted play" (*Letters*, II, 244), a "sentimental farce" ("Ode on Indolence," 54), in which his own role as a "pet lamb" patronized by the literary crowd came to annoy him. Wordsworth's haunting doubts as to the self's real presence in its public image find expression, to take but one instance, in his description of Bartholomew Fair, in book XII of *The Prelude:* "a phantasma, / Monstrous in colour, motion, shape, sight, sound!" (687–688). His fascination with solitary figures that lack apparent intentionality or deliberateness in their actions derives from the same constitutional skepticism. As for Coleridge, the ambulatory corpses of the crew members in "The Rime of the Ancient Mariner" are but one indication of his recurring dread of bodily self-dissociation, a dread reflected in similar experiences in daily life. One Friday evening in November 1803, for example, he confided to his notebook, "In this, dim Light London appeared to me as a huge place of Sepulchres thro' which Hosts of Spirits were gliding."[58]

Feelings of emptiness and insubstantiality, and the corresponding derealization of the embodied self, both one's own and others': this is the negative moment in the dialectic of visionary solipsism, the price that must be paid for identifying the self wholly with a mind that imaginatively appropriates the world as its own and transforms it so as to reflect the contours of its own inchoate being. These negative effects lead, in the three poets considered here, to frequent and at times desperate reactions against visionary solipsism, moments in which the poet strives to win some kind of recognition as a real and individuated being in the world. He needs to feel that the mental abstraction he calls a "self" is really present to the awareness of others, and that he views the world as a temporally and spatially determined being in it. He needs assurance that he has a particular role to play, with a particular destiny.

Although this search for recognition, for the reflection of one's real presence in the responses of witnesses, does represent in one sense an anxious flight from visionary solipsism, it is more accurate to say that visionary solipsism seems to compensate for the poet's prior fear of not properly belonging to the world, a fear he otherwise seeks to allay through real or imagined confrontations. The tense encounters that appear in the work of Wordsworth, Coleridge, and Keats represent attempts to make a place for the self among others, but on the poet's own terms. These confrontations reveal an abnormal fascination with and fear of the eye as an instrument of public self-confirmation and definition: for all three poets, the self that is engaged in direct confrontations is, on the one hand, individuated and affirmed as real thereby, but on the other is nearly always felt to be taken away from itself by the eye of the person confronted, especially if that person is unsympathetic or a stranger.

As a result, each poet tries to exercise some control over the situations in which his identity is to be realized and defined, or, as in Gray's "Elegy," over the attitudes of those who define it. This control is ultimately verbal or narrative, for it is through retrospection on real encounters or the imagining of fictitious ones that the poet seeks to identify himself by redefining the circumstances, and even the audience, in or before which his identity becomes concrete. Only in this way can the Romantic poet overcome the "ontological insecurity" that his sublime imaginative gifts inevitably entail. Only thus can he make for himself a place in the world where what is recognized as real corresponds to what is felt to be true.

The Romantic's quest for self-knowledge, then, can best be understood as the quest for an intimate yet authoritative audience: to use Keats's words, it is the search for a proper "greeting of the Spirit" from another or others so as to realize an ideal, interiorized self-image that the poet fears the world will otherwise deny or deface. The dark underside of this anxious investment of power in the Other to bring the self into being is the poet's feeling that he has to a great extent lost control over the self made manifest in any social situation, and that the Other possesses as great a power to rob him of himself, to distort or misinterpret or paralyze the true self, as to bring it to life.

Romantic poetry, as Geoffrey Hartman characterizes it, is a flight into "anti-selfconsciousness," but also, as paradoxical counterpoint, a search for right recognition.[59] Both impulses stem from the same basic anxiety over self-representation and misprision in the eyes of the world. The resistance to self-consciousness, which leads ultimately to visionary solipsism, can take the form of physical retreat or mental withdrawal. Or the poet can disown the public self by *making* it a complete Stranger to others, a *poète maudit*, an inscrutable mask that will defend from too close scrutiny the very being it misrepresents. Sometimes, as in the case of Coleridge, resistance can take the form of an imposition of something like mesmeric power on the poet's audience, a power that commands its own recognition. But despite his tendencies to defend himself from the gaze of others, the poet cannot for long keep the self aloof or in isolation. He is torn between his uneasy feeling that the wholly self-possessed mind lacks reality, and his fears over the loss of self-possession incurred by accepting the self as an object whose meaning depends on recognition from others.

These anxieties and ambivalences are shared in part by Byron, Shelley, and Blake, but seem less pressing in their work. Solipsistic experiences of the world do not appear very prominently, if at all, in Byron's poetry, nor, despite the posturing of *Childe Harold,* do empathic self-projections, though the poet possessed a healthy appreciation of *theatrum mundi.* The phenomenal world made "unreal," conceived as a "veil," is of course central to Shelley's thought, but less as something immediately felt than as something mediately assumed, a fascinating philosophical concept. Shelley's poetry also lacks that intense anxiety surrounding confrontations which we find so prominently in Wordsworth, Coleridge, and Keats. More often than not, the eye of another offers an invitation to Shelley, revealing the presence of an "epipsyche," a soul like his own. Of all the Romantic poets, Shelley seems the least agitated by others' observations or opinions of him, the most secure in his understanding of his role as poet.

Blake, of course, is a special case: a prophetic, not a solipsistic visionary, a mythmaker, an apocalyptic revolutionary with a hearty distrust for reveries and dream-states. Although he was indeed concerned with expunging the "Negation," the "spectrous" phenomenal self, he rejected entirely the idea of a hidden spirit or soul full of secret desires, a principle of self separated from the world it observes. The body purely as object is but the fallen manifestation of the Poetic Genius or Imagination, the whole man and "prolific" source of all explicit and "bounded" human images of the world, including the image of humanity itself. This Poetic Genius, as Blake makes clear, is a power that takes a unique form in a civilization's history and arts. Thus, Blake's vision of redemption, like Hegel's conception of the phenomenological dialectic, is expressed in the form of an historically evolving social aggregate: as Hegel looked to the State, as the final expression of the Absolute, Blake looked to the rejuvenated City, the scene of Wordsworth's most disturbing encounters with others.[60]

Wordsworth, Coleridge, and Keats, then, most clearly exemplify in their work the principal features of visionary solipsism and Romantic reactions to it. On the one hand, they exhibit the poet's tendency to identify solely with mind, and thus to make of the perceived world something unreal, something lacking substantiality apart from the mind; feelings of alienation from the phenomenal, embodied self; and derealization of the embodied selves of others. On the other hand, they reveal an ambivalent need for definitive self-recognition from others who are either sympathetic or are to be made, somehow, nonthreatening. Shelley, Byron, and Blake manifest this temperament in a more fragmentary way. For that matter, in any one of the poets under discussion, the complete array of these features manifests itself but rarely in any one work. This is so because the need for definitive self-embodiment in carefully controlled situations is not compatible with the tendency toward imaginative visionary experiences, but derives from the anxieties generated by such tendencies. In any case, whether the Romantic writer seeks inner revelation or outer recognition, self-elision or self-expression, he faces the task of overcoming the contradictions in his divided self.

One final note. In the chapters that follow it will soon become clear that I have not excluded from my discussions biographical or psychological determinants of identity, indeed, that at times such determinants become the focus of my argument, and are assigned an importance equal to that of class, culture, or intellectual milieu as underlying causes of the visionary solipsism that appears in the work of Wordsworth, Coleridge, and Keats. My justification is that a large part of what makes a person outstandingly characteristic of his or her time is precisely the degree of resonance that obtains between that person's individual history and the cultural assumptions of the historical period in which he or she lived. All three of these poets, for instance, had to come to terms with the early loss of their parents (in Coleridge's case, the de facto loss of his mother), and these early experiences of loss led, apparently, to deeply rooted convictions of the insubstantiality of the self and doubts about its place in the world. What matters in this book, however, is the *terms* in which such convictions were expressed, and how such terms were *meant to be interpreted* in the context of the individual's society and culture.

Formerly, experiences of what I call visionary solipsism were often termed "mystical"; and the "Presence that is not to be put by" (to borrow Wordsworth's phrase), which the mystic apprehended, took its meaning as Divine Presence from a firm theological and institutionalized religious outlook that obtained in the wider society, not just in the private mind of the saint. After Decartes, Newton, and Locke, with the secularization of the world and the isolation of the mind in its "dark room," such meanings could not retain their widespread currency, but become increasingly a matter of *individual* conviction, and less definite as a result. Divinity became, to Wordsworth's perplexity as well as joy, a vague "something far more deeply interfused" and at the same time a "something in myself."

Furthermore, as J. Hillis Miller observed in *The Disappearance of God*, the gradual realization of the withdrawal of the Divine Presence from His own creation led to doubts, not only about the "reality" of that creation but about the "reality" of the perceiving self *in* that creation.[61] In the everyday family life and polite social relations of the nineteenth-century middle classes, such self-doubts could, by and large, be quelled by the constant and immediate recognition, approval, and concern expressed by intimates—thus, the increasing importance placed on the home as a place of refuge from the outside world. The doubts persisted, nonetheless. That is why, when the personal trauma of early parental loss coincided with great artistic gifts, the works that resulted gave rise to innumerable echoes in the collective consciousness of English nineteenth-century society, a society whose Great Parent had abandoned it. And, in turn, this sense of cosmic abandonment resonated in the heart of each artist. Not only did the poet's own biographical and psychological situation lead him to respond in the way he did, and as intensely and seriously as he did, to the problems of identity posed by his age, but precisely those inescapable and intractable problems of identity posed by his age lent universal significance to the particular origins and development of the poet's struggle to achieve a sure sense of identity in a world now crowded with strangers.

2

Wordsworth: Making a Place in the World

There was a Boy; ye knew him well, ye cliffs
And islands of Winander!
—*Prelude*, V, 364–365

THERE WAS a boy, and in the evening he would visit the shores of
Windermere Lake to blow "mimic hootings to the silent owls, / That
they might answer him" (*Prelude*, V, 381–388).[1]

> Then sometimes, in that silence while he hung
> Listening, a gentle shock of mild surprise
> Has carried far into his heart the voice
> Of mountain torrents; or the visible scene
> Would enter unawares into his mind,
> With all its solemn imagery, its rocks,
> Its woods, and that uncertain heaven, received
> Into the bosom of the steady lake.

Though ostensibly referring to another, these lines were originally
written, in 1798, about Wordsworth himself.[2] The reason for the
later change of person is difficult to determine, but David Ferry, noting that the boy in the *Prelude* version dies young, takes the episode to
show a perversely benevolent response to the painful fact that the
mystical glories of the childhood state of mind must end with the
entry into adult life. It is better that the boy should not live to see a
manhood so spiritually stultified.[3]

Ferry was one of the first to remark on the mystical features of this
passage, identifying the boy, along with the little girl of "We Are
Seven" and the Idiot Boy, as one of Wordsworth's "heroes of the
mystical imagination." Ferry pointed out that this was a state
of mind Wordsworth deemed wholly incompatible with the demands
of adult life: "these children are Wordsworth's formulation for a state
of being which resists and refuses the involvements incumbent on us
as adult mortals . . . They have so little of time, of the finite, about
them."[4] They exemplify Wordsworth's "hostility to man's commit-

ment to the ordinary functions of life."[5] My comments hereafter are indebted to Ferry's remarks, and to similar views expressed by others,[6] but I wish to go beyond the simple observation of Wordsworth's misanthropy (if it is that) and consider its consequences for the poet's sense of identity. For in the end, and despite his "sublime egotism," the poet had to make for himself a real place in the temporal and finite world he tried so hard to shun—a place in history, which is to say, in the world of others.

Numerous critics have traced Wordsworth's dreamlike experiences, his oceanic moments of oneness with the landscape or the universe, to inherently subjective or "mystical" tendencies, and detected in them an intensified form of imaginative projection and perceptual transformation.[7] Like the Windermere boy's quiet incorporation of the sights and sounds of nature, these sublime moments represent instances of visionary solipsism. "The visible scene" begins to "enter unawares into [the] mind," and the world appears as unreal as a dream, that is, something in the self and not beyond it or surrounding it.

One need not deny the spiritual depth of such experiences in order to consider their psychological structure or origins. For Wordsworth, and for his readers, they are part of the mystery of his "visionary mind" (*Prelude*, III, 526). But they also derive from a certain configuration of consciousness, what A. D. Nuttall cites as the poet's psychological inheritance from Berkeley and Hume: "solipsism as an experience." Nuttall uses this phrase when he considers Wordsworth's note to Isabella Fenwick on the "Intimations" ode. Here, the poet traces his "visionary gleam" (56) back to youthful experiences of "idealism":

> I was often unable to think of external things as having external existence, and I communed with all that I saw as something not apart from, but inherent in, my own immaterial nature. Many times while going to school have I grasped at a wall or tree to recall myself from this abyss of idealism to the reality. At that time I was afraid of such processes. In later periods of life I have deplored, as we have all reason to do, a subjugation of an opposite character, and have rejoiced over the remembrances, as is expressed in the lines—
>
> "Obstinate questionings
> Of sense and outward things,
> Fallings from us, vanishings," *etc.*[8]

Nuttall observes that Wordsworth's reaction "has an argumentative structure of its own," that "this boy is clutching at the stones of the wall . . . to refute" their apparent unreality: *"Esse est obstare,* to be is to resist pressure or penetration."[9] Nuttall then raises an interesting question: Why should the reality of the world be any more accessible to touch than to sight, when all the senses are here subject to the same solipsistic doubt? Those of us who are sensitive to Wordsworth's horror, despite its absurdity, may have experienced something like it ourselves, in still moments, in undistracted silence, alone. There is something about the world simply as seen—unheard and untouched—that is fantastic, that plants a doubt. The question is, a doubt as to what?

A first response might be, doubt as to the objective reality of what one sense alone perceives, unconfirmed by information from the others. But what is so distinctively reassuring about tactile sensations? What can touch, as merely one more among the senses, restore to this boy that his "questioning" sight cannot?[10] Not the reality of the world, or not only that, but Wordsworth's sense of himself as something *in* the world. It is the unreality of the boy's own "immaterial nature" that terrifies him, the suspicion that *he* is not there, as a being embodied in the world he only watches. Reaching out to touch the wall ratifies not only the existence of the wall that is touched, but of the self *as a physical thing that touches,* that encounters resistance and *is touched* in return. Tactile sensations draw the immaterial self back into its real material form. What Nuttall calls "solipsism as an experience" is symptomatic of a felt lack of physical embodiment in a world which is perceived, but not inhabited.

Much later, such experiences were to give rise to quite different feelings. In the period at which he wrote the "Intimations" ode, Wordsworth says, he had come to deplore a "subjugation of an opposite character," a feeling of oppression by "sense and outward things" so severe that he "rejoiced over the remembrances" of these terrifying moments teetering on the brink of nothingness. The poet's change of attitude reflects a gradual shift in the focus of his anxieties as he matured and, gradually, secured his place in the world.

"The Abyss of Idealism"

As a child, Wordsworth had felt that sense of his place shaken, in no small measure, by the early and unexpected death of his mother and, a short time later, his father as well. Richard J. Onorato has provided the finest statement of and argument for the impact of those events on Wordsworth's poetic development. In particular, the poet's early loss of his mother, the primary source of his childhood identity, led to Wordsworth's "recurrent search in solitude and Nature for 'the life of things,' an absent reality, the sense of which was retained deeply within as soul."[11] One need not lean too heavily on psychological theory, however, to understand the importance of a consistent and continuous parental presence in the growth of a sure sense of oneself, and of the conviction that one belongs in the world and will find acceptance there. Perhaps only for Coleridge, among the English Romantics, does the absence of the mother have more drastic consequences on the poet's later development of identity. Even if it was not the primary cause of Wordsworth's tendencies to solitude and inwardness, the loss of his mother seems, early on, to have exacerbated his innate subjectivism and imbued him with an anxious sense of his own immateriality.

By the time he wrote the Intimations ode in 1802–1804, however, Wordsworth had outgrown such anxieties. He had come to feel, like Gray's elegiac speaker, more uneasy at the thought of subjection to outwardness than at the possibility of the world's or his own ideality, and he extolled the powers of an Imagination that, in the words of the ode, questions "outward things," pointing beyond them to "that immortal sea" of Being "which brought us hither" (163–164). Clearly, the "abyss of idealism," however frightening in boyhood, had given Wordsworth ample evidence of the "indomitableness of the Spirit within," and it is that sense of inner certainty and immortality for which the poet longs in middle age—so much so, indeed, that he minimizes its accompanying terrors. That the threat of unreality was now, in retrospect, outweighed by its compensations suggests that by 1804 Wordsworth had surrendered so much of the self to "outward things" that the "abyss of idealism" no longer had power to drag him hence. It had become a safe object of longing for a poet whose place in the world, while still embattled, was nonetheless secure.

That sense of assurance in his identity as a poet had not come easily, and was not retained without constant support from his close circle of friends and admirers. In fact, Wordsworth had first found his place, and a purpose as well, not in the visionary fields of poesy but in the streets and salons of revolutionary France, an early and hard test of his involvement in "outward things." That test was made more difficult because it came close on the heels of the adolescent flowering of his solipsistic imagination, poor preparation for a commitment to the course of world events. At Cambridge, even amidst the din of collegiate life, Wordsworth, "turning the mind in upon itself," could "spread [his] thoughts, / And spread them with a wider creeping," until he "felt / Incumbencies more awful, visitings / Of the upholder, of the tranquil soul, / Which underneath all passion lives secure / A steadfast life" (*Prelude,* 1805, III, 112–118). "I had a world about me—'twas my own, / I made it; for it only lived to me / And to the God who looked into my mind" (1805, III, 144–146). Soon, he was to be thrown into a world shaped by others whose ends, as it turned out, were neither his nor his God's, and certainly not the ends of the "tranquil soul" within him.

In the traumatic aftermath of his idealistic commitment to the French Revolution, Wordsworth tried to shun society and its demands on the public self; after difficult struggles to maintain his mental balance, he came, more than ever before, to value rather than fear his constitutional solipsism as an escape from what he called, in the opening lines of *The Prelude,* "the burthen of my own unnatural self, / The heavy weight of many a weary day / Not mine" (I, 21–23). Here he associates the "unnatural self" with public life and events, with "the vast city," for instance, where he "long had pined / A discontented sojourner" (I, 7–8). Wordsworth's strong sense of confinement and self-limitation in the presence of others appears most clearly in the 1805 version of these lines, where he describes himself as "A captive . . . coming from a house / Of bondage, from yon city's walls set free, / A prison where he hath been long immured" (I, 6–8).

The opposite of the "unnatural self" constricted and confined by society and its demands is not difficult to find in Wordsworth's writings: it is the being that, instead of acting on the assumed expectations or judgments of others, surrenders itself to a spontaneous harmony with natural powers working from within. The conflict is clearly expressed in "Expostulation and Reply," where Wordsworth refuses to take "lying down," as it were, the good-natured teasing of his busy and bookish friend Matthew:

"Why, William, on that old grey stone,
Thus for the length of half a day,
Why, William, sit you thus alone,
And dream your time away?

"Where are your books?—that light bequeathed
To Beings else forlorn and blind!
Up! up! and drink the spirit breathed
From dead men to their kind.

"You look round on your Mother Earth,
As if she for no purpose bore you.

The poet refutes this conventional judgment of his apparent idleness and affirms the value of such reverie: its "purpose" is hidden from people like Matthew, who judge such things from physical appearances:

"The eye—it cannot choose but see;
We cannot bid the ear be still;
Our bodies feel, where'er they be,
Against or with our will.

"Nor less I deem that there are Powers
Which of themselves our minds impress;
That we can feed this mind of ours
In a wise passiveness.

The true self cannot be determined from without because it is essentially disembodied—passive, detached, and observant, not active and deliberate. Its ends do not answer the expectations of others, but derive from the "Powers" at work within it. The true self has nothing to do with the realm of human activities. It emerges from what Wordsworth calls, in "Tintern Abbey," that "blessed mood" in which all physical action is arrested and the poet becomes completely a spiritual or mental entity (40–49)—

that serene and blessed mood,
In which the affections gently lead us on,—
Until, the breath of this corporeal frame
And even the motion of our human blood
Almost suspended, we are laid asleep
In body, and become a living soul:
While with an eye made quiet by the power
Of harmony, and the deep power of joy,
We see into the life of things.

This passage describes a quintessential moment of visionary disembodiment. As the body is "laid asleep"—not sensorily dulled but rather physically stilled, almost to the point of catalepsy—the poet is freed of his sense of physical limitation and "the burden of the mystery . . . the heavy and the weary weight / Of all this unintelligible world, / Is lightened" (37–40). The language recalls the sense of un-

burdening we feel in the lines Wordsworth quotes from the Intimations ode— *"fallings* from us, *vanishings."* The "burden" of a mysteri-
ous world opaque to thought, moreover, reminds us of the "burthen"
of the "unnatural self" in that world, a creature that is itself opaque
to others, like Matthew, and, we may assume on the evidence of
"Expostulation and Reply," thereby made to feel *answerable* for its
purpose on earth.

Instead of placing itself among things and others that demand a
reply, and thus enforce self-consciousness, Wordsworth's visionary
mind tends to embrace all things. It infuses the universe—made otherwise "unintelligible" by the innumerable contrarieties of others'
aims, intentions, and judgments—with its own harmonious and joyful intelligence writ large. At Cambridge, "To every natural form,
rock, fruit or flower, / Even the loose stones that cover the highway,"
the young man from Cumberland "gave a moral life": "I saw them
feel, / Or linked them to some feeling. The great mass / Lay bedded
in a quickening soul, and all / That I beheld respired with inward
meaning" (*Prelude,* 1805, III, 124–129). When "we see into the life
of things," we see our own life, our own "quickening soul," *in*
things.

This is what many readers have identified, adverting to Keats's
phrase, as Wordsworth's "egotistical sublime." "Through a violent
alteration in the sense of spatial identity," writes Albert O. Wlecke,
"the mind experiences itself as having expanded to a state of divinity" and "phenomena come peculiarly to appear as if they had their
origin in the mind." Often, in such experiences, "the world of ordinary sensation takes on the character of a world that is dreamed."[12]
Frederick Garber calls such instances of egotistical sublimity "an imposition of self upon that which is not self." They represent "in part a
protective gesture which makes familiar what is potentially dangerous."[13]

Garber is certainly correct insofar as this gesture makes *safe* what is
otherwise dangerously constrictive. In such visionary dislocations all
outward and unnatural constraints on the poet's identity, all things
that reinforce a sense of being among things, are appropriated by a
formative, wholly mental power that is taken to be as completely his
own as a dream. But the landscape of dream is both intimate and uncanny. The principal effect, if not the principal aim, of the "egotistical sublime" is not to make familiar what is strange but to make
strange what is familiar, quotidian. The Highland lass of "The Solitary Reaper";[14] the "two well-dressed Women" of "Stepping Westward"; the girl "who bore a pitcher on her head," walking against

the wind atop Penrith Beacon in book XII of *The Prelude,* all are common people made unfamiliar, as other-worldly as the wall that the boy, William, reached out to touch. As Wordsworth himself writes of the Penrith Beacon episode, "I should need / Colours and words that are unknown to man, / To paint the visionary dreariness" of that scene (*Prelude,* XII, 254–256).

Precisely because these unusual visionary effects are not consciously willed, Wordsworth does not recognize in them the workings of his own mind. Indeed, they are not, strictly speaking, "his" but rather the work of "Powers / Which of themselves our minds impress," a divine, not human, revelation. It is his sense of the uncanny that strikes the poet as the surest sign of other-worldly intervention. The dreamscape and the figures in it etch upon his passive mind a cryptic, often indecipherable message that he must struggle to understand because *he* means nothing thereby: the imaginative "Powers" of mind working *in* him do. And yet, in all cases, the meaning that emerges turns out to be personally significant.

By disengaging the self from the world and thus making the everyday strange and dreamlike, the "egotistical sublime" accomplishes two things: it shows itself to be impersonal and universal, even Godlike, in its power to make the world intelligible, and at the same time it shows itself to be a radically individual, even unique possession, thus distinguishing its owner from all others. Visionary solipsism, the avenue to self-transcendence, becomes self-affirming and self-referring. Wordsworth feels like "a renovated spirit, singled out" in such experiences (*Prelude,* I, 52) even as he comes into contact with omnipresence and the absolute—his own mind unrestricted by finitude. To the visionary, the world appears as both "something in myself" and "a prospect of *the* mind," not just "my mind." For a moment, "this mind of *ours*"—at work eternally in all of us—makes its presence known in the otherwise finite being he calls "myself."

But with the world held firmly in an infinitely expanding Mind, what outside that mind can confirm the reality of this finite being it has "singled out"? As the Fenwick note demonstrates, Wordsworth's experiences of self-expansion and dispersion were rooted in an alienation bordering on despair. What is missing is a strong sense of individual substantiality, the assurance that comes from an understanding that the self so divinely gifted has received more mundane recognition as a person. That is one reason for Matthew's appearance in "Expostulation and Reply": unlike visionary, dreamlike figures in the landscape of the mind, Matthew, with his teasing, scolding, and exhortations, approaches and confirms, by his very criticism, the poet's real presence in the world *as a poet.*

That Matthew does not confirm it in quite the way Wordsworth desires makes little difference to the outcome of the confrontation and serves, in fact, to emphasize Matthew's apparent independence as a source of recognition. He is not just a mouthpiece for the poet. In any event Wordsworth does get the last word and the upper hand in the argument, in effect silencing Matthew, and he does so in a public forum, the poem itself. If, as Nuttall contends, *esse est obstare,* Matthew's initial negative reaction to the poet's presence confirms all the more the reality of that presence, just as the resistance of a wall confirms the embodied limits of the boy's identity. Others must be truly other, outside the mind, even somewhat intractable, if the poet is to count as real and not illusory in their eyes, if their challenge to his "being there" is to prove substantial enough to make his being there "matter," in both senses of the word. To have its say and take its place as something definite in the world whose reality is confirmed by others, *the* mind must make room for other minds.

There is, of course, little sense of anxiety in Wordsworth's encounter with Matthew—we are told he is the poet's "good friend," and we understand him to be speaking facetiously. Nonetheless, he is there to evoke, or to provoke, the enunciation of a central Wordsworthian doctrine and, in his subsequent silence, to bear tacit witness to its truth. In other encounters Wordsworth's sense of anxiety is more pronounced. But whether slight or severe, the uneasiness we sense in these confrontations can be traced to Wordsworth's understanding that here the true or natural self, the abstract and passive self, risks betrayal, misprision, or repudiation for the sake of a real confirmation. Why else should one ever abandon "wise passiveness" to dispute with fools and knaves? Belonging to the world of others, except in circumstances to be defined by the poet as conducive to the pursuance of his public role as poet, always carries with it the threat of an enforced inauthenticity, the imposition of a false self incongruent with one's sense of the "Spirit within." Indeed, so sensitive is the poet to possible misinterpretations of his lassitude that he goes on, in the next poem of *Lyrical Ballads,* "The Tables Turned," to extend his defense without allowing poor Matthew so much as a word in reply.

Wordsworth records, or stages, such confrontations in his poetry, I believe, because he achieves thereby a confirmation of his own self-understanding, even if, at times, he must strain to find it. His sensitivity to his imagined audience is unusually acute, considering his own repeated emphasis on the value of solitary thought, but even so, he was not always certain that the responses his poetry elicited were the responses he sought. In light of the written record of his confrontations, Wordsworth's mature career appears, among other things, as an extended attempt to test the reality of the immaterial self by placing it in situations where initially ambiguous, unanticipated, or hostile reactions are overcome and the shared world is made safe for the expression of the true self. Thus, in most of the face-to-face encounters set down in his verse, one senses Wordsworth's need for audiences, or intimates, that can be persuaded to accept him in the role he feels compatible with his inner sense of himself as a "gifted" poet: spontaneous, magnanimous, sincere, prophetic.[15] Only with such assurances can the self in the world remain *both* certain of its being there and true to the transcendent powers working within it. When such assurances are lacking in confrontations, Wordsworth nearly always seeks to elicit them or to impute, anticipate, or even dictate others' responses so as to assure himself of being recognized as the person, and poet, he takes himself to be.

The Vicissitudes of Embodiment: Two Beggars

Before turning to direct confrontations in Wordsworth's poetry, I would like to look more closely at the poet's anxieties over embodiment as expressed in his images of the social self. We notice first of all that the self among others is nearly always portrayed as false and forced—an actor or automaton. In the Intimations ode, for instance, the poet characterizes the social self by drawing on metaphors of the theater, describing how each fragment of the "dream of human life" shapes the sensibility of the six-year-old child as he grows to adulthood (98–108):

> Then will he fit his tongue
> To dialogues of business, love, or strife:
> But it will not be long
> Ere this be thrown aside,
> And with new joy and pride
> The little Actor cons another part;
> Filling from time to time his "humorous stage"
> With all the Persons, down to palsied Age,
> That life brings with her in her equipage;
> As if his whole vocation
> Were endless imitation.

The child's "exterior semblance doth belie" his "Soul's immensity" (109–110). That Soul, Wordsworth goes on to say, too soon "shall have her earthly freight," staggering under the "weight" of "custom," "Heavy as frost, and deep almost as life!" (127–129).

The grand metaphor of life as a stage is, of course, older than Jacques, going back to the Roman notion of *theatrum mundi*. But we have the feeling that for Wordsworth, at times, it is more than a metaphor. The poet so often feels his own soul crushed by its "earthly freight" and the imposed "weight" of "custom" (the phrases recall again the "heavy and the weary weight" of this "unintelligible world," "the heavy weight of many a weary day / Not mine") that he tends naturally to perceive social life in general that way, as borne down and petrified by the "frost" of conventional roles and expected patterns of behavior. In crowds, particularly, Wordsworth found epitomized the plight of the self burdened by its own embodiment. Ironically, his very tendency toward solipsism contributed to such instances of derealization: anonymous, detached observation of the passing scene could often give rise to experiences in which people became dreamlike images in the mind's eye, phantoms or puppets lacking true subjectivity.

"I was the Dreamer, they the Dream," he writes of the "motley spectacle" of Cambridge life in the third book of *The Prelude* (30–31). And (570–576)

> At this day
> I smile, in many a mountain solitude
> Conjuring up scenes as obsolete in freaks
> Of character, in points of wit as broad,
> As aught by wooden images performed
> For entertainment of the gaping crowd
> At wake or fair.

To the solipsistic Dreamer "the surfaces of artificial life" (III, 562) could often seem a hideous parade of empty masks and mimes, forms without substance. People who pass in the streets become "a second-sight procession, such as glides / Over still mountains or appears in dreams" (*Prelude*, VII, 633–634). Of his early experiences of London he writes (VII, 626–629),

> How oft, amid those overflowing streets,
> Have I gone forward with the crowd, and said
> Unto myself, "The face of every one
> That passes by me is a mystery!"[16]

In the midst of this unreal spectacle, a visionary moment occurs when Wordsworth chances upon a blind beggar. The man seems an image of the self utterly reduced, in the gaze of others, to its exteriority. The poet stands transfixed (VII, 637–649):

> Amid the moving pageant, I was smitten
> Abruptly, with the view (a sight not rare)
> Of a blind Beggar, who, with upright face,
> Stood, propped against a wall, upon his chest
> Wearing a written paper, to explain
> His story, whence he came, and who he was.
> .   .   .   .   .
> . . . an apt type
> This label seeemed of the utmost we can know,
> Both of ourselves and of the universe;
> And, on the shape of that unmoving man,
> His steadfast face and sightless eyes, I gazed,
> As if admonished from another world.

Here Wordsworth encounters a man made into a thing— "propped," "unmoving," and labeled like a specimen of plant, insect, or mineral. The beggar inspires not pity or compassion but metaphysical horror, and the source of that horror is the man's inability to respond coherently to the immediate presence of the crowd around him. For the poet of *The Prelude,* tracing the growth of his "Poet's Mind," telling his own "story," what is appalling about the image is not the beggar's destitution but his helplessness and dependency on his unseen audience, his utter loss of self-determination.[17] Given up entirely to his outward appearance, and the label that characterizes it, he stands with "upright face," "steadfast face" turned toward the crowd, as though in need of it. But because he is sightless, the beggar cannot refute, influence, turn aside from, or even acknowledge those who judge the plausibility of his story and the severity of his need. There is no way for him to challenge the accuracy of their interpretation or to assure himself that he is being "read" right. Like Gray's young poet in the chronicle of the Swain, he has been summed up by a tale told *about* him, a record of acts and appearances that misses the inner man.

Confronted with this spectacle, Wordsworth "gazed / As if admonished from another world": "an apt type / This label seemed of the utmost we can know / Both of ourselves and of the universe." That the blind beggar serves to "admonish" Wordsworth in a fashion which the man himself cannot possibly intend confirms the episode as an instance of visionary solipsism. From out of the poet's dream of London life comes a figure that has been appropriated by the imagination as personally significant. As an "apt type" or symbol of the limitations placed on embodied beings, the beggar speaks to Wordsworth's deepest fears of depersonalization. Through this figure he questions his oft-asserted faith that there must be more to the self than this false exterior. In the eyes of the world, perhaps, there is not.

Such self-admonishment serves to remind us that the poet's unfailing urge to renounce "outward things / Done visibly for other minds" (*Prelude*, III, 176–177) and to search out those "points" we have "within our souls / Where all stand single" (III, 188–189), where we exist as independent and not as public persons, represents in large part a reaction against his very dependence, as a poet, on "other minds." In his own choice of vocation Wordsworth continually risked adverse judgments of his work, risked losing his certainty of identity to the imposed expectations of the audience whose approval he sought. Wordsworth so feared this dependency that in his poetry the two moments in the dialectic of full self-realization often become mutually exclusive: either we transcend embodiment completely, situating the true self in those hidden "points" where we stand alone and not for others, or the self becomes a mere epiphenomenon, like the blind beggar, and life itself a "Parliament of Monsters" or a "blank confusion" (*Prelude*, VII, 718, 722), like the spectacle of Bartholomew Fair.

In short, our being for ourselves seems in Wordsworth's view antithetical and not correlative to our being for others (*Prelude*, IV, 354–357).

> When from our better selves we have too long
> Been parted by the hurrying world, and droop,
> Sick of its business, of its pleasures tired,
> How gracious, how benign, its Solitude.

That we find our better selves alone, and not in the crowd, and that the better self is to be identified in some way with a transcendent "power of harmony" to which one surrenders "in a wise passiveness," is evidenced by "The Old Cumberland Beggar."

Here, Wordsworth creates a solitary whose natural isolation frees him from the burden of the unnatural self, making his embodied identity an authentic image of the "better self" that transcends our individuation as persons. The old man does not acknowledge any attempt to label or define that image in human terms, according to conventional expectations or notions of usefulness or purpose. Though depersonalized, like his London counterpart, the Cumberland beggar differs in one major respect: he has no "story" he wants to tell. Rather, a story is told through him, by natural powers working within and on him. He takes the meaning of his existence not from a summary scrap of paper, which offers him up to the objectifying gaze of anonymous passersby, but rather from the "eye of Nature," a consciousness that supercedes both his own and ordinary society's understanding of his place in the universe. That "eye," as it turns out, is the visionary poet's as well.

Wordsworth begins, characteristically, with a painstaking description of a sight, not a true encounter—a man, like the blind beggar, observed but not approached or addressed (1–15):

> I saw an aged Beggar in my walk;
> And he was seated, by the highway side,
> On a low structure of rude masonry
> . . . . .
> . . . The aged Man
> Had placed his staff across the broad smooth stone
> That overlays the pile; and, from a bag
> All white with flour, the dole of village dames,
> He drew his scraps and fragments, one by one;
> And scanned them with a fixed and serious look
> Of idle computation. In the sun,
> Upon the second step of that small pile,
> Surrounded by those wild unpeopled hills,
> He sat, and ate his food in solitude.

Nuttall, echoing other critics, writes that these lines are, "no doubt . . . full of tenderness, . . . but all the tenderness is lavished on the act of seeing, none on the human figure himself . . . So far from being interested in the human predicament, [Wordsworth] is really moved above all by the inhumanity of the figure before him, by its stillness, by its continuity with the surrounding landscape."[18]

That sense of inhumanity is enhanced by Wordsworth's keeping his distance. Throughout the poem the Cumberland beggar remains less a person encountered than a something seen, something held in mind—in short, something quite close to "visionary." And like the blind beggar, who is also reduced by the poet's appropriative imagination to the level of the phenomenal, the peripatetic old man seems to lack individual will or power of choice. Thus he feeds the birds, but only by accident (16–21):

And ever, scattered from his palsied hand,
That, still attempting to prevent the waste,
Was baffled still, the crumbs in little showers
Fall on the ground; and the small mountain birds,
Not venturing yet to peck their destined meal,
Approached within the length of half his staff.

In describing this feeble attempt to *"prevent* the waste" the poet
comes as close as he can to ascribing intentionality to this figure. The
old man lacks that responsiveness to his environment that implies
consciousness. To all appearances he is unconscious. The "sauntering
Horseman . . . stops,—that he may safely lodge the coin / Within the
old Man's hat" (26–29); "She who tends / The toll-gate . . . if on the
road she sees / The aged Beggar coming, quits her work, / And lifts
the latch for him that he may pass" (32–36). The postboy's warning
shouts may go unnoticed, but that will not prevent him from passing
the Beggar "gently by, without a curse / Upon his lips or anger at his
heart" (42–43). We do not feel that the beggar ignores others: that
would itself be a way of "taking notice" which would call forth from
those who observe and accost him an angry response. We have no
reason to believe the beggar knows that others even exist, or that they
expect him to know. Rather, as the poem proceeds, he becomes almost an elemental power, as unaware of the people around him as a
passing stream or a floating cloud (45–58):

. . . On the ground
His eyes are turned, and, as he moves along,
They move along the ground; and, evermore,
. . . . .
. . . one little span of earth
Is all his prospect. Thus, from day to day,
Bow-bent, his eyes for ever on the ground,
He plies his weary journey; seeing still,
And seldom knowing that he sees, some straw,
Some scattered leaf, or marks which, in one track,
The nails of the cart or chariot-wheel have left
Impressed on the white road,—in the same line,
At distance still the same.

The white road in which the cart wheel nails have left their impressions provides an apt image of this man's mind, if so it can be
called: a Lockeian tabula rasa impinged upon by atoms of perception in time's "one track." There is no one inside, however, to observe

these qualia or to act on them. The beggar is absorbed in a vacant kind of "seeing" that does not know it sees, a perfect, if extreme, example of wise passiveness. Unresponsive to the scene before and around him, he moves along the road, mechanical, unreflective, purposeless, "free" (171–185):

> —Then let him pass, a blessing on his head!
> And, long as he can wander, let him breathe
> The freshness of the valleys; let his blood
> Struggle with frosty air and winter snows;
> And let the chartered wind that sweeps the heath
> Beat his grey locks against his withered face.
> Reverence the hope whose vital anxiousness
> Gives the last human interest to his heart.
> May never HOUSE, misnamed of INDUSTRY,
> Make him a captive!—for that pent-up din,
> Those life-consuming sounds that clog the air,
> Be his the natural silence of old age!
> Let him be free of mountain solitudes;
> And have around him, whether heard or not,
> The pleasant melody of woodland birds.

Wandering, breathing, circulation: the most unconscious of living processes constitute the extent of the beggar's freedom.[19] Like the poet in "Tintern Abbey," he seems "laid asleep in body." His "hope" is not fastened to any goal that could betray an overt intention or a desire that might result from choice. The beggar does not have freedom *of* choice, but freedom *from* choice.

At first glance, the London beggar seems to be similarly free from choice and similarly depersonalized. But the London beggar's identity has been surrendered to the crowd, the audience to whom he turns his "upright face" and shows his "label." He depends as much for the sustenance of his identity as for that of his body on *their* choices, *their* decision whether to accept or reject his "story." The alms given the Cumberland beggar, however, seem merely ancillary to his existence. With his face turned to the ground, seeking and responding to no one, he *looks* to no one for help except, perhaps, Nature herself. It is Nature who makes his choices for him to further her own ends—even the crumbs which he has accidentally dropped to the ground constitute the birds' *"destined* meal." The Cumberland beggar's autonomic freedom reflects his transcendent instrumentality: he lives to no purpose, answers to no conventional story, that we can frame.

The beggar's only purpose, apparently, is passive—to suffer. The choices Nature makes for him—inflicting on him her "frosty air and winter snows," her "chartered wind that sweeps the heath"—turn him into an appropriate object of compassion and charity. In this way he becomes a public "record" of the past "which together binds / Past deeds and offices of charity / Else unremembered, and so keeps alive / The kindly mood in hearts which lapse of years . . . make slow to feel" (89–94). In an important sense, then, *Nature* tells a story through the record of kind acts its treatment of the beggar has elicited, a record inscribed on the figure itself: a tale of hardship which continues to stir the hearts of the community and remind them of past generosity. In view of the old man's power to elicit pity and sympathy, Wordsworth castigates politicians who would draft Poor Laws for putting such indigents to work: "Deem not this Man useless—Statesmen!" (67). We must, the poet implies, accept the man for what he is and what Nature intends him to be: an exemplum.[20]

Leaving aside the questionable logic of Wordsworth's defense of destitution,[21] we see that his notion of the man's "use" is a sharply reduced one. We can hardly call it something the beggar does or contributes on purpose. The last stanza enjoins us to "let him pass" almost as we would let a beautiful stream pass by without hindrance of dam, sluice, or wheel that might turn it to some practical end: it is there to refresh the soul, not grind our corn. As the passive instrument of a higher power, the Cumberland beggar *is used* to improve virtue, to edify and uplift the soul. That transcendent function is literary. As a text to be read or a record to be deciphered, the beggar loses his proper humanity, to which ordinary categories of usefulness may properly apply.

The poet ends by imagining the Cumberland beggar as a thing that has his being's heart and home "in the eye of Nature," not society (186–197):

> . . . if his eyes have now
> Been doomed so long to settle upon earth
> That not without some effort they behold
> The countenance of the horizontal sun,
> Rising or setting, let the light at least
> Find a free entrance to their languid orbs.
> · · · · ·
> . . . and, finally,
> As in the eye of Nature he has lived,
> So in the eye of Nature let him die!

The beggar's lack of subjectivity is redeemed by his subsumption into an order fixed in the sight of a higher mind. Thus, his physical existence is understood to be at one with his spiritual being, and to transcend in its significance the world of mutual solicitations and acknowledgments where persons are brought into focus by *each other's* needs, addresses, and responses. He does not move in that world but with the "tide of things" impelled by a power whose visionary organ is here represented by the "horizontal sun," the only thing to which the old man turns his face upright.

Nature's eye, furthermore, is the poet's, as is the actual text or record—this poem—in which the old man takes on his metasocial significance. Perhaps in no other poem does Wordsworth end up so completely in the role that Coleridge later cited as most characteristic of his attitude toward others: *spectator ab extra* or *spectator, haud particeps*—"a contemplator, rather than a fellow sufferer or co-mate."[22] It is precisely Nature's kind of disembodied seeing that the poet has come to assume. By the end of the poem he has so distanced himself from the person he observes, and so firmly appropriated him as a mental image, that he can pray that the beggar "have around him, *whether heard or not,* / The pleasant melody of woodland birds." If that melody is not heard by the old man, then for whom is it conceived to be pleasant?[23] In these few words the Cumberland beggar takes his place firmly in the peaceful landscape of the picturesque, a mental landscape. Though the old man may not hear the birds, the poet (and, presumably, Nature and the reader) can. The lines confirm our sense that the beggar, who first appears to share the same world as the poet, has been transformed into a visionary object. Indeed, he has a special relevance to Wordsworth's situation as an artist of Nature: for to the extent that the old man can surrender himself completely to natural processes of thought and action, he is free of caring what the world thinks of him.

Self and Other: The Captive Audience

As visionary figures, both the blind beggar of London and the Cumberland beggar demonstrate what David Ferry calls Wordsworth's sense of "an extraordinary freedom" from "obligations to the actual circumstances and conditions of what he sees," "the freedom to ignore whatever is irrelevant to his sublime egotism."[24] Both figures speak particularly, on a visionary level, to one of Wordsworth's profoundest concerns: his sense of himself as a poet in a world that belongs to others. The blind beggar's vulnerability to his unseen audience corresponds to the writer's sense of vulnerability before his anonymous and unseen readers. He fears what they will *make* of him. But if this image reflects the poet's terror of becoming another's object, open to others' misinterpretations or rejections of his story, the image of the Cumberland beggar represents freedom from such oppression. Far from betraying any sense of indebtedness to his benefactors, he appears, instead, as Nature's gift to them: his life is the very record or text of a story by which Nature knits the community together in filial love and sympathy. Such a transvaluation of the significance of the phenomenal self can take place only when the individual does not try to tailor his life's story to others' expectations or assumptions, but lets the natural "Powers" within him direct its course.

In the end, the question of true identity is, for Wordsworth, intimately connected to the question of the springs of spontaneous or impulsive action, behavior that does not anticipate the responses of others. Consider, for instance, the terms in which Wordsworth describes his feelings of liberation from the "vast city" in *The Prelude*'s first few verse paragraphs. He fastens his attention on things that wander and float, passive objects impelled not by choice but by chance (14–18, 27–31):

> With a heart
> Joyous, nor scared at its own liberty,
> I look about; and should the chosen guide
> Be nothing better than a wandering cloud,
> I cannot miss my way.

> whither shall I turn,
> By road or pathway, or through trackless field,
> Up hill or down, or shall some floating thing
> Upon the river point me out my course?
> Dear Liberty! . . .

A "wandering cloud," a "floating thing"—Wordsworth rejoices in the kind of liberty he attributes to the Cumberland beggar, the liberty of choosing not to choose. To surrender one's choices in life, and in art, to natural powers is to be directed by a transcendent *telos*. Indeed, this moment is vatic, as the poet affirms when he stops to reflect on the day these lines were first uttered (50–54):

to the open fields I told
A prophecy: poetic numbers came
Spontaneously to clothe in priestly robe
A renovated spirit singled out,
Such hope was mine, for holy services.

In Wordsworth's recollection not even his words were spoken with premeditation—he did not speak, but was spoken through. Like the Cumberland beggar, he became a part of Nature, her instrument.

The portraits of the Cumberland beggar and the London beggar suggest that for Wordsworth the possibility of throwing off the "unnatural" or false self depends on the extent to which he can remain "passive," unself-conscious, and spontaneous in poetic expression. He must try not to anticipate others' expectations of his use, and ignore the possibility of his story being misread. Only in the eye of Nature will he find the rationale, the final end, which makes useful or meaningful the choices, the vexing accidents, the visitings of a "peculiar grace," as it is called in "Resolution and Independence," that add up to an integrated life, a life not lived merely for and among others (*Prelude*, I, 344–351).

How strange that all
The terrors, pains, and early miseries,
Regrets, vexations, lassitudes interfused
Within my mind, should e'er have borne a part,
And that a needful part, in making up
That calm existence that is mine when I
Am worthy of myself! Praise to the end!
Thanks to the means which Nature deigned to employ.

Even in his petty sins of boyhood Wordsworth detected the guiding hand of a higher power. Thus, when he describes the famous boat-stealing episode in book I of *The Prelude,* the poet cannot help asserting parenthetically that he was "led by her" (357) to the boat, and taught a lesson by her "severer interventions" (355), which made a nearby mountain seem, to his guilty mind, a pursuer and avenger. Nature, through her "Powers" working from without as well as from within, preempts the individual will for its ulterior purposes. We need only trust her spontaneous promptings, however ill-conceived they may appear at first, to become what we were meant to be. "Nature never did betray," he tells Dorothy in "Tintern Abbey," "the heart that loved her" (122–123).[25]

Such, at least, was the desideratum. But Wordsworth was, in fact, the least spontaneous of the Romantic poets. As he reminds his "Friend," Coleridge, to whom *The Prelude* is addressed, referring to the lines that had originally come "spontaneously to clothe" his renovated spirit, he is "not used to make / A present joy the matter of a song" (46–47). In the "Preface" to *Lyrical Ballads* he cautions that "the spontaneous overflow of powerful feelings" which makes poetry must be "recollected in tranquility" before composition can begin (I, 148).[26] First, one must compose oneself. This ambivalence over the spontaneity he espoused shows the extent of Wordsworth's sensitivity to what others would make of such apparently uncontrolled expressions of feeling. Ideally, like the Cumberland beggar, he wanted to rise above petty considerations of what others thought about the powers that, working through him, had "singled" him out. Professionally and constitutionally, being a poet as well as a visionary, wearing his "label" like the blind beggar for all to see, he depended more than he wished on others and their opinions.

This audience anxiety appears quite early in Wordsworth's life, in his description, for instance, in book IV of *The Prelude*, of walks around Windermere during his Hawkshead schooldays, when, taking his dog to warn him of the approach of strangers, he would compose aloud. His comparison of himself to a murmuring river brings to mind the Cumberland beggar, similarly turned inward and similarly depicted as a perambulating natural force (118–130):

And when at evening on the public way
I sauntered, like a river murmuring
And talking to itself when all things else
Are still, the creature trotted on before;
Such was his custom; but whene'er he met
A passenger approaching, he would turn
To give me timely notice, and straightway,
Grateful for that admonishment, I hushed
My voice, composed my gait, and, with the air
And mien of one whose thoughts are free, advanced
To give and take a greeting that might save
My name from piteous rumours, such as wait
On men suspected to be crazed in brain.

To the stranger, the unself-conscious, spontaneous poet appears not inspired, but insane.[27]

The incidence and importance of face-to-face confrontations in

Wordsworth's poetry, often fraught with Kierkegaardian "fear and trembling," bespeak a deep-rooted need for recognition *in propria persona*, despite the poet's professed love of solitude and even at the risk of rejection or misunderstanding. In nearly all such encounters the embodied significance of the spontaneous or natural self, initially put in question by the eye of another, is finally confirmed by the other's response to the poet's actions. Wordsworth turns to others, as he reached out to touch a wall, for an assurance of his otherwise inchoate, evanescent, and immaterial identity, an assurance he expects his readers, as silent witnesses, to approve.

An example of such self-confirmatory encounters appears in "Simon Lee the Old Huntsman; with an Incident in which he was Concerned." Here what begins as a "tale" describing the poet's spontaneous act of compassion for another's suffering ends by gently castigating the reader's impulse to turn that suffering into a sentimental anecdote. And yet the final effect of the poem, I submit, is to suggest that the poet himself has registered a certain callousness toward his subject: Wordsworth's zealous demonstration of charity toward the "Old Huntsman" does make us, in the end, uncomfortable—not for ourselves but for him.

The poem opens with three stanzas recounting Simon's jocund youth and subsequent decline into old age (1–28).

> In the sweet shire of Cardigan,
> Not far from pleasant Ivor-hall,
> An old Man dwells, a little man,—
> 'Tis said he once was tall.
> Full five-and-thirty years he lived
> A running huntsman merry;
> And still the centre of his cheek
> Is red as a ripe cherry.
>
> No man like him the horn could sound,
> And hill and valley rang with glee
> When Echo bandied, round and round,
> The halloo of Simon Lee.
> . . . . .
> He all the country could outrun,
> Could leave both man and horse behind;
> And often, ere the chase was done,
> He reeled, and was stone-blind.
> And still there's something in the world

At which his heart rejoices;
For when the chiming hounds are out,
He dearly loves their voices!

But, oh the heavy change!—bereft
Of health, strength, friends, and kindred, see!
Old Simon to the world is left
In liveried poverty . . .

The description of Simon's hardships continues, with graphic details of his "body, dwindled and awry" (34) and his "ankles swoln and thick" (35), until the poet pauses, at line 61, to address the reader (57–72):

Few months of life has he in store
As he to you will tell,
For still, the more he works, the more
Do his weak ankles swell.
My gentle Reader, I perceive
How patiently you've waited,
And now I fear that you expect
Some tale will be related.

O Reader! Had you in your mind
Such stores as silent thought can bring,
O gentle Reader! you would find
A tale in every thing.
What more I have to say is short,
And you must kindly take it:
It is no tale; but, should you think,
Perhaps a tale you'll make it.

What will follow is, the poet asserts, not a tale, as he demonstrates by stepping into the poem himself and taking part in the "incident" in which Simon Lee was concerned: the poet, with one blow, severs the root of a rotten stump at which the old man has been working long and tediously (81–88):

"You're overtasked, good Simon Lee,
Give me your tool," to him I said;
And at the word right gladly he

Received my proffered aid.
I struck, and with a single blow
The tangled root I severed,
At which the poor old Man so long
And vainly had endeavoured.

The "incident" is meant to destroy the reader's comfortable assumptions of aesthetic disinterestedness, his position as a mere observer. However we may sympathize, pain should not be only watched, or even pitied, but relieved. The poet provides that object lesson for his passive reader's edification, and he does so, apparently, without hesitation and without being expected to. We are made to understand, by its very suddenness, that the act arises from the impulse of the natural self.

But the poet's impulsiveness, taken in a different light, appears peremptory. In the stanza just quoted the bald assertion of the first line registers an insensitivity to that pride of the old man's which the first three stanzas establish so vividly in the reader's mind: this was once a "tall" man, "a running huntsman merry," who "all the country could outrun, / Could leave both man and horse behind"—"No man like him the horn could sound." Instead of showing some regard for Simon Lee's proud and vigorous history, the poet's sudden interposition in his "tale" rather reinforces our sense that the old man has become merely pitiable, with no lingering trace of valor to command respect. It takes little effort to imagine the difference in tone between "You're overtasked, good Simon Lee" and a question as to whether or not Simon Lee is overtasked, or a statement emphasizing the difficulty of the *task* rather than the weakness of the *man*. If such a reading seems overnice, consider the imperative that follows, which adds to the feeling that the speaker is being too abrupt and also suggests a further reason for our discomfiture: by his command—"Give me your tool"—the poet establishes control over the situation and defines it in terms of the kind of behavior to be expected of the participants.

Wordsworth wants to prove more here than the superiority of practical charity. He wants to prove himself, to *show* his "use" in a concrete way. This explains why the poet cannot resist putting himself forward as exemplar, despite the fact that his doing so lends the whole narrative something of the flavor of preaching down and, worse, makes this spontaneous "incident" look staged. The poet not only insists that what he presents is truth, not fiction, but also that, by taking up Simon's mattock, he partakes of that reality, and becomes real thereby. Yet this reality of which the poet becomes a part is qualified by that artificial form of expression which represents it, and which is the poet's own work to begin with.

We come away from "Simon Lee" feeling less chastened for our disinterestedness in his tale than puzzled and disturbed by the way the poet has appropriated Simon in his own tale of himself. And not only Simon: "O Reader! *had* you in mind . . ."—but you have not, implies the speaker. "O gentle Reader! you *would* find . . ."—but you do not, the poet suggests. Anonymous, helpless, silent, the "gentle Reader," much like Matthew in "Expostulation and Reply," submits to be enlightened. Thus Wordsworth creates in his own mind a fictive audience of converts to his brand of benevolence.

Whether we identify with the "gentle Reader" or not is beside the point. Chances are we do not—we always assume it is someone else whom poets reprimand. But we wonder why the reader must be invoked at all. The answer lies in Wordsworth's need to feel that his demonstration of compassion is recognized by others who can be brought to agree with his assessment of it. His act of charity is also an act of self-affirmation, for which, Wordsworth tells us, he receives more than his due acknowledgment (89–96):

> The tears into his eyes were brought,
> And thanks and praises seemed to run
> So fast out of his heart, I thought
> They never would have done.
> —I've heard of hearts unkind, kind deeds
> With coldness still returning;
> Alas! the gratitude of men
> Hath oftener left me mourning.

In the end Wordsworth seems more moved by his own act of pity than by Simon's helplessness. Here, in the last stanza, our attentioin to the old huntsman's hard case is deflected by that which measures both its severity and the depth of Wordsworth's concern: the intensity with which the old man expresses his gratitude.

In "Simon Lee," as in "Expostulation and Reply," the poet shows very little of what we might call performance anxiety. When Wordsworth feels he is losing control over the way others view him, however, when he feels confirmation is lacking or that repudiation threatens, he does all in his power to convince himself of the former, or to forestall the latter. The "Preface" to the *Lyrical Ballads,* in which the poet tries to reason his reader into approbation of his "experiments," is a major case in point, to which I will turn momentarily.

A more dramatic example is Wordsworth's description of his encounter with the discharged soldier in book IV of *The Prelude*. As with the "incident" in "Simon Lee," the poet wishes to prove his "use"— or usefulness—by a spontaneous act of charity. The person he confronts, however, shows much less awareness than does Simon of his grim situation or of the poet's benevolent intentions. As a result, Wordsworth must struggle to evoke the response that will confirm the embodied reality of those intentions. The episode, which concludes the book, takes place during Wordsworth's first summer vacation from Cambridge, after a long day of "strenuous idleness" (377) and a night of partying (384–391):

> No living thing appeared in earth or air,
> And, save the flowing water's peaceful voice,
> Sound there was none—but, lo! an uncouth shape,
> Shown by a sudden turning of the road,
> So near that, slipping back into the shade
> Of a thick hawthorn, I could mark him well,
> Myself unseen . . .

The ensuing description of the "shape" is ghostly and gruesome enough to justify Wordsworth's initial reaction: he hides and watches. But the poet's withdrawal "into the shade" is also an act of virtual disembodiment that does nothing to mitigate the uncanniness, the other-worldly quality of the soldier's appearance. It can only intensify and prolong that eerie moment during which the figure, the road on which he appears, the moonlit hills, the whole world becomes as unreal as a dream, "a prospect in the mind." That sense of somnolent unreality, and its dependence on furtiveness, is stressed in the text of 1805 (IV, 385–395):

> Thus did I steal along that silent road,
> My body from the stillness drinking in
> A restoration like the calm of sleep,
> But sweeter far. Above, before, behind,
> Around me, all was peace and solitude;
> I looked not round, nor did the solitude
> Speak to my eye, but it was heard and felt.
> O happy state! what beauteous pictures now
> rose in harmonious imagery; they rose
> As from some distant region of my soul
> And came along like dreams . . .

In the 1850 version Wordsworth writes that he is concerned, after all, not so much with depicting a person as with presenting "a mere image" (358) of "Solitude." In this solipsistic, visionary mood, "the soul of that great Power," as it "is met / Sometimes embodied in a public road" (365–366), displaces, in effect, the soul ordinarily taken to be embodied in the human image. As in the case of the blind beggar of London and the Cumberland beggar, personality is submerged in a visionary personification that reflects the power of the appropriative imagination to assign transcendent meanings to the objects of its perception. The poet's aim is to describe a thing stripped of its mundane associations: not a soldier, but an "uncouth shape . . . clothed in military garb" (398), like a manikin.

In the soldier, then, consciousness must be inferred. A Cartesian judgment must be exercised. For the moment, the soldier is merely a "desolation, a simplicity" (401), the shell of a self: "Of stature tall" (390), "stiff, lank, and upright," "meagre" (392), "pallid, ghastly" (394–395). "Propped" up by a milestone (396), he resembles the corpse of the drowned man described in book V—"bolt upright . . . with his ghastly face, a spectre shape / Of terror" (449–451).[28] Like a ghoul, the soldier utters not words but "low muttered sounds" (404). The impression of living death continues as Wordsworth comes near (407–415):

> . . . From self-blame
> Not wholly free, I watched him thus; at length
> Subduing my heart's specious cowardice,
> I left the shady nook where I had stood
> And hailed him. Slowly from his resting-place
> He rose, and with a lean and wasted arm
> In measured gesture lifted to his head
> Returned my salutation; then resumed
> His station as before.

The gesture is mechanical, "measured" as if performed by a clock-work figure. A few lines later Wordsworth describes the soldier walking next to him: "I beheld, / With an astonishment but ill-suppressed, / His ghostly figure moving at my side" (431–433). Here, as always, Wordsworth shows his genius for choosing the right words: the indefiniteness of "figure" and "moving" implies the presence of an animated cadaver, not a man walking.

Although we have no reason to doubt that Wordsworth's "self-blame" is largely a matter of conscience, nor that his later offer of help is sincere, the method by which he aids the soldier and his feelings in doing so are curious enough to suggest that his motives are not unmixed with the simple desire to humanize the image before him and, more important, to extract some show of recognition that the poet is the man's benefactor: Wordsworth needs an expression, however slight or ambiguous, of thanks. By that expression the soldier will characterize himself in a way congruent with Wordsworth's need to demonstrate that he is a compassionate person, and the poet will feel at ease.

Wordsworth begins by asking the man's "history" (416–425):

> . . . the veteran, in reply,
> Was neither slow nor eager; but, unmoved,
> And with a quiet uncomplaining voice,
> A stately air of mild indifference,
> He told in few plain words a soldier's tale—
> That in the Tropic Islands he had served,
> Whence he had landed scarcely three weeks past;
> That on his landing he had been dismissed,
> And now was travelling towards his native home.
> This heard, I said, in pity, "Come with me."

But as they walk, Wordsworth pursues the man's tale with a relentlessness that he himself seems to think borders on the prurient (434–438):

> Nor could I, while we journeyed thus, forbear
> To turn from present hardships to the past,
> And speak of war, battle, and pestilence,
> Sprinkling this talk with questions, better spared,
> On what he might himself have seen or felt.

What is the purpose of this interrogation? On one level we sympathize with Wordsworth's compulsion to make conversation. We have all felt similarly discomfited in the presence of strangers. But why drag forth these painful reports of past hardships, of war and pestilence?

The poet is struggling, first of all, to understand this "uncouth shape" as a sensibility, a conscious presence which *has* "seen" and "felt" and thus can be understood to be responding to Wordsworth's real presence. He is trying to conjure mind in a manikin. But he is also attempting to place the soldier in the reassuring role of one who is in need, so that Wordsworth can, with confidence, assume his own role as benefactor. A parenthetical phrase like "in pity" (425) not only apprises the reader of the poet's motivations, but more firmly positions the soldier in the realm of the human, as someone *in need* of pity.

Already the poet can sense, with growing unease, the soldier's inability to play along with the scenario that Wordsworth is struggling to realize. "In all he said," reports the poet, "there was a strange half-absence, as of one / Knowing too well the importance of his theme, / But feeling it no longer" (441–444). The soldier appears ignorant of his own identity and unresponsive to the poet's, as "unmoved" by and "indifferent" to his tale as to Wordsworth's offer of help. He does not acknowledge, by tone of voice or any outward sign, that he is in fact the character in the story which Wordsworth has drawn from him, and which is now recounted in, and thus made a part of, the poet's own story—*The Prelude*. Unlike Simon Lee, he resists inclusion in the poet's tale of himself.

Consequently, Wordsworth feels vulnerable, offering unsolicited aid while the object of his charity remains aloof. The unresponsiveness of the man places the meaning of the poet's embodied self in jeopardy. Wordsworth seeks another source of reassurance (444–451):

> . . . Our discourse
> Soon ended, and together on we passed
> In silence through a wood gloomy and still.
> Up turning, then, along an open field,
> We reached a cottage. At the door I knocked,
> And earnestly to charitable care
> Commended him as a poor friendless man,
> Belated and by sickness overcome.

The soldier has now been publicly identified.

We never find out how the cottager reacted at finding the soldier deposited on his doorstep and commended to his keeping in this manner. In the 1805 version the poet makes it quite clear that there was no other choice, for in the village "all were gone to rest, the fires all out, / And every silent window to the moon / Shone with a yellow glitter. 'No one there,' / Said I, 'is waking' " (451–453). In this text Wordsworth describes the cottager as "a labourer" who dwells "behind yon wood," one who, he assures the soldier, "will not murmur should we break his rest, / And with a ready heart will give you food / And lodging for the night" (455–459).

Nothing in either this version or that of 1850, however, indicates that Wordsworth even knows the man's name. The cottager remains indoors during the poet's speech, and when the door is unbarred, no description of him ensues, no exchange of words takes place. The cottager is a vague presence throughout the episode—not a participant in the scene unfolding before his locked door, but its captive, and sympathetic, audience. That he is sympathetic is the one thing that we do know about this man and that Wordsworth can count on. He will not "murmur" at this interruption of his sleep, but will respond "with a ready heart." He is to Wordsworth's "commendation" what the "gentle Reader" is to the incident in "Simon Lee." Unprotesting, quick to enter into the feelings expressed by the poet, the cottager is the perfect "kindred Spirit," whose agreement with the poet's characterization of the soldier can be taken for granted. Quite aside from the "charitable care" he can provide, the cottager is invoked as a witness for Wordsworth's enactment of his identity.

But the poet has not yet received confirmation from the object of his care; there is more still to be witnessed (452–456):

> Assured that now the traveller would repose
> In comfort, I entreated that henceforth
> He would not linger in the public ways,
> But ask for timely furtherance and help
> Such as his state required.

Wordsworth's reproof is unmerited. We are led to wonder how this man could have approached him to ask for "timely furtherance and help" when the poet had immediately, on seeing the soldier, retreated into the shadow of the hawthorn bush. Wordsworth's entreaty is meant less to point the man a better way than to exhort him to behave in accordance with his "state," and with what Wordsworth assumes him to be: "a poor friendless man" in need of the "timely furtherance and help" that the poet offers. In his reproof Wordsworth asserts his identity as Good Samaritan at the expense of the soldier's self-containment (456–459):

> ... At this reproof,
> With the same ghastly mildness in his look,
> He said, "My trust is in the God of Heaven,
> And in the eye of him who passes me!"

The ambiguity of the last line leaves much room for speculation. The soldier seems to be saying that his wants and needs should be obvious without his having to entreat a passerby for help. But his enigmatic words can be understood in still another, more flattering sense. They admit that this "passserby" has repaid the soldier's trust without having to be asked, much like God in Heaven, for whom not even a sparrow falls to the ground unnoticed. The lines recall the final words of "The Old Cumberland Beggar": "As in the eye of Nature he has lived, / So in the eye of Nature let him die!" Here too, an equivalence is suggested between the eye of the poet and the eye of a beneficent, transcendent power.[29] The soldier is saying, in effect, that he *does* answer to what Wordsworth's "eye" has made of him.

What complicates things for Wordsworth in this case is that the soldier does not remain part of a "prospect in the mind." If the poet is to help, he must step forward, and his "visionary mind" cannot maintain its sense of bodily displacement if it is made conscious of its embodiment by the eye of another. By approaching the soldier Wordsworth jeopardizes that hermetic, imaginative mode of perception on which his spiritual identity depends. When the soldier says that his trust is in "the eye of *him who passes me,*" that spiritual identity is concretely reaffirmed, at least to the poet's satisfaction: he is the one who has passed. That Wordsworth hid at all only makes more apparent his understanding of the soldier's power to call him into the "humane world" to which Ferry says he is ordinarily so hostile,[30] and to make him accountable for the meaning of his being there. On the cottage doorstep the poet gives that account (460–468):

The cottage door was speedily unbarred,
And now the soldier touched his hat once more
With his lean hand, and in a faltering voice,
Whose tone bespake reviving interests
Till then unfelt, he thanked me; I returned
The farewell blessing of the patient man,
And so we parted. Back I cast a look,
And lingered near the door a little space,
Then sought with quiet heart my distant home.

Gone is the mechanical, clockwork response: not "a measured gesture," from "an uncouth shape," but a *"patient* man," who *"touched* his hat . . . with his lean hand." The shape is finally invested with a personality, with will and sensibility. His voice falters, betraying emotion, and his "tone" of voice suggests "reviving interests / Till then unfelt." Though the soldier himself does not say so, Wordsworth can assume that the man is interested in all that he was before indifferent to—himself, his past, his fate, and his benefactor.

The ambiguity and indirectness of Wordsworth's description of the soldier's replies make it clear that what is important for the poet is not *what* the man says, but *that* he can now be understood to feel and perceive, to *be there* for Wordsworth in the manner he has anticipated. I suspect that this is the reason for the poet's otherwise disquieting final line, "Then sought with quiet heart my distant home." Edward Bostetter, in *The Romantic Ventriloquists,* spoke for many readers when he expressed his uneasiness with this bland assurance of spiritual tranquility. It comes as a shock, he wrote, because "quiet" is "simply an inadequate and inhibiting word," appearing at the end of such an episode: "The turmoil aroused by the tale is not resolved or reconciled dramatically into a higher serenity, as in a tragedy, but simply *pronounced* resolved."[31]

In this sense, the last line matches perfectly the rhetorical tone of Wordsworth's "commendation." For it is not the turmoil aroused by the man's plight that is here resolved, but the turmoil aroused by his unresponsiveness to Wordsworth's overtures of assistance. As in "Simon Lee," the poet is more moved by his having done the right thing than by the sufferings of his beneficiary. Wordsworth's "quiet heart" is a sign that his anxiety over misinterpreted intentions has been quelled. Now that thanks is given, his identity is confirmed. Like Jacob wrestling with his angel, Wordsworth has struggled with this ghost, making it familiar by obtaining its blessing and, in so doing, making his idea of himself a reality.

Being and Doing: The Poet in the "Preface"

It is not my intention to belittle Wordsworth by drawing attention to his uncertainties in confrontations or to the ways he seeks to alleviate his anxieties over self-representation by various forms of manipulation. Certainly, these tendencies are immaterial to any assessment of his stature as a poet. But these troubling indications of self-doubt are important to our understanding of how Wordsworth conceived himself as both a visionary and a poet, a *"spirit* singled out" and a *public* man.

It is not a question of what Wordsworth does in confrontations, or of what we would have him do—he does, in each case, the right thing: he helps those who need his help. It is more a question of why and how—what motivates his actions, how he feels in performing them, and what effects they, and the responses they evoke, have on his self-understanding. In all of Wordsworth's confrontations two demons are laid to rest: the inhumanity and strangeness of the Other (which is the price exacted by visionary power) and Wordsworth's own sense of insubstantiality, his uncertainty about motives and dispositions that, lacking embodiment for another, must otherwise go unrecognized and unconfirmed.

If Wordsworth's exchanges with others often seem cryptic, ambiguous, slightly beside the point, or simply insensitive, it may be because for him the point of confrontation is to find self-assurance in a hostile world. In the meeting with the discharged soldier, as in the encounter with Simon Lee, it is not enough that Wordsworth act benevolently to be convinced of his benevolence. The act must be acknowledged by its object and witnessed by an audience before its "agent" can be sure of having manifested himself correctly. We feel uneasy at Wordsworth's uneasiness, his initial retreat and hidden watching, his persistent questions, "better spared," his commendation of the man on the cottage doorstep: all these taken together suggest that the poet is anxious above all to control a situation in which his inmost identity is exposed, or rather, proposed.

In general, Wordsworth finds it difficult to take his place in the world unless and until he has made it habitable on his own terms. Comments in the 1815 *Essay, Supplementary to the Preface* of his collected works suggest that, by the age of forty-five, Wordsworth was satisfied that he had found, or rather, made such a place for himself. After reviewing the rise and fall of writers' reputations over the previous four centuries, he concludes that "every author, as far as he is great and at the same time *original*, has had the task of *creating* the taste by which he is to be enjoyed: so has it been, so will it continue to be" (III, 80). And he adds, "As far as concerns myself, I have cause to be satisfied. The love, the admiration, the indifference, the slight, the aversion, and even the contempt, with which these poems have been received ... must all, if I think consistently, be received as pledges and tokens, bearing the same general impression, though widely different in value;—they are all proofs that for the present time I have not laboured in vain; and afford assurances, more or less authentic, that the products of my industry will endure" (III, 80).

For Wordsworth, as demonstrated in "Expostulation and Reply," even negative notice is better than none. But the negativity, the "indifference, the slight, the aversion, and . . . contempt" made Wordsworth anxious to differentiate and mold his audiences. Ultimately, he was to appeal to the "People," a frank metaphysical idealization, an audience "philosophically characterised," rather than to the "Public," which comprised real persons, for a vindication of his poetic identity. How does poetry survive, he asks, but through the "People"?

> The voice that issues from this Spirit, is that Vox Populi which the Deity inspires. Foolish must he be who can mistake for this a local acclamation, or a transitory outcry—transitory though it be for years, local though from a Nation. Still more lamentable is his error who can believe that there is any thing of divine infallibility in the clamour of that small though loud portion of the community, ever governed by factitious influence, which, under the name of the Public, passes itself, upon the unthinking, for the People. Towards the Public, the Writer hopes that he feels as much deference as it is entitled to: but to the People, philosophically characterised, and to the embodied spirit of their knowledge . . . his devout respect, his reverence, is due. (III, 84)

As Patrick Crutwell has observed, Wordsworth "must have an audience but must have it on his own terms only": the "People" was "a dream-public—the sort of public that many a self-conscious, minority writer has dreamed of—whose taste was, miraculously, both unlettered and correct."[32]

The need to transform his audience reflects Wordsworth's broader need, expressed in his handling of confrontations, to exert control over the circumstances surrounding his encounters with others. *The Prelude* itself, conceived as a way of presenting to the reader the credentials of the philosopher-poet who had conceived the epic *Recluse;* the "Advertisement" to the 1798 edition of *Lyrical Ballads;* the extensive notes in later editions; Wordsworth's scene-setting titles and subtitles—all indicate uncertainty as to how his poetic performances, his self-embodiment in language, will be received. They surround the poetry like a magnetic field enveloping an alien planet, reorienting, or disorienting, his readers' compasses.

The "Preface" to the 1800 edition of *Lyrical Ballads* represents an early stage in Wordsworth's long journey toward the creation of his ideal audience, that "embodied spirit" of the Deity which, by 1815, he had apparently managed to internalize, and in the presence of which, gradually, he had come to establish a sense of his identity independent of what "the Public" made of it. Dorothy, as will become apparent, had no small part in these developments, providing almost the sole encouragement to Wordsworth during the bleak years immediately following his revolutionary involvements. It was she, the literal "embodiment" of his idealized audience, who, he later wrote, "preserved me still / A Poet" (*Prelude*, XI, 346–347).

Indeed, one way to understand Wordsworth's motivations in writing the "Preface" is to recall that he had no one except Dorothy, and of course Coleridge, to articulate for him, as he had for the Cumberland beggar, his use or purpose as a part of nature. The very line, "Deem not this man useless!" is echoed in the verse-essay "On Man, On Nature, and On Human Life" written in 1798, just before the first edition of *Lyrical Ballads* appeared and just as Wordsworth was about to begin work on *The Prelude*.[33] There, after describing his high aims for the long philosophical poem he had but vaguely conceived at this point, and invoking the "prophetic Spirit" to descend and bestow "A gift of genuine insight," Wordsworth adds (*Poetical Works*, V, 93–99),

> ... And if with this
> I mix more lowly matter; with the thing
> Contemplated, describe the Mind and Man
> Contemplating; and who, and what he was—
> The transitory Being that beheld
> This Vision; when and where, and how he lived;—
> Be not this labour useless.

"You look upon your Mother Earth / As if she for no purpose bore you": the "Preface" is another, more extended reply to the Matthews of this world. Nature *has* a purpose for this "transitory Being," Wordsworth is convinced, though he is not sure that others will read it right. To make that purpose understood, to explain, qualify, reinterpret the "label" he wears, to make others see him as the poet he claims to be and not, as on the shores of Windermere, someone "craz'd in brain," he must answer suspicions about his performance as a poet. He must "advance / To give and take a greeting" that will prove he is not only conscious of what the role demands but also conscious of what repudiating it means. Unlike the blind beggar of London, Wordsworth refuses to be victimized by the audience to which he turns for sustenance. He will make the self real on his terms, and make others accept those terms, by drawing up a new contract with his reader.

> It is supposed, that by the act of writing in verse an Author makes a formal engagement that he will gratify certain known habits of association; that he not only thus apprises the Reader that certain classes of ideas and expressions will be found in his book, but that others will be carefully excluded. This exponent or symbol held forth by metrical language must in different eras of literature have excited very different expectations . . . I will not take upon me to determine the exact import of the promise which, by the act of writing in verse, an Author in the present day makes to his Reader: but I am certain it will appear to many persons that I have not fulfilled the terms of an engagement thus voluntarily contracted. I hope therefore the Reader will not censure me, if I attempt to state *what I have proposed to myself to perform,* and also, (as far as the limits of a preface will permit) to explain some of the chief *reasons* which have determined me in the choice of *my purpose* . . . that I myself may be protected from the most dishonourable accusation which can be brought against an Author, namely, that of an indolence which prevents him from endeavouring to ascertain what is his duty, or, when his duty is ascertained, prevents him from performing it.   (I, 122: italics added)

What is noteworthy about this famous passage from the 1800 "Preface" is that Wordsworth changes what he admits to be, traditionally, an understood "engagement" between the poet and the reader into a new contract between the poet and himself—something "I have proposed *to myself* to perform." He then offers to let his audience in on this private agreement and the "reasons" and "purpose" behind it. In this way the reader will know how to interpret the poet's performance and what the new terms of this contract are. The reader will also in some way understand that, if the poetry is to succeed as poetry under these new terms, he or she must sacrifice some of his or her independence as a person possessed of expectations that are not shaped by the poet himself: the reader will have to adopt the poet's concept of poetry. In the "Preface" Wordsworth attempts to transform his audience from "the Public" into "the People," from a group of strangers into an intimate circle of "kindred Spirits."

First and foremost, Wordsworth, like Gray's elegist before him, wants us to understand his intentions: the purpose behind the personae, the mind behind the masks, the life behind the lines. "The poems in these volumes," he writes, "will be found distinguished at least by one mark of difference" from more meretricious works that depend on "poetic diction" for effect: "each of them has a worthy *purpose*" (I, 124). "My descriptions of such objects as strongly excite [my] feelings, will be found to carry along with them a *purpose*" (I, 126). "I proposed to myself to imitate, and, as far as is possible, to adopt the very language of men" (I, 130). "I shall request the Reader's permission to apprize him of a few circumstances relating to their *style,* in order, among other reasons, that I may not be censured for not having performed what I never attempted" (I, 130). "Purpose," "attempted"—and of course "censure" and "perform": we hear ringing through the "Preface" the Prufrockian refrain, "That is not what I meant at all; / That is not it, at all."

It is easy enough to understand Wordsworth's nervousness about the clarity of his intentions when we consider that in order "to imitate, and, as far as is possible, to adopt the very language of men," or "to bring [his] language near to the language of men," even if he fits it to "metrical arrangement" (I, 130, 132), the poet must repudiate many of those hallmarks of the profession by which he has always identified himself as a poet. Formerly, one had practiced the use of certain tools and techniques, like any professional aspiring to be recognized as such. Wordsworth himself learned his craft, like his predecessors and contemporaries, by zealous imitation of the best models, notably Spenser and Milton, and there is considerable uncertainty as to whether he achieved as rustic, natural, and "real" a diction as he professed to seek.[34] Nonetheless, his blanket condemnation of traditional "poetic diction" (I, 130) and structure, of the artificial "family language" (1850; I, 131) by which poets aroused in their readers certain formal expectations, is strikingly new. It places the "Preface"— however tame it may appear to us and however conventional, in fact, the poems it introduces—at the very forefront of the line of great nineteenth-century manifestos, a forerunner of the coming avant-garde and its scandals. For Wordsworth's aim is not, like his predecessors', to meet the public's expectations, or to vindicate his performance by appeal to conventional canons of taste, but to free himself of such trammels, to *consciously* create the taste that his poems will satisfy.

Wordsworth's aversion to such tools of the trade as "poetic diction" and conventional language stems in large measure from his aversion to the idea of the poet as a "professional," one who "professes" to play an understood part with respect to others. As he makes clear in the 1850 edition of the "Preface," the poet cannot be expected to behave in accordance with any such predetermined public role. In fact, he should not be defined in terms of behavior or performance at all: "What is a Poet? To whom does he address himself? And what language is to be expected from him?—He is a man speaking to men: a man, it is true, endowed with more lively sensibility, more enthusiasm and tenderness, who has a greater knowledge of human nature, and a more comprehensive soul, than are supposed to be common among mankind: a man pleased with his own passions and volitions, and who rejoices more than other men in the spirit of life that is in him" (I, 138).

Here, the author has shifted the grounds of an argument about poetics from the topic of poetry (an activity, and thus open to judgment) to the topic of the poet's spiritual or mental faculties (a state of mind, open not to judgment, but only to empathy or dispathy). He is de-emphasizing the poet's role as a writer in favor of the poet's role as a sensibility. The major points made here are anticipated by Gray. Thus, Gray's "mute, inglorious Milton" would qualify, in Wordsworth's definition, as a poet, and so would the speaker of the "Elegy" himself, but not because of his written performance. The difference between the poet and other people is internal, not external, something felt, not something done. He is a "man speaking to men," true, but as Wordsworth has just indicated by rejecting meter as the point of distinction between poetry and prose (I, 132), it is not the poet's speech that particularly distinguishes him. Moreover, this something felt within is quantitatively, not qualitatively, distinctive. The poet is "more" lively, "more" enthusiastic and tender, has a "greater" knowledge of human nature, and a "more comprehensive soul." The poet is not a different kind of man from his fellows, however different in race, station, training, or profession: he is simply "more" of one. Further on, Wordsworth states as much. "Among the qualities enumerated as principally conducing to form a Poet, is implied nothing differing in kind from other men, but only in degree" (I, 142).

Thus the "true" self in each of us, that point at which we all "stand single" is, paradoxically, identical, and lies deeper than the differentiation of persons that results from the adoption of social roles, a point Wordsworth is at pains to make clear in the 1850 edition: "The Poet writes under one restriction only, namely, the necessity of giving immediate pleasure to a human Being possessed of that information which may be expected from him, not as a lawyer, a physician, a mariner, an astronomer, or a natural philosopher, but as a Man" (1850; I, 139). "Immediate pleasure" refers to an enjoyment that is not mediated by strictly personal interests extrinsic to the "Man" within, to "this mind *of ours.*" We are identical on the level of undifferentiated consciousness in a shared experience—the poem—and the poet is he who would usher us into this universal fellowship of "human Being." Since it is the poet who defines the standards by which his performance is to be judged, questions of judgment or of poetic performance become moot. The burden of *being* judged, in fact, shifts to the reader—*do* we, *can* we empathize? If these do not seem like poems to me, perhaps it indicates not the poet's failure to write poetry but my own failure as a "Man."

In Wordsworth's view we must, as readers, put off our proper selves, which stand and are recognized in the world, as mariners, lawyers, astronomers, or professors of English, and become disembodied minds, like the poet himself. Indeed, my consciousness of my proper self as something situated in the world does become muted, if not altogether obliterated, as I read, and in the same way the identity of the poet may evaporate in imaginative contemplation of his subject: "So that it will be the wish of the Poet to bring his feelings near to those of the persons whose feelings he describes, nay, for short spaces of time, perhaps, to let himself slip into an entire delusion, and even confound and identify his own feelings with theirs" (I, 138).

To "throw his voice," as it were, into such creations as the mad mother of "Her Eyes Are Wild" or the loquacious narrator of "The Thorn" is perhaps as close as Wordsworth can come to the condition of Keats's "camelion Poet," a thing of "no self," continually going out into others' identities by a sort of transmigration of soul. And it is probably as close as Wordsworth wants to come. We do him a disservice by comparing him in this respect with Keats's or Coleridge's idea of the poet, because so very often Wordsworth turns to face, address, and prepare the audience he would play for. He may do this within the poem itself (as in "Simon Lee" or "Michael"), or in prefatory remarks or subtitles describing the situation in which the reader is to imagine the lines being spoken (as in "Lines, Left upon the Seat of a Yew Tree which Stands near the Lake of Esthwaite, on a Desolate Part of the Shore, Commanding a Beautiful Prospect"), or in extended notes on the assumed character of the narrator (as in "The Thorn").

Wordsworth is uncomfortable with the idea of an audience completely beyond his power to manipulate outside the boundaries of his persona. The ambiguity of identity inherent in Keats's conception of the poet would not exhilarate but terrify him. Although Wordsworth can "impersonate" characters like the credulous old sea captain of "The Thorn," he is careful to "show himself in the wings," as it were, to make sure that this role is recognized as such and that his proper self is understood to be playacting. He is careful to spell out, outside the text, what he *means* by this self-display. It is precisely to forestall criticisms like Coleridge's in the *Biographia Literaria*[35] that the poet includes a few words in the "Advertisement" to the first edition of the *Lyrical Ballads,* in 1798, concerning "The Thorn": "The poem of the Thorn, as the reader will soon discover, is not supposed to be spoken in the author's own person: the character of the loquacious narrator will sufficiently shew itself in the course of the story" (I, 117).

If so, why explain it here? Nor was this enough. In notes to subsequent editions of the poem Wordsworth describes the background of the supposed speaker, "captain of a small trading vessel," "past the middle-age of life," "retired upon an annuity . . . to some village or country town of which he was not a native"[36] All this minutely fitted machinery is meant to provide a dramatic context for the speaker so that we can know what to expect of him as a certain kind of character, and not as a poet. Wordsworth, furthermore, tells us what to expect of the poet himself as creator of this character: *"It appeared to me proper* to select a character like this to exhibit . . ."; *"It was my wish* in this poem to show . . ."; *"I had two objects to attain . . ."; It seemed to me* that this might be done by . . ."; *"I hoped* that . . . it would appear . . ."[37] Again and again Wordsworth tells us what he meant by these performances, what we should expect of him here, how we must react if the poem is to work properly. This is hardly the mark of a protean or "camelion" poet, one who is everywhere embodied in his creations but whose "intentions" are nowhere so precisely—or so anxiously—articulated.

"In order entirely to enjoy the Poetry which I am recommending," Wordsworth writes in the "Preface," "it would be necessary to give up much of what is ordinarily enjoyed" (I, 156). And he enjoins us to give it up. If Wordsworth's poetry does not please his audience in the "ordinary" way, the fault lies not with the poetry, nor with the poet, but with the "ordinary" expectations of what is or should be enjoyable. Though he denies that his decision to write a preface was "principally influenced by the selfish and foolish hope of *reasoning* [the reader] into an approbation of these particular Poems" (I, 120), that is precisely what Wordsworth tries to do. As in the encounters depicted in his poetry, where Wordsworth comes face to face with the possibility that his intentions may be "misread," he attempts to reeducate his "reader," the person he confronts or before whom he enacts his sense of himself. He will preempt the Other's responses to his presence, appropriate the Other in his own scenario, or characterize the Other in such a way as to assure himself that he is recognized properly. The boy who gropes to feel himself touching a wall understands that the self can be made real only in the world. So does the man, whatever his professions of spiritual strength. But the man also understands that, in the world, the self runs the risk of being made false.

From Partisan to Poet: The Road to "Tintern Abbey"

The "Preface" was the product of a lifetime of hesitation and self-doubt, the literalizing of Wordsworth's deepest anxieties of being "misread" by a world of strangers. It was an afterthought necessitated by the burst of originality, the almost reckless disregard for the prevailing canons of taste, that was *Lyrical Ballads.* But how did he arrive at this, his most radical and challenging poetical self-embodiment, and particularly, at the doctrines of "wise passiveness" and spontaneity, the love of solitude and what he calls in "Tintern Abbey" that "sense sublime / Of something far more deeply interfused" (95–96) which the *Ballads* convey with almost missionary zeal? Having observed Wordsworth's discomfort with his audiences, both fictional and real, we are now in a better position to trace the development of his sense of poetic identity from his Cambridge years, through the publication of the *Ballads* and the "Preface," to the composition of the "Intimations" ode, and to understand the relation of that sense of identity to Wordsworth's sense of his destined role in society. This period spans the crisis that precipitated his decision to become a poet—his experiences with the French Revolution—and the gradual loss of visionary powers that is the theme of "Tintern Abbey" and "Resolution and Independence."

Wordsworth's natural sensitivity to others' opinions was exacerbated at a serious turning point in his life, at that precarious age when, as a young adult, he had first posed for himself the questions he was later to pose for the Leech-gatherer in "Resolution and Independence": "How is it you live? and what is it you do?" The poet was about to embrace a life among things and others and to establish himself in the continuum of history. "Shall I ever have a name?" he confided to his notebook in 1788.[38] In the three years following Wordsworth's encounter with the soldier on the lonely Windermere road, the emotional crisis precipitated by his experiences during the Revolution heightened the diffident Cambridge boy's uncertainties over self-embodiment in committed expressions of intent and purpose, pity and compassion, love and loyalty. Of this time, he writes (*Prelude*, XI, 105–109),

> O pleasant exercise of hope and joy!
> For mighty were the auxiliars which then stood
> Upon our side, we who were strong in love!
> Bliss was it in that dawn to be alive,
> But to be young was very Heaven!

Wordsworth was "an active partisan" (XI, 153) of the Revolution. He was "led to take an eager part / In arguments of civil polity" (XI, 77–78) and, as Mary Moorman points out, he admired the Republican cavalry officer, Michel Beaupuy, precisely because the man was *acting* on his convictions.[39] Beaupuy was "one whom circumstance / Hath called upon to embody his deep sense / In action, give it outwardly a shape, / And that of benediction, to the world" (IX, 400–403). Indeed, Wordsworth looked upon the earth as his "inheritance, new-fallen," and relished the prospect of "mould[ing] it and remould[ing] . . . half pleased with things that are amiss, / 'Twill be such joy to see them disappear" (XI, 146, 150–152). "Now was it," he writes (XI, 136–144),

> that *both* found, the meek and lofty
> Did both find helpers to their hearts' desire,
> And stuff at hand, plastic as they could wish,—
> Were called upon to exercise their skill,
> Not in Utopia,—subterranean fields,—
> Or some secreted island, Heaven knows where!
> But in the very world, which is the world
> Of all of us,—the place where, in the end,
> We find our happiness, or not at all!

The place, too, where we find our real self.

It was the English declaration of war on revolutionary France that first blighted this inheritance, alienating Wordsworth from his fellow countrymen.[40] "Not in my single self alone, I found / But in the minds of all ingenuous youth, / Change and subversion from that hour," he writes (X, 268–299):

. . . No shock
Given to my moral nature had I known
Down to that very moment; neither lapse
Nor turn of sentiment that might be named
A revolution, save at this one time;
. . . . .
. . . I rejoiced,
Yea, afterwards—truth most painful to record!—
Exulted, in the triumph of my soul,
When Englishmen by thousands were o'erthrown,
Left without glory on the field, or driven,
Brave hearts! to shameful flight. It was a grief,—
Grief call it not, 'twas anything but that,—
A conflict of sensations without name,
Of which *he* only, who may love the sight
Of a village steeple, as I do, can judge,
When, in the congregation bending all
To their great Father, prayers were offered up,
Or praises for our country's victories;
And, 'mid the simple worshippers, perchance
I only, like an uninvited guest
Whom no one owned, sate silent, shall I add,
Fed on the day of vengeance yet to come.

With the declaration of war, Wordsworth's dormant but long-standing self-doubts were brought to a crisis. For the first time since he had become involved in the great debate over the Revolution, he felt the crushing weight of nation and class on the heart's *sanctum sanctorum.* "Like an uninvited guest," he understands himself to be unowned, excluded and unrecognized among his own people, who are in this passage represented not as an abstract populace, not as "the People," but as neighbors and fellow congregants. Thus was Wordsworth's identification with his native land placed in opposition to all he had embraced as an "active Partisan."

In books X and XI of *The Prelude,* as the poet describes his growing doubts about the Revolution, it becomes clear that what he was suffering was not only an emotional crisis but a crisis of profession, in the most literal sense. "Before my time," he wrote, "like other youths" prompted by "what there is best in individual man" (XI, 78–83), Wordsworth had taken his stand and wagered his identity on the outcome of history. He had assumed that the aspirations of a free and freedom-loving England would naturally coincide with those of France, in whose "People," he writes, "was my trust" (XI, 11). Now, among Englishmen who had declared their enmity with France, he felt his commitment as a son of Liberty challenged by his allegiances as a son of Albion. One or the other of these identities would have to be suppressed, and at first it was the defender of France.[41]

Events had cast Wordsworth's public professions of revolutionary sympathy in a new light: to speak now for France was to become a traitor to his country. Yet not to speak was to betray the true self which, alone in the crowd, looked forward to the "day of vengeance" that would vindicate it. How easily that self, once expressed, had become ensnared by circumstances, torn away from itself by what others do and say, feel and express! "Oh! much have they to account for, who could tear, / By violence, at one decisive rent, / From the best youth in England their dear pride, / Their joy, in England" (X, 300–302), which is to say, their pride and joy in being English.

But history was to give another turn to the screw: the Reign of Terror fed on the hysteria incited by the newly declared war (X, 331–338):

> In France, the men, who, for their desperate ends,
> Had plucked up mercy by the roots, were glad
> Of this new enemy. Tyrants, strong before
> In wicked pleas, were strong as demons now;
> And thus, on every side beset with foes,
> The goaded land waxed mad; the crimes of few
> Spread into madness of the many; blasts
> From hell came sanctified like airs from heaven.

"Domestic carnage now filled the whole year / With feast days," writes Wordsworth. "Head after head, and never heads enough / For those that bade them fall" (356–357, 362–363).

The Terror strained Wordsworth's loyalties almost to the breaking point. His vivid nightmares at this time, movingly described in book X, show that the young man who had given himself up to the course of events now felt, not simply mistaken in his beliefs, but guilty in his having voiced them. He feels more than horror and revulsion at the crimes of Robespierre; he feels responsibility, as one who pled for the cause (X, 397–415):

> Most melancholy at that time, O Friend!
> Were my day-thoughts,—my nights were miserable;
> Through months, through years, long after the last beat
> Of those atrocities, the hour of sleep

To me came rarely charged with natural gifts,
Such ghastly visions had I of despair
And tyranny, and implements of death;
And innocent victims sinking under fear,
And momentary hope, and worn-out prayer,
Each in his separate cell, or penned in crowds
For sacrifice, and struggling with forced mirth
And levity in dungeons, where the dust
Was laid with tears. Then suddenly the scene
Changed, and the unbroken dream entangled me
In long orations, which I strove to plead
Before unjust tribunals,—with a voice
Labouring, a brain confounded, and a sense,
Death-like, of teacherous desertion, felt
In the last place of refuge—my own soul.

The "treacherous desertion" Wordsworth feels in his soul is the desertion of self-certainty. His heart is simply not in these pleas and orations; they are mere sophistries. The young man's zeal for "what there is best in individual man" has betrayed him into commitments that, because of circumstances beyond his control, have had unintended effects, self-contradicting results.

France's invasion of Belgium, Italy, and other neighboring countries in 1793–1794 and during the years following drove Wordsworth, at last and completely, into the moral and emotional desert of rationalization. In order to convince himself of a commitment he felt increasingly unsure of, Wordsworth again gave voice to it, embracing with renewed zeal his former role of "active partisan." But now, ironically, the feelings that had first informed his hopes and loyalties had withered, leaving only the partisan's shell. It was now as a defender of France rather than as a patriot of England that Wordsworth felt his public persona becoming less and less representative of his true feelings. Once more, as during the years of the Terror, he struggled not just with disappointment, but against shame, the growing awareness that he had been put in a false position. In the French invasions, he read the "doom" of liberty (XI, 211–222),

With anger vexed, with disappointment sore,
But not dismayed, nor taking to the shame
Of a false prophet. While resentment rose
Striving to hide, what nought could heal, the wounds
Of mortified presumption, I adhered
More firmly to old tenets, and, to prove

Their temper, strained them more; and thus, in heat
Of contest, did opinions every day
Grow into consequence, till round my mind
They clung, as if they were its life, nay more,
The very being of the immortal soul.

The "heat of contest" can relieve, momentarily, "the shame / Of a false prophet." The opinions expressed in such debates take on a life of their own, becoming in effect a defensive mask to which Wordsworth clings for his sanity. Here is a portrait of Blake's "negation," the unalterable pose of the terrified public man, which is mistaken for "the very being of the immortal soul." One feels Wordsworth's desperation to retain the integrity and continuity of his identity in the eyes of others, those eyes through which he viewed himself, perhaps for the first time in his adult life, as something real. He had made himself a place in the world. To abandon it now was to make of the self a phantasm.

Wordsworth's attempts at rationalization must not be dismissed simply as tokens of hypocrisy or cowardice or vanity. In the role of "prophet" and "partisan" he had indeed committed his mind and "immortal soul" to something material, and boldly defined. He had entered history, had made himself responsible for his opinions and activities. Now, trapped by events, he would *have* to respond, though his "reasonings," he says, were "false" (XI, 289–305),

From their beginnings, inasmuch as drawn
Out of a heart that had been turned aside
From Nature's way by outward accidents,
And which was thus confounded, more and more,
Misguided and misguiding. So I fared,
Dragging all precepts, judgments, maxims, creeds,
Like culprits to the bar; calling the mind,
Suspiciously, to establish in plain day
Her titles and her honours; now believing,
Now disbelieving; endlessly perplexed
With impulse, motive, right and wrong, the ground
Of obligation, what the rule and whence
The sanction; till, demanding formal *proof,*
And seeking it in every thing, I lost
All feeling of conviction, and, in fine,
Sick, wearied out with contrarieties,
Yielded up moral questions in despair.

"Precepts," "maxims," "creeds," "impulse, motive, right and wrong," "obligation," "sanction,": this is, indeed, the vocabulary of "moral questions," matters referring, ultimately, to the relationship between who we are and what we do. One can detect the inchoate poet of spontaneity here, recoiling from this, "the soul's last and lowest ebb" (307), spurning those "lordly attributes / Of will and choice" that have led him into a paralyzing labyrinth of self-doubt. They have become "but a mockery of a Being / Who hath in no concerns of his a test / Of good and evil" (311–313), and who, "to acknowledged law rebellious, still, / As selfish passion urged, would act amiss; / The dupe of folly, or the slave of crime" (318–320).

The problem with consciously assuming the burden of being in the world is that, in Keats's words, "things cannot to the will be settled." If we act at all, we embrace things and their waywardness and inevitably open ourselves to the possibility of having acted amiss. And if we have acted self-consciously, with forethought, we run the risk of seeing our purposes perverted, our commitments overturned, our professions of loyalty become our indictments. The meaning of one's identity is indeed taken away from one as it is embodied: the self in the world is made false, to the point where the true self cannot be recognized for what it is.

The Revolution was not the only object of Wordsworth's devotion during these years. As Paul Sheats observes, the bleak poems of the Racedown period, which reflect the most intense relapse of Wordsworth's emotional crisis following the outbreak of hostilities between England and France, reveal the deeper anguish he must have suffered over his forced abandonment of his mistress, Annette Valon, and his illegitimate daughter, Caroline, who were awaiting his return to Orleans. Noting the recurring patterns of guilt and fear, centering on a crime toward a wife or lover, that appear in "Guilt and Sorrow" and later Racedown poems, Sheats contends that "Wordsworth began to regard Annette with fear and guilt in 1795," and suffered "the anguish of a man who is trapped, by forces he had trusted, into betraying and destroying what he loved."[42]

Though a victim of circumstances, Wordsworth could not throw off the weight of guilt. He had acted willingly, purposefully, and his actions had resulted in a dereliction of duty he both was and was not responsible for. By 1795 Wordsworth's involvement in the life of "sense and outward things" had become insupportable. It was not what he had *meant* it to be.

From the faces of his accusers—the unjust tribunals, the fellow congregants, the compatriots, the haunting visages of the abandoned wife or lover in the Racedown poems, all of whom hold up to him the image of a self that can no longer be integrated with his earliest hopes, expectations, and intentions—Wordsworth flees to the one person who can confirm for him the image of the true self he had meant, all along, to make real. It is she who will tell him the "name" of his profession, his "office upon earth" (XI, 333–347):

> . . . Then it was—
> Thanks to the bounteous Giver of all good!—
> That the beloved Sister in whose sight
> Those days were passed, now speaking in a voice
> Of sudden admonition—like a brook
> That did but *cross* a lonely road, and now
> Seen, heard, and felt, and caught at every turn,
> Companion never lost through many a league—
> Maintained for me a saving intercourse
> With my true self; for, though bedimmed and changed
> Both as a clouded and a waning moon,
> She whispered still that brightness would return,
> She, in the midst of all, preserved me still
> A Poet, made me seek beneath that name,
> And that alone, my office upon earth.

Formerly a "Poet only to myself, to man / Useless" (X, 233–234), Wordsworth now shares his aspirations with a person as understanding of his true self as any on earth. Like the moon obscured by clouds, the true Wordsworth had not been recognized—least of all, perhaps, by himself. Now he finds his "purpose," the meaning of his existence, becoming clearer in Dorothy's sight.

In *The Prelude* the "Poet" dismisses the "active partisan" as an unnatural, forced, and self-conscious misrepresentation of the true self: it turned out to be not what he had meant it to be because it had never been what he *was meant* to be. Wordsworth's fated identity is to be found only by appealing to an intention higher than the merely personal, though only another person, and only one in particular, Dorothy, can confirm its reality. What Wordsworth feels he was meant to be has its source in "Nature's self" (349), from which his "heart . . . had been turned aside . . . by outward accidents" (290–291). But She will make him whole again only "by all varieties of human love / Assisted" (XI, 350–351).

In 1795 what Wordsworth found most healing in the "Soul of Nature" (XII, 93, 102) was its majestic and sublime "counterpoise" to the "spirit of evil" in humankind. That countervailing power helped maintain for him "a secret happiness" (XIII, 41–43) in a place safe from outwardness, free of the insupportable pain that arose from "outward accidents" (XII, 24–34):

And you, ye groves, whose ministry it is
To interpose the covert of your shades,
Even as a sleep, between the heart of man
And outward troubles, between man himself,
Not seldom, and his own uneasy heart:
Oh! that I had a music and a voice
Harmonious as your own, that I might tell
What ye have done for me. The morning shines,
Nor heedeth Man's perverseness; Spring returns,—
I saw the Spring return, and could rejoice,
In common with the children of her love.

Wordsworth reaches back to his boyhood dream-states in the presence of unpeopled Nature, alone on the verge of the abyss of idealism, and forgets his own "uneasy heart" (XII, 93–100):

O Soul of Nature! excellent and fair!
That didst rejoice with me, with whom I, too,
Rejoiced through early youth, before the winds
And roaring waters, and in lights and shades
That marched and countermarched about the hills
I daily waited, now all eye and now
All ear . . .

It is to those solipsistic "visitings of imaginative power" (XII, 203) that Wordsworth turns, those times when he "in Nature's presence stood, as now . . . / A sensitive being, a *creative* soul" (XII, 206–207). In *The Prelude* Wordsworth attempts not only to discover the meanings of those "visitings" but to establish the temporal continuity of the immaterial self over the course of a lifetime in which it had betrayed itself into becoming a thing in the world of things, subject to the judgments of history, and of others. The self that is true does not, and has never, committed itself to a human place and time, nor to the dictates of reason or judgment, those faculties that generally inform purposeful action. Instead, the true self is to be identified with the mind that, looking back at certain "spots of time," can exult at the imaginative and spontaneous mastery over the senses demonstrated therein (XII, 208–223):

> There are in our existence spots of time,
> That with distinct preeminence retain
> A renovating virtue, whence, depressed
> By false opinion and contentious thought,
> Or aught of heavier or more deadly weight,
> In trivial occupations, and the round
> Of ordinary intercourse, our minds
> Are nourished and invisibly repaired;
> A virtue, by which pleasure is enhanced,
> That penetrates, enables us to mount,
> When high, more high, and lifts us up when fallen.
> This efficacious spirit chiefly lurks
> Among those passages of life that give
> Profoundest knowledge to what point, and how,
> The mind is lord and master—outward sense
> The obedient servant of her will.

Such "spots of time" are the stones in the streambed of *The Prelude* along which the true self warily steps its way back through the tumult of history, of "false opinions and contentious thought," and much "of heavier or more deadly weight." They are, invariably, solipsistic in structure, that is, in each of them the boy or the young man who isolates himself from others—rowing a stolen boat on a moonlit lake, skating away from his playfellows, wandering away from his adult guide during a ride, or losing the trail along the Simplon Pass—displaces his mind's own "powers" or "motions" or "visionary dreariness" into his surroundings, obliterating the embodied boundaries between self and world and appropriating that world as the contents of his own dream.

In turning to Nature the poet turns, in the most fundamental sense, to the self as mind, not embodied in the world and as if for others, but embodying the world and others in it. In turning to Dorothy, however, Wordsworth turns to the only person who is intimate enough with that true self to confirm and encourage its expression as a Poet, to give it a sense of its own reality as concrete and convincing as that momentarily achieved by the "active partisan" of former years.[43] In short, the turn toward Nature and away from others represented a groping for essence, and the turn toward

Dorothy, and later, Coleridge, a compensatory groping for presence. However independent and withdrawn the "egotistical sublime," it could not subsist indefinitely without assurances of its reality—without them the poet would face the terrors of the interior abyss, what David Perkins has called the "nightmare subjectivism" of Wordsworth's Racedown years.[44] Throughout the dark period of this waking nightmare it was Dorothy who kept Wordsworth in touch with the real world, making it once more habitable for the true self. By 1798 Wordsworth was prepared to reenter that world, but only conditionally: he would be the poet he had always *been meant* to be, not the poet others expected him to be.

The *Lyrical Ballads* of 1798, with the "Advertisement" of the poet's intentions, was the result. Here, as the later "Preface" of 1800 asserts, was a concerted attempt to break with the conventional orthodoxies of decorum, the picturesque, the "family language" and "poetic diction" by which poets had, up to then, been identified. Throughout the *Ballads,* Wordsworth betrays his divided need to be his own, natural man and yet to seek assurances that he *is* the man he would be. Although the "Lines, Left upon the Seat of a Yew Tree" warn against the destructive self-indulgence of a misanthropic solitude that finally alienates the human heart from human concerns, *Lyrical Ballads* in general extols the imagination's power to break free of the ordinary patterns of perception and expression expected by others. The "Anecdote for Fathers," "We are Seven," "The Idiot Boy," and "The Thorn" are all cases in point, in which we are allowed to glimpse ways of making sense of the world and of talking about it that defy the categories of logic and the facticity of the understanding. In such deviations from norms of seeing and knowing and speaking appears the true self, and the true poet is he who sees the world, and can talk about it, like a child, a rustic, or even an idiot boy.

But as poems like "Expostulation and Reply," "The Tables Turned," "To My Sister," and "Simon Lee" make clear, the poet still needs to see himself through others' eyes—he needs his captive audience. If the *essence* of the poet depends on the singularity of his vision, the real *presence* of the poet is insured by his audience's acceptance of him as a poet. The two impulses coexist in uneasy tension throughout *Lyrical Ballads,* and nowhere more so than in "Lines Composed a Few Miles above Tintern Abbey, on Revisiting the Banks of the Wye during a Tour, July 13, 1798." Here, facing the contradictory claims of essence and presence, Wordsworth begins that process of disentangling himself from solipsism which was to eventuate, in 1802, in "Resolution and Independence" and, over the course of the following two years, the valedictory Intimations ode.

In "Tintern Abbey" the poet relinquishes his power to place the world in the self as he seeks to place himself in the world. That search for a sense of reembodiment is prompted by the radical discontinuity Wordsworth feels between the mind he once possessed and the mind he now possesses. Although the poet begins with an attempt to connect his present self with the self of five years ago by reviving in memory "the picture of the mind" left by this particular view of the Wye valley,[45] that attempt at establishing an experiential or perceptual continuity of consciousness over time fails: the poet is, in his own words, "chang'd, no doubt, from what I was." Instead, he resorts to anchoring the true self, that volatile, evanescent entity, to the place where it had last physically manifested its love of Nature so long ago. In lieu of spiritual continuity Wordsworth opts for bodily continuity. He reaches, figuratively, to touch a wall. He turns, as in 1793 and during the ensuing years, to Dorothy.

Long before his sister appears in the poem, however, Wordsworth introduces us to an insistent series of both sensory and self-localizing affirmations (1–22):

Five years have past; five summers, with the length
Of five long winters! and again I hear
These waters, rolling from their mountain-springs
With a soft inland murmur,—Once again
Do I behold these steep and lofty cliffs,
That on a wild secluded scene impress
Thoughts of a more deep seclusion; and connect
The landscape with the quiet of the sky.
The day is come when I again repose
Here, under this dark sycamore, and view
These plots of cottage-ground, these orchard-tufts,
Which at this season, with their unripe fruits,
Are clad in one green hue, and lose themselves
'Mid groves and copses. Once again I see
These hedge-rows, hardly hedge-rows, little lines
Of sportive wood run wild: these pastoral farms,
Green to the very door; and wreaths of smoke
Sent up, in silence, from among the trees!
With some uncertain notice, as might seem
Of vagrant dwellers in the houseless woods,
Or of some Hermit's cave, where by his fire
The Hermit sits alone.

The use of *deixis*—referring to absent objects as though they were present, to hypothetical events as though they were fact—is pronounced throughout this passage. "Again I hear / *These* waters . . . Once again / Do I behold *these* . . . cliffs," "I again repose / *Here,* under *this* dark sycamore, and view / *These* plots . . . *these* orchard-tufts," "Once again I see / *These* hedge-rows . . . *these* pastoral forms." The demonstrative pronouns, like rhetorical gesticulations, reach toward a world out there, at hand. The perceptual assertions—"I hear," "I behold," "I see"—almost make us wonder whether there might be some doubt. In particular, the position of the phrase "Do I behold . . ." at the beginning of a line plants a vestigial interrogative in the reader's mind. We have the impression of a man groping his way out of a dream—that "more deep seclusion" which the cliffs themselves, and the lonely Hermit as well, imply.

What the poet "sees," *insists* he sees, are "beauteous forms" that "have not been . . . as is a landscape to a blind man's eye" (22–24). Once out of sight, they have not been out of mind. On the contrary, they have often arisen before him during these five years, a picture vividly remembered. Indeed, so firmly have these "forms" (the vagueness of the diction keeps us from thinking of them as objects, as things outside the mind) been appropriated, says the poet, that their "sensations sweet" have passed "even into my purer mind / With tranquil restoration" (27–30). Thus absorbed by a consciousness purified of all the weighty distractions of its embodiment in the here and now, "in lonely rooms, and 'mid the din / Of towns and cities" (25–26) such forms confer "another gift, / Of aspect more sublime, that blessed mood" in which we "become a living soul" (36–46).

The "picture of the mind" in which these beauteous forms are preserved, then, has persisted as a solipsistic vision. From this dream of the world Wordsworth now attempts to awaken (58–61):

And now, with gleams of half-extinguished thought,
With many recognitions dim and faint,
And somewhat of a sad perplexity,
The picture of the mind revives again.

Is this the world, or the mind itself?[46] "Do I wake or sleep?" Keats would ask at this point, and leave the question unanswered. Wordsworth reassures himself immediately, in the very next line—"While *here* I stand"—not the world in the self, but the self in the world, embodied, substantial.

It is clear from what Wordsworth says next in "Tintern Abbey"

that the poet of five years before was less interested in distinguishing
between the mind and what it beholds (72–85):

> . . . For nature then
> (The coarser pleasures of my boyish days,
> And their glad animal movements all gone by)
> To me was all in all.—I cannot paint
> What then I was. The sounding cataract
> Haunted me like a passion: the tall rock,
> The mountain, and the deep and gloomy wood,
> Their colours and their forms, were then to me
> An appetite; a feeling and a love,
> That had no need of a remoter charm,
> By thought supplied, nor any interest
> Unborrowed from the eye.—That time is past,
> And all its aching joys are now no more,
> And all its dizzy raptures.

The poet of 1793 sought to lose his sense of himself in Nature, min-
gling his own appetites, feelings, and love with the landscape surrounding him. But he was at that time "more like a man / Flying
from something that he dreads, than one/Who sought the thing he
loved" (70–71). The self of 1793 wished, above all, to escape the
world of outwardness that had entrapped it, to flee the social, political, and historical arena.[47] It is a stranger to the Wordsworth of 1798,
who cannot "paint" it, who no longer experiences its "aching joys"
and "dizzy raptures."

By 1798 the poet has already begun to outgrow visionary solipsism, what he later calls, in the "Intimations" ode, "the visionary
gleam." Still, here as in that poem, he finds a philosophic recompense (85–102):

> . . . Not for this
> Faint I, nor mourn nor murmur; other gifts
> Have followed; for such loss, I would believe,
> Abundant recompense. For I have learned
> To look on nature, not as in the hour
> Of thoughtless youth; but hearing oftentimes
> The still, sad music of humanity,
> Nor harsh nor grating, though of ample power
> To chasten and subdue. And I have felt
> A presence that disturbs me with the joy

Of elevated thoughts; a sense sublime
Of something far more deeply interfused,
Whose dwelling is the light of setting suns,
And the round ocean and the living air,
And the blue sky, and in the mind of man:
A motion and a spirit, that impels
All thinking things, all objects of all thought,
And rolls through all things.

For the "dizzy joys" and "aching raptures" of *"thoughtless* youth" Wordsworth is compensated by an *awareness* of that "presence which is not to be put by," that "Immortality" in the light of which, he later writes, the infant "Philosopher"—"Mighty Prophet! Seer Blest!"—lives without knowing it. Receiving these "other gifts" of philosophical insight, Wordsworth leaves behind visionary solipsism as an experience and takes it up as the profoundest object of contemplation. He comes to understand that this "motion" and "spirit" reside not only in Nature but in "the mind of man," and that "all the mighty world / Of eye, and ear" is a composition that eye and ear themselves "half-create" (105–106). He can now "recognise," where before he could only feel, "In nature and the language of the sense, / The anchor of my purest thoughts, the nurse, / The guide, the guardian of my heart, and soul / Of all my moral being" (107–111). He now *understands* how profoundly suffused by his own consciousness and desire—by his own "purest thoughts," "heart," and "soul"—is the mental "picture" of the world he beholds. *The Prelude,* which he begins writing in earnest the next year, goes on to build an edifice of identity on that new power of reflection. But Wordsworth has come to know the basis of his communion with Nature, its partial source in "the mind of man," only now that he begins to find it more and more difficult to abandon himself to that communion. The "picture of the mind" revives, but it no longer has the power to replace the world of objects, or to interiorize them.

In "Tintern Abbey" Wordsworth seeks to reestablish his real, embodied presence in the world as he comes to terms with the loss of those experiences to which he once resorted as an escape from it, experiences in which he can recognize the true self that, ironically, he feels to be no longer part of him. The problem for Wordsworth here, as in *The Prelude,* is to reconnect the present with that former self which he now only knows and can no longer experience. The solution is *not* to revive the "picture of the mind," seeking some resemblance between the contents of consciousness then and now, for such an identification of contents will only cast into greater relief the disparity between modes of apprehension: gone is the "appetite," the "feeling" and "love," the joys and raptures.[48] They have left their "recognitions dim and faint," some "present pleasure," but also "a sad perplexity," a sense of disappointment we as readers feel the more strongly for Wordsworth's denials—"Not for this / Faint I."

To reestablish contact with the self that was, Wordsworth must prove to himself that he is still, as he was then, a "lover" of Nature, and that proof depends on his "warmer love" (154) being articulated, acted upon, and then recognized by another (102–105):

> . . . Therefore am I still
> A lover of the meadows and the woods,
> And mountains; and of all that we behold
> From this green earth . . .

"From," not "*Of* this green earth": the lover is now an embodied part of the world he apprehends. The proof of Wordsworth's identity with his past self must come in the form of presence, not essence, of *being there as he was before.* Wordsworth cannot recapture the self that incorporated the landscape; therefore, he will reassume the position of the self that was last incorporated *in* the landscape. He will retrace the path of the former self through this valley, "re-collect" and locate it at the very spot where five years before, "like a roe," he had "bounded o'er the mountains, by the sides / Of the deep rivers, and the lonely streams, / Wherever nature led" (67–70). By putting himself back in its last known place, Wordsworth reinhabits the self of five years ago on the verge of its escape from the world of men.

In so doing, he reenacts the love of Nature his being there signified. For the present self is not merely localized, it is characterized— "a lover." Professions of presence are not enough to assure the poet of *what* his being there, returning there, *means.* "Therefore am I still / A lover . . .": again the syntax suggests a question. His sense of presence and of what that presence signifies must be validated from without, by others. But the world of others is still held at a distance, still repulsed. Wordsworth cannot yet accommodate the "evil tongues, / Rash judgments," "the sneers of selfish men," those "greetings where no kindness is," and "the dreary intercourse of daily life" (128–131), which before had driven him away. He insists on keeping humanity at arm's length, composing a tranquil symphony out of once

"harsh" and "grating" experiences: "the still, sad music of humanity" is but the close up dissonance of life harmonized at a distance by
that grander "motion" and "spirit" which subsumes all minor, con-
flicting motives, "impels / All thinking thing," and "rolls through all
things," and which is now Wordsworth's object of philosophical contemplation.

If the world of others is kept at a distance, how can Wordsworth
reenter it? How can the reality of the embodied self find recognition
there? Wordsworth singles out a sympathetic representative. As in
the "Preface" of 1800, as in the confrontation with the discharged
soldier, as in the "incident" with Simon Lee, the poet seeks to limit
and control the audience before whom the self will appear and become real. Here, he calls on his most dependable witness, his "dearest
Friend" (115), his "dear, dear Sister" (121).

Dorothy, the reader suddenly learns, has been standing near at
hand during the utterance of the first half of the poem. Wordsworth's
unexpected appeal to an intimate bystander, it has been observed,
suggests doubts or second thoughts, as though the poet were unsure
whether the "other gifts" that have replaced his youthful raptures
are indeed "abundant recompense" for their loss.[49] He wants a cor-
roborative opinion. But it soon becomes clear that Wordsworth is not
only unsure of his opinions: he is unsure of the reality of the self who
holds them. He wants more than agreement—he wants another person to confirm his own presence on the scene. Thus his first few words
to his sister refer to her, himself, and their physical situation: "For
thou art *with me here* upon the banks / Of *this* fair river" (114–115,
italics added).

In turning to this sister for self-assurance, however, Wordsworth
compromises something of her independence (116–121):

> . . . and in thy voice I catch
> The language of my former heart, and read
> My former pleasures in the shooting lights
> Of thy wild eyes. Oh! yet a little while
> May I behold in thee what I was once,
> My dear, dear Sister! . . .

"There is a subtle and persistent confusion of Dorothy with himself
that impedes the intended simplicity of the conclusion," writes
Richard Onorato. "It is difficult to see him looking at Dorothy ('my
dear, dear Sister!') as herself, as someone particular and other."[50]

Indeed, Dorothy is not Other, at least, not wholly so. She has become a projected self-image, the safest, most intimate audience he could conceive. Dorothy is "the People" made present, the very sibling embodiment of the reader to whom the "Preface" of 1800 is addressed, the Wordsworthian counterpart to Gray's "kindred Spirit." She is there to make whole the identity of a poet, and in the years that follow it is she, the most admiring and encouraging representative of his unknown audience, who continues to assuage Wordsworth's fears and suspicions of that audience until its etherealized, timeless essence becomes the surest, and most intimate, mirror of his self-reflection. It is Wordsworth's paramount need to *make sure* that he is recognized by Dorothy in the right way, as the person he wants to believe he still is, that ultimately destroys her independence as a person. Furthermore, Dorothy's independence cannot be asserted except in an overt response to his claims. This is not forthcoming. Instead, we have only the poet's insistence that she will remember, and remember as he wants her to, that he is still "a lover of Nature" (139–146):

> . . . when thy mind
> Shall be a mansion for all lovely forms,
> Thy memory be as a dwelling-place
> For all sweet sounds and harmonies; oh! then,
> If solitude, or fear, or pain, or grief,
> Should be thy portion, with what healing thoughts
> Of tender joy wilt thou remember me,
> And these my exhortations! . . .

This is a curious and disturbing hope. Given the image of Dorothy as a young version of Wordsworth—(she was, after all, only a little less than two years his junior), imbibing Nature's "quietness and beauty," being fed "with lofty thoughts" (127–128), enjoying "all lovely forms," "all sweet sounds and harmonies"—we would expect that when meeting with distress in later years, she would refresh herself with thoughts of her own former joys, as Wordsworth has just done, and not with the memory of her brother and his "exhortations." "Remember me"—it is the cry of Hamlet's father's ghost. It is the cry of a man who fears he is not really there (146–155):

> . . . Nor, perchance—
> If I should be where I no more can hear
> Thy voice, nor catch from thy wild eyes these gleams

Of past existence—wilt thou then forget
That on the banks of this delightful stream
We stood together; and that I, so long
A worshipper of Nature, hither came
Unwearied in that service: rather say
With warmer love—oh! with far deeper zeal
Of holier love . . .

Here, in the final lines of "Tintern Abbey," we return to the simul-
taneous articulation of Other, world, and self: "Nor . . . wilt *thou* then
forget / That *on the banks of this delightful stream / We stood* together."
What is to be made real of the self here and now, in its "unwearied
service" on the banks of the Wye, are its otherwise intangible charac-
teristics, its "warmer love," "far deeper zeal / Of holier love" for Nature. And it is somehow "saying" or affirming out loud Wordsworth's
"warmer love" and gaining Dorothy's understood agreement to
what's said ("rather say" is another way of asking her to agree) that
makes the poet's intangible feelings fully manifest. What is to be
realized in the world and preserved in another's consciousness, then,
is the *persistence* of this ghostly self *as embodied in the scene*. Wordsworth's physically being here for his sister proves that his "genial
spirits" have not "wearied" but have withstood, and will continue to
withstand, "decay." Though his visionary gifts are waning, his devotion to Nature, which also has its source in the true self, remains
strong. "These steep woods and lofty cliffs, / And this green pastoral
landscape," asserts the poet, are now "to me / *More* dear, both for
themselves and for thy sake!" (157–159; italics mine). Dorothy will
remember them, and the poet to whom they remained so dear.

"Resolution and Independence": The Last "Spot of Time"

The encounters with the blind beggar and the Cumberland beggar,
and the descriptions of the London crowds and Bartholomew Fair,
demonstrate how the "egotistical sublime" can assert its ontological
primacy at the expense of others' personalities and its own sense of
presence. In "Tintern Abbey" this visionary process is partially re-
versed: the poet acknowledges, even asserts, his presence in the world
as the "picture of the mind" escapes the mind and once more comes
to enclose the poet himself. Even so, the "burthen" of the "unnatural
self" has not been fully assumed, for Dorothy is only an Other manqué, an unprotesting witness to the poet's self-realization.
    The old Leech-gatherer of "Resolution and Independence" repre-

sents the last significant step in this evolution of the Other. No study of Wordsworth's recorded confrontations and his gradual acceptance of his own embodiment—and historicity—would be complete without some consideration of this profoundly disturbing figure. The Leech-gatherer appears initially, like Dorothy, as an image of the poet. But unlike Dorothy, he represents the poet Wordsworth must become, rather than the person he has been. Also, unlike Dorothy, the old man comes eventually, and with great difficulty, to be recognized as an independent consciousness. When that recognition takes place, the poet is forced to come to terms with his own presence in the world and for another. But in place of the desperate "exhortations" that mar Wordsworth's self-assurances in "Tintern Abbey," "Resolution and Independence" ends with the good-humored laughter of a man finally at ease with himself, and with his finitude.

That the old man at first appears—like the beggars, like Dorothy—as an image of the poet is evidenced by his situation, his speech, and his manner. "I seemed to see him pace / About the weary moors continually, / Wandering about alone and silently" (129–131), writes the poet, who is also "a Traveler . . . upon the moor" (15), wandering, like the old man, "far from the world" (33), and wanting nothing to do with the "ways of men, so vain and melancholy" (21). But the Leech-gatherer is a version of the poet sobered and matured by years of hardship and solitude: his eyes do not reveal Wordsworth's "former pleasures," his voice does not bespeak "the language" of the poet's "former heart." Rather, the old man's speech is vatic, the speech of a bard, experienced, weighty, and deliberate. His words "each in solemn order followed each," "a lofty utterance," "choice word and measured phrase, above the reach / Of ordinary men: a stately speech" (93–96). Stirring the pond with his staff, looking "fixedly . . . upon the muddy water, which he conned, / As if he had been reading in a book" (79–81), the old man resembles an aged oracle, studying the arcane language of nature's entrails and ashes in "a pool bare to the eye of heaven" (54).

There are many clues to suggest that the transformation of this disturbing figure into a self-referential image is the result of its appropriation by Wordsworth's visionary imagination. "Bare to the eye of heaven," for instance, recalls the "eye of Nature" in which the Cumberland beggar lives and dies, and the "visionary" powers which the poet there assumes. Indeed, the arrangement of lines in which this phrase appears, and the homonyms—"bare to the *eye* of heaven / *I saw* a Man before me unawares" (54–55)—strengthen the suggestion of an identity between the heavenly "eye" and the poet's initially distanced "I." In addition, the otherworldliness and eerie, unreal quality of the Leech-gatherer's demeanor and speech are emphasized throughout the following stanzas. He is like a man "met with in a dream" (110). In the old man, then, much as in the ambulatory Cumberland beggar, Wordsworth beholds a visionary image of the poetic self in an ideal visionary state, the being of wise passiveness seen from without and so much at one with his environment that he seems almost inanimate. Unlike the old Cumberland beggar, however, the Leech-gatherer does not leave Wordsworth reassured as to the advantages of having become, over so many years, a thing of Nature.

The Leech-gatherer's resemblance to the old Cumberland beggar is reinforced by his apparent, and in this case disturbing, loss of conscious presence. He simply *"was,"* wrote Wordsworth to Sara Hutchinson, "a figure presented in the most naked simplicity possible."[51] It is the phenomenal "Man" (55)—the word capitalized so as to deemphasize personality—that fills the poet's eye: the old man is likened to "a huge stone" (57) that only "seems a thing endued with sense," or a "sea-beast" (61–62), "not all alive, nor dead, / Nor all asleep" (64–65), nor all, it seems, human. He lacks initially that which would make him entirely a person and not merely an emblematic image or a phantasm of a human being: his own mind.[52]

The Leech-gatherer is one of the best examples of the way in which Wordsworth's solitaries, when exalted, as Frederick Garber contends, to the level of "absolute humanness" or "absolute being,"[53] appear diminished in their own understanding of themselves as individuals. The old man offers answers, of course, to the questions the poet puts to him: "What occupation do you there pursue?" (88). "How is it that you live, and what is it you do?" (119). But these answers are matters of fact, not figuration—"He told, that to these waters he had come / To gather leeches, being old and poor" (99–100). The old man's replies are not, at first, acknowledged as pertinent to his significance in the visionary landscape, a landscape in the poet's mind (127–131):

> While he was talking thus, the lonely place,
> The old Man's shape, and speech—all troubled me:
> In my mind's eye I seemed to see him pace
> About the weary moors continually,
> Wandering about alone and silently.

Throughout the encounter, the poet's reiterated questions remain unmodulated by the faintest recognition of what, in fact, the old man is saying.

The Leech-gatherer has such a difficult time breaking out of the poet's mind's eye and making his real presence felt precisely because, like the blind beggar, the Cumberland beggar, and the discharged soldier, he appears in a world suddenly appropriated by the poet's imagination for the purpose of self-enlightenment (106–112):

> The old Man still stood talking by my side;
> But now his voice to me was like a stream
> Scarce heard; nor word from word could I divide;
> And the whole body of the Man did seem
> Like one whom I had met with in a dream;
> Or like a man from some far region sent,
> To give me human strength, by apt admonishment.

The dreamlike feeling described here is a sign of visionary solipsism, and the "far region" of this man's origins is the terra incognita of Wordsworth's own soul. Like Wordsworth's other solitaries, the Leech-gatherer turns out to be the instrument of a higher power, a "peculiar grace, / A leading from above, a something given" (50–51) working through the poet's appropriative mind to educate or enlighten him as to his vocation. As we would expect, this visionary instrument shows no awareness of his visionary function in the encounter.

But what "admonishment" is the Leech-gatherer expected to deliver? This question cannot be answered without reference to Wordsworth's description of his state of mind in the first seven stanzas of the poem, just before he comes upon the old man. Here he captures the gladness of solitude in its "summer mood" (37), that youthful state of soul in which one takes an immediate, unself-conscious delight in the glories of Nature. In this state, Wordsworth likens himself to her "blissful creatures" (16–21):

> I saw the hare that raced about with joy;
> I heard the woods and distant waters roar;
> Or heard them not, as happy as a boy:
> The pleasant season did my heart employ:
> My old remembrances went from me wholly;
> And all the ways of men, so vain and melancholy.

In stanza five he reiterates these sentiments (29–33):

I heard the sky-lark warbling in the sky;
And I bethought me of the playful hare:
Even such a happy Child of earth am I;
Even as these blissful creatures do I fare;
Far from the world I walk, and from all care.

Here is a moment—"far from the world," from "the ways of men"—similar to that described in "Tintern Abbey," "when like a roe" the poet "bounded o'er the mountains," and in the opening lines of the Intimations ode, when "the earth and every common sight . . . did seem / Apparelled in celestial light, / The glory and the freshness of a dream." It is a revisitation of Wordsworth's most primitive and youthful experiences of visionary joy, in which the finite self constricted by a hostile society is wholly forgotten and the being within expanded to embrace all of creation—"By our own spirits are we deified," he writes. "We Poets in our youth begin in gladness" (47–48). This is life lived entirely in the present moment, what Keats later called "a Life of sensations rather than of Thoughts!"[54]

But at this point, thoughts begin to intrude: "fears and fancies thick upon me came; / Dim sadness—and blind thoughts, I knew not, nor could name" (27–28). He continues (34–42),

. . . there may come another day to me—
Solitude, pain of heart, distress, and poverty.

VI

My whole life I have lived in pleasant thought,
As if life's business were a summer mood;
As if all needful things would come unsought
To genial faith, still rich in genial good;
But how can He expect that others should
Build for him, sow for him, and at his call
Love him, who for himself will take no heed at all?

Wordsworth has become conscious of his embodied self, and such "taking heed" immediately calls to mind the imagined presence of others: "How can He expect that *others* should . . . at his call / Love him?" The question is not only, as in the Gospel of Matthew (6:25–34), "What shall I put on?" but also "What *am* I for others, and of *what use* to them?" The third-person pronoun, "He," capitalized like the "I" it replaces, reinforces our sense that Wordsworth is here seeing himself from without, as another would, and judging himself accordingly.

What he fears, however, is no longer the attention but the neglect of others. For the anticipated admonishment is directed at the poet's sudden dejection over his own finitude and mortality, and the loss of his powers of self-deification (43–49):

> I thought of Chatterton, the marvelous Boy,
> The sleepless Soul that perished in his pride;
> Of Him who walked in glory and in joy
> Following his plough, along the mountain-side:
> By our own spirits are we deified:
> We Poets in our youth begin in gladness;
> But thereof come in the end despondency and madness.

Chatterton and Burns (the "Him" of line 45) were the Romantic epitomes of poets who died poor, obscure, despised, and alone.

The Leech-gatherer is another version of the Cumberland beggar, but seen with new eyes. Gone is the enthusiasm for solitude, for becoming an object of Nature, for living life in her "eye." Wordsworth has come to realize to what extent the self depends on others for its sustenance in the widest sense: not only physical but emotional and spiritual support, self-assurance and self-esteem. Solitude, up to now valued as the means whereby we are put in touch with the "better self" within us, the self "deified," here shows its negative, outward side: it leads eventually to "pain of heart" and "poverty" for the embodied self to which we must inevitably return.[55]

Wordsworth's questioning the value of solitude in the spring of 1802 is especially significant in light of his decision, at this time, to marry Mary Hutchinson.[56] He was ready to make a commitment to someone from outside the safe circle of familial attachments; he was reaching beyond Dorothy to the wider world, although it can be plausibly argued that the Hutchinson sisters had by this time been thoroughly assimilated to the household at Grasmere, as much "family" as Dorothy herself. The decision to marry coincided with Wordsworth's growing awareness, expressed, as I have noted, as early as "Tintern Abbey," that he was losing his visionary powers. Solitude without the compensation of visionary joy, even in the company of Dorothy, must have seemed a bleak and lonely prospect when extrapolated over a lifetime.

So despondent does Wordsworth become over this prospect of life in the world, deprived of his visionary gifts and without the ameliorating sympathy and self-affirmation of others, that in "Resolution and Independence" he immediately, upon considering it, disassumes his own embodiment, retreating into a state of visionary solipsism. The finite self he will not accept, the fearful state of embodiment he must reject, is personified in the dreamlike, depersonalized figure of the Leech-gatherer on the lonely moor: the old man becomes an objective image of the poet of nature, but now seen from without, literally, *as* a third person in the poet's visionary mind. The questions Wordsworth puts to this phantasmal self-image, concerning the man's "occupation" and how he lives, seem motivated by the need to reassure himself that such a life can be endured. But the old man's answers are not reassuring (99–105):

> He told, that to these waters he had come
> To gather leeches, being old and poor:
> Employment hazardous and wearisome!
> And he had many hardships to endure:
> From pond to pond he roamed, from moor to moor;
> Housing, with God's good help, by choice or chance;
> And in this way he gained an honest maintenance.

This is not what the poet wants to hear (113–119):

> My former thoughts returned: the fear that kills;
> And hope that is unwilling to be fed;
> Cold, pain, and labour, and all fleshly ills;
> And mighty Poets in their misery dead.
> —Perplexed, and longing to be comforted,
> My question eagerly did I renew,
> "How is it that you live, and what is it you do?"

On a mundane level, the Leech-gatherer can offer no comfort to the solitary and wandering poet of nature. And yet, Wordsworth reiterates his questions as though he were asking for something more than comfort, as though he were waiting for the *visionary* significance of the man to emerge. In the third-to-last stanza Wordsworth records, for the first time, the Leech-gatherer's exact words of reply,[57] as if to suggest that the "apt admonishment" meant for him lies here (120–126):

> He with a smile did then his words repeat;
> And said, that, gathering leeches far and wide
> He travelled; stirring thus about his feet
> The waters of the pools where they abide.
> "Once I could meet with them on every side;
> But they have dwindled long by slow decay;
> Yet still I persevere, and find them where I may."

This speech becomes significant only in light of the Leech-gatherer's visionary correspondence to the poet and the implicit correspondence between their "occupations," which has been the topic of Wordsworth's earnest questioning. The old man stirs the waters of the pools "bare to the eye of heaven" just as the poet stirs the waters of his imagination. Here then is the Leech-gatherer's symbolic, and exemplary, admonition: "persevere," *be* resolute and independent. In the face of his dwindling powers of self-deification and growing isolation, the poet must persist in his search for visionary joy during the life remaining to him, however impoverished and alienated from the human community that search may leave him.

But if this is indeed Wordsworth's "apt admonishment," he does not seem to have gathered much "human strength" from it. He is still, in the next stanza, "troubled" by the "old Man's shape and speech." And yet, ironically, he continues to pursue his thoughts within himself—that is, Wordsworth remains in a state of sublimely egotistical solipsism, which can only eventuate in the isolation and neglect that he fears.

The Leech-gatherer, meanwhile, "having made a pause, the same discourse renewed." The man confronting the poet persists in responding to his questions on the most ordinary level, offering him every opportunity to "come to" and respond in a way that shows he is listening to what is said, not to how it is said, or for its hidden message. Whatever Wordsworth's conscious or unconscious intent, the Leech-gatherer demonstrates another kind of perseverance than that which the poet so obscurely apprehends at the visionary level: the persistence of a mind outside his own, inviting him to return to a shared world, pressing him to acknowledge his own embodied presence there. As Anthony E. M. Conran has observed, in this poem we are presented with "the comedy of a solipsist faced with something outside himself."[58] But it is an existential comedy at best, for the something outside is also a some*one*, an Other that the poet cannot assimilate to the demands of his inner self (134–140):

> And soon with this he other matter blended,
> Cheerfully uttered, with demeanour kind,
> But stately in the main; and when he ended,
> I could have laughed myself to scorn to find
> In that decrepit Man so firm a mind.
> "God," said I, "be my help and stay secure;
> I'll think of the Leech-gatherer on the lonely moor!"

The final message of the poem comes not from some "far region," but from the world at hand, "admonishing" Wordsworth to accept his place there. Two important changes occur in the demeanor of the Leech-gatherer at the end of "Resolution and Independence," both of which encourage that acceptance. First, the old man, for the first time in the encounter, appears "cheerful" and "kind," no longer "grave" and "stately." He has become more approachable and personable, at least in the poet's eyes, certainly less forbidding in appearance and therefore, presumably, more accepting of the poet's presence. Second, and more important, it is not until this stanza that the old man takes the initiative and turns to topics of conversation, "other matter," not prompted by Wordsworth's own desperate questions. For the first time the old man behaves in a manner that suggests he is not "sent" there simply as a symbolic comment on the poet's visionary preoccupations. He has a "firm mind" of his own: the individual consciousness that gently keeps asserting itself in the "decrepit Man" finally forces Wordsworth to accept him as independent and to see himself as this man sees him. The poet becomes, finally, self-conscious, and accepts his own proper embodiment for another.

Through his verbal "resolution and independence," then, his persistence in speaking for himself, the Leech-gatherer has broken free of the poet's dream of the world and brought him face-to-face with himself in all the ludicrousness of his single-minded interrogation: he is an object worthy of scornful laughter. That the poet feels impelled to laugh is one measure of his acceptance of himself as others see him. It is also one measure of his abandonment of visionary power and its exacting isolation. He was never, so far as his poetry can reveal, to experience another "spot of time" to match this encounter with the Leech-gatherer on the lonely moor.

"The Light of Common Day"

It is a matter of debate, and perhaps more of taste, whether or not Wordsworth's poetic inspiration began to taper off soon after his marriage to Mary Hutchinson in 1802, or somewhat later.[59] *The Prelude,* beyond books I and II, which date from 1798–1799, was substantially completed during 1804–1805, and constitutes more a retrospective than a contemporary chronicle of Wordsworth's visionary moments. The Intimations ode was written over the course of two years, 1802–1804, as were the most memorable of the sonnets. The "Ode to Duty" was written in 1804, "Stepping Westward" and "The Solitary Reaper," 1805, "Elegiac Stanzas," 1806, and "Laodamia" as late as 1814. The stars in Wordsworth's poetic firmament thin out considerably beyond the publication of the *Poems* of 1807, as we near the western horizon of his life.

The question is why. What lies behind Wordsworth's drastic decline in poetic power, what Willard Sperry, some fifty years ago, called the poet's "anti-climax"? Sperry surveyed the reasons suggested by critics of the 1930s and found none of them convincing.[60] My own feeling is that Wordsworth's growing sense of familial and historical self-possession accelerated the fading of the "visionary gleam." In the Intimations ode, the metaphysical complacency of *The Excursion,* and the stoicism of "Ode to Duty" and "Elegiac Stanzas," we find a sensibility that has come to terms with the conditions of its existence, a soul that has found its real "place" in the world. For Wordsworth, the flight from embodiment, which had provided the spur to his most important inspirations, had come to an end. He had his intimates—Dorothy, Mary and Sara Hutchinson, Coleridge; his followers—De Quincey, Crabb Robinson, the "Lake School"; his "People"—audience "fit" though "few." With solid assurances of his place, his role, his identity as a poet, Wordsworth felt less urgently the need to seek refuge in visionary solipsism, until finally that "celestial light" faded into "the light of common day." What remained of his former audience-anxiety was an extreme sensitivity to the slightest criticism of his work.

I offer this analysis as conjecture, but it seems to square with the facts of Wordsworth's later life. He went on to secure a government post—distributor of stamps for Westmoreland—in 1813, and worked assiduously for the Tory cause. He was named poet laureate in 1843. Mary bore him five children, three of whom survived to adulthood. He became a professed Anglican and wrote on ecclesiastical themes. Certainly, these developments, in and of themselves, are not necessarily fatal to a poet's inspiration, and none of them can be said to have presented insurmountable obstacles to sublimity in the form of distractions, debilitating worries, or simply demands on a poet's time. But this poet based his identity as a poet on his convictions of the self's interiority, and on the mystical, dreamlike rapport with Nature to which such convictions can give rise. Domesticity, bureaucracy, and established religion provided for Wordsworth a snug web of clearly defined relationships in which the self could be expressed without fear of betrayal, and from which it no longer needed to withdraw. In these forums the poet could find acceptance and esteem, satisfying the very tastes that he had, by 1807, helped make acceptable. By the end of his middle years Wordsworth had learned to content himself with the role of priest, rather than prophet, of the imagination. He had come down from the mountain; he had a congregation to look after now.

3

Coleridge: Speaking Dreams

O! What a life is in the eye! what a strange
and inscrutable essence!
—"Hexameters," 28

COLERIDGE, in his massive and omnivorous erudition, the subtlety of his observations, the restlessness of his intellect, and the bedevilling undependability of his autobiographical anecdotes, is perhaps the most daunting of the Romantics to treat justly in the scope of a single chapter. Four works, however, show clearly the principal features of visionary solipsism and some typical Coleridgean reactions to it: "Kubla Khan," "Frost at Midnight," "This Lime-Tree Bower My Prison," and "The Rime of the Ancient Mariner" all present figures of the poet in an imaginatively dominant role in confrontations and "conversations." "Christabel," the fifth work treated at some length here, is a special and much more psychologically complex representation of the process of self-definition through submission, though it derives from the same fundamental insecurities over the substantial reality of the true self. By way of introduction to these poems,[1] and along the way, some attention to Coleridge's other works will prove necessary.

The Life of the Eye

Like his friend and partner in the *Lyrical Ballads,* Coleridge tended to identify closely with the self within. Unlike Wordsworth, he never quite reached the point where he could feel sure enough of his audience to create a firm place in the world for the "real" expression of that true self. In a notebook entry of October 1803, a year or two after his poetic output had slowed to a trickle, he wrote, "But yet tho' one should write Poetry, Draftsman's-ship & Music—the greater & perhaps nobler certainly all the subtler parts of one's nature, must be solitary—Man exists herein to himself & to God alone / —Yea, in how much more only to God—how much lies *below* his own Consciousness."[2] Coleridge here sounds very much like Gray's elegiac poet, whose soul, abiding in the "bosom of his Father and his God," can never be satisfactorily disclosed to the senses.

Such feelings explain something of Coleridge's notorious difficulties with executing his grandiose projects, whether in poetry or prose: no artistic or philosophical activity could fully represent the self within—its intentions, its "nature," its vision. Even consciousness remained partly ignorant of its "subtler parts." By 1805 Coleridge had come to feel strongly the "fragmentary character of Action, & its absolute dependence on Society, a majority, &c" for its illusion of "Truth."[3] The self at work in the world seemed to be a mere fabrication of prevailing opinion. All but immobilized by such self-doubts, Coleridge still hoped for deliverance from them. In a notebook entry of May 1804, echoing lines from his own unfinished poem "Christabel," he prays, "Let me live in *Truth*—manifesting that alone which *is,* even as it *is,* & striving to be that which only Reason shows to be lovely."[4]

Unhappy with the inadequacy of the real self to manifest the true, Coleridge could not, however, ignore the fluid, amorphous, indefinite condition of the self within, which impelled it to seek recognition. He was acutely sensitive to audiences and their (presumed) demands, driven by a pronounced, at times pathological, and in all cases tormenting dependency on others' approval. His fears of offending, his uncertainties over his own motivations, his low self-esteem have all been amply rehearsed in commentary on his life and works. As Kelvin Everest observes, with Coleridge "the problem of audience is central" and his "chameleon-like relationship with every kind of audience . . . is a manifestation of the need to belong."[5] The letters offer many instances of Coleridge's inability to write what he really thinks when he thinks his correspondent will disapprove of or deny it. Responding to what he believes is expected of him, Coleridge even deceives himself in trying to deceive others, warming to the task of rationalizing his conduct, not only for the benefit of his correspondent but for his own sake as well.[6]

Coleridge's sense of self fed voraciously on others' impressions of him. But one often has the feeling, in reading his letters and notebooks, that it is not just his self-esteem that the poet wishes to reinforce by accommodating his audience. It is his very sense of manifest existence. A notebook passage of December 1804, written while he was filling the post of Public Secretary in Malta, far from home and friends, reveals the characteristic emptiness Coleridge felt constantly threatening him from within, and his need for continual recognition and support from without:

$$\overline{W+D+MW}+SH+\overline{HDSC} = STC$$
$$= \text{Ego contemplans.}^7$$

"Wordsworth + Dorothy + Mary Wordsworth + Sara Hutchinson + Hartley, Derwent, Sara Coleridge [Coleridge's children]" add up to "Samuel Taylor Coleridge." "Ego contemplans," as Kathleen Coburn points out in her notes to this entry, means "personal identity," according to the *Biographia Literaria,* and Stephen Potter, more than half a century ago, observed that "STC" was Coleridge's characteristic appellation for his public identity.[8] Apparently, Coleridge's sense of self at this time had become so perilously feeble and ephemeral that it had come to depend almost wholly on what his children and closest friends made of him. And not only friends—in a later notebook entry, he asserts that "only by meeting with, so as to be resisted by, *Another,* does the Soul become a *Self*": "What is Self-consciousness but to know myself at the same moment that I know another, and to know myself by means of knowing another, and vice-versa, an other by means of & at the moment of knowing my Self. Self and others are as necessarily interdependent as Right and Left, North and South."[9]

Coleridge seems to have felt the self to be volatile and unfocused without the presence of others, a feeling of inner uncertainty that can be traced back through his boyhood experiences at Christ's Hospital to his earliest childhood. Walter Jackson Bate has observed that Coleridge's dependency on his older siblings, coupled with the early death of his father and what amounted to abandonment by his mother, resulted in a strong "need to ingratiate himself . . . and with it, as corollaries, a readiness of guilt, a chronic fear of disappointing others, and a fascinated admiration for people of firm—or at least apparently self-sufficient—character."[10] Coburn, too, in her commentary on the *Notebooks,* suggests that "the lost or orphan child and the dying or absent mother come too frequently into Coleridge's poems to be insignificant images."[11]

As children, we naturally tend to internalize our parents, making their spectral presences part of our own mind's eye. As we grow older, these presences help to validate the reality of the true self as it is imaged or embodied internally, in self-reflection, regardless of how others perceive us. This internalization of a parental presence as the surest mirror of self-consciousness does not seem to have been completed in Coleridge's case, a failure to which I shall return when I discuss "Christabel." He considered himself even at the age of thirty-seven and all during the years his mother was still alive "a deserted orphan," "an orphan Brother."[12] As a result, says Geoffrey Yarlott, the poet spent a good deal of his adult life searching for " 'sheet-anchor' men," "father-figures": Southey or Poole or Wordsworth or Gillman, the doctor into whose care he finally committed himself, a hopeless opium addict. His dearest friends seemed to him complete unto themselves, and thus sure and independent sources for his own self-validation.[13]

In his poetry Coleridge's anxieties over dependency most often appear as a reaction *against* the limitations of embodiment. Like Wordsworth, he centered his work on moments in which the world becomes internalized as dream, moments presaging a sudden expansion of the self beyond its apparent physical limits. "Frost at Midnight," as I have mentioned, begins with such a moment, experienced in solitude "so calm, that it disturbs / And vexes meditation with its strange / And extreme silentness" (8-10). In this "hush of nature," "inaudible as dreams," the poet's "idling spirit / By its own moods interprets" objects, like the fire-film on the grate, which it has made its own, "every where / Echo or mirror seeking of itself" (17, 20-22). Out of this initial imaginative appropriation of the world surrounding him grows the poet's climactic vision of nature's "shapes and sounds intelligible" (59), the "eternal language" (60) of God, "Great universal Teacher!" (63).

Transforming the world into dream, as here, more often than not prepares the way for a mystical union with, or a revelation of, what the poet calls in "The Eolian Harp" "the one Life within us and abroad." In "This Lime-Tree Bower My Prison" he conveys some sense of such an experience as he imagines his friend, Charles Lamb, standing on the Quantock hills, "as I have stood," "silent with swimming sense" (39-43),

> ... yea, gazing round
> On the wide landscape ... till all doth seem
> Less gross than bodily; and of such hues
> As veil the Almighty spirit, when yet he makes
> Spirits perceive his presence.

"Religious Musings" makes clear Coleridge's understanding that the "Spirits" who perceive the presence of this "Almighty Spirit" share, on a metaphysical level, in the being of that Spirit. The "one Life" is indeed both "within us" *and* "abroad" (105–114):

> There is one Mind, one Omnipresent Mind,
> Omnific. His most holy name is Love.
> Truth of subliming import! with the which
> Who feeds and saturates his constant soul,
> He from his small particular orbit flies
> With blest outstarting! From himself he flies,
> Stands in the sun, and with no partial gaze
> Views all creation; and he loves it all,
> And blesses it, and calls it very good!
> This is indeed to dwell with the Most High!

In such raptures, we make "The whole one Self! Self that no alien knows! / Self, far diffused as Fancy's wing can travel! / Self, spreading still! Oblivious of its own, / Yet all of all possessing!" (154–157). Thus does the soul, "by exclusive consciousness of God / All self-annihilated . . . make / God its Identity: God all in all! / We and our Father one!" (42–45).

The Neoplatonic and Spinozistic background of Coleridge's transcendental flights hardly requires documentation at this late date: the "one Life" is Coleridge's world soul, the *anima mundi,* the *en kai pan,* of which all of us are parts, "Parts and proportions of one wondrous whole!" (128).[14] To truly feel one's identity with this Oversoul, one need only put off "his own low self" (152)—no easy task, if he is made conscious of that "low self" by others and their demands.

If we look at Coleridge's poetic work as a whole, this "outstarting" from the "small particular orbit" of selfhood, this dispersion of the soul, appears to be a reaction against the constrictions of the self-for-others. Certainly the most famous, or notorious, instance of the sobering effects of another's dyspathy on the poet's visionary excursions occurs in "The Eolian Harp," just as Coleridge reaches the apex of metaphysical speculation (44–52):

> And what if all of animated nature
> Be but organic Harps diversely fram'd,
> That tremble into thought, as o'er them sweeps
> Plastic and vast, one intellectual breeze,
> At once the Soul of each, and God of all?
> But thy more serious eye a mild reproof

Darts, O beloved Woman! nor such thoughts
Dim and unhallow'd dost thou not reject,
And biddest me walk humbly with my God.

Here, in the earliest of the conversation poems, we find one of the central, recurring events of Coleridge's poetry: the abrupt and anxious confrontation with the eye of another. "The Eolian Harp" was written in 1795, on the eve of Coleridge's dutiful (and disastrous) marriage to Sara Fricker. The misery that lay ahead for the newlyweds is almost entirely unheralded here, except for the obvious discomfort the poet feels at Sara's unsympathetic reaction to what she could only have taken to be metaphysical web-spinning, if not heresy. It may indeed be that, as Paul Magnuson observes, Coleridge "cannot step toward a truth by perceiving through Sara's alien eyes"—that because "she does not see as he does, she blocks his further progress."[15] Clearly, Coleridge looked to others for assurance of the truth of his opinions.

But Sara's eye does more than "reject" the poet's musings—it "darts." It threatens the very life and soul of what it sights, like the Ancient Mariner's crossbow: that too is something "sighted," and its dart kills the albatross, a dovelike symbol of the human soul. What is fixed by Sara's evil eye, here and now, as "a sinful and most miserable man" (62) had but a moment before imagined himself "thus, my Love!" (34–43),

    . . . as on the midway slope
Of yonder hill I stretch my limbs at noon,
Whilst through my half-clos'd eye-lids I behold
The sunbeams dance, like diamonds, on the main,
And tranquil muse upon tranquility;
Full many a thought uncall'd and undetain'd,
And many idle flitting phantasies,
Traverse my indolent and passive brain,
As wild and various as the random gales
That swell and flutter on this subject Lute!

We recognize the experience as an instance of visionary solipsism, something very close to Wordsworth's "wise passiveness." The "half-clos'd eye-lids," the sense of solitude (he imagines himself on "yonder hill," alone), tranquility in physical repose, and most of all the reduction of the sensorium to mental states, to thoughts and "phanta-

sies" that haunt the poet's "passive brain"—these render the experience much like what he was to describe as a more constant, and
troubling, state of mind in a letter to Sara seven years later: "I seem
to exist, as it were, almost wholly within myself, in *thoughts* rather
than in *things.*"[16] In "The Eolian Harp" the experience of solipsism
leads finally to the feeling of oneness with the "intellectual breeze"
that animates the poet's mind with images, just as the breeze
through the window animates the Eolian lute with sound.

Sara's eye fells the poet as he soars heavenward—it brings him
"to" himself. From internal evidence, it does not appear that he regrets being shot down in this manner: "Well hast thou said and hol-
ily disprais'd / These shapings of the unregenerate mind," he tells his
"Heart-honour'd Maid" (54–55, 64). It is quite possible that he feels
himself soaring too close to the Shelleyan "intense inane," skirting
the edge of that insubstantiality which so vexed and frightened him
in later life. It is also possible that he feels he has, in fact, come close
to heresy. I tend to side with those who find Coleridge's recantation
to be inconsistent with the overall tone of the poem—it sounds too
much like the kind of pious afterthought to which he was prone
whenever he realized his respondent was reacting negatively.[17]

The recantation is also inconsistent with Coleridge's self-portraits
manqué, for in nearly every other poem of his maturity he depicts his
poet figures as overcoming the threatened expropriation of the self in
the eye of another by an exertion of imaginative—or of what, I shall
argue, can aptly be termed mesmeric—power over the mind of his
listener. With this power the poet seeks to appropriate, literally to
"keep in mind," the world from which others emerge to threaten
him, and to establish, to his satisfaction, an empthic unity with them
on the level of the volatile self as mind, the "one Life" that permeates
and shapes creation. In this way poetry itself becomes a reenactment
of the primal creation of a world held in the Divine Mind. The poet's
word becomes the Word—*Logos.*

"Kubla Khan": Mesmerism and Logos

"Kubla Khan" has long been read as a poem about the workings of
the imagination and the mission of the youthful poet as imagination's prophet.[18] The walled-off gardens, the stately pleasure-dome,
the romantic caverns, the sacred river, the lifeless ocean, all have
their analogues in the creative mind and the operations of the unconscious. The poem is also fraught with tensions: order as opposed

to disorder, life against death, culture against nature, will against impulse. Indeed, it is precisely Coleridge's ability to reconcile these opposites, to create "unity" out of "multeity" in a poem about the synthetic processes of the creative imagination, that has so fascinated modern critics.[19]

But the opposition that is most highlighted by its place at the very end of the poem is that between the poet and others (37–54):

> A damsel with a dulcimer
> In a vision once I saw:
> It was an Abyssinian maid,
> And on her dulcimer she played,
> Singing of Mount Abora.
> Could I revive within me
> Her symphony and song,
> To such a deep delight 'twould win me,
> That with music loud and long,
> I would build that dome in air,
> That sunny dome! those caves of ice!
> And all who heard should see them there,
> And all should cry, Beware! Beware!
> His flashing eyes, his floating hair!
> Weave a circle round him thrice,
> And close your eyes with holy dread,
> For he on honey-dew hath fed,
> And drunk the milk of Paradise.

Once initiated into the mysteries of divine creation and poetic re-creation, the poet stands outside the "all" which he confronts. There is no place for such a man among his fellow beings, as part of what Coleridge calls, in "Dejection: an Ode," "that inanimate cold world allowed / To the poor loveless, ever-anxious crowd" (51–52). Because his vision cannot be ratified by consensus, the poet transformed by his own vision must remain apart from the reality others share or sacrifice to it both his vision and the true self which beheld that vision.

What is the nature of this true self? It is, first and foremost, a being withdrawn and made whole in opposition to others.[20] The first two stanzas of the poem, particularly, represent a turning inward and away, the creation of an inner order, a private garden walled off, like a dream, from a world "out there." By such introversion the private self reaches transcendent sources of imaginative power—the "deep romantic chasm" and its "mighty fountain" flinging up "the sacred river" of an imaginatively fertile and divinely creative consciousness. Such imaginative retreats, in Keats's *Lamia* and Tennyson's "Palace of Art," lead to nightmarish self-enclosures, but for the moment, in the first blush of Romanticism's maturity, the private self into which the poet would retire also provides a haven from outward struggles (29–30):

> And 'mid this tumult Kubla heard from far
> Ancestral voices prophesying war!

It is to a consideration of this strife beyond the boundaries of the self that the poem proceeds in the last lines.

If to venture out of the private parks and palaces of the mind is to become engaged in a struggle to the death for dominance, a "war," then in "Kubla Khan" that war comes figuratively to pass in the confrontation between the poet and his audience.[21] The poet hopes to win this struggle by a process of contagion. He envisons the damsel—"a personification of [his] imagination . . . in its peculiar independence from his conscious control," as Kathleen M. Wheeler describes her[22]—hears her song, and then, reenacting "within" him, within the precincts of his own mind, that "symphony and song," the poet sings so that others *cannot help* hearing . . . and seeing: "And all who *heard* should *see* them there."

What Coleridge depicts is the potential creation of a hallucinatory reality for all who "hear" the poet's music "loud and long."[23] The horizons of that reality are established by the poet-figure's "flashing eyes," its contents, by his words. It is, so to speak, *his* "mind's eye" that sets the boundaries of perceived reality, and in the process commands his audience's suspension of disbelief. Like the Ancient Mariner, who "holds" the Wedding-Guest "with his glittering eye," the poet "hath his will": the theater of his dream ("within me") becomes the theater of his listener's waking awareness "out there"—in the world we share.[24]

"Kubla Khan" is an instance of what Edward Bostetter calls "a dream of power."[25] But it is a dream that demands recognition, both for itself and, more important, for its creator. The poem ends with a scenario of acknowledgment, of awe and veneration. The cry, "Beware! Beware!" is an implicit admission of the poet's visionary power, an expression of that supernatural fear which properly at-

tends manifestations of a divine "Presence." In imagined confrontations like this Coleridge satisfies the urge both to repudiate the "low
self" and to command recognition of the visionary being by which,
momentarily, it is possessed. The embodied self, with its "flashing
eyes" and "floating hair," now registers the power and presence of
the infinite being that works through it, rather than the finite being
that answers to an earthly name.

As variants of visionary solipsism, Coleridge's portraits of imaginative dominance differ somewhat from Wordsworth's "egotistical sublime," which tends to dissolve in confrontations with others as the
true self struggles to materialize in their eyes. Coleridge's poet stead-
fastly resists reciprocity in confrontations, seeking to draw others into
the visionary gardens of his own imagination. In "Kubla Khan" they
respond with wariness and "dread." The youthful poet's floating hair
threatens like Medusa's snakes: his hearers are afraid that they will
turn to stone, that they will lose their powers of will and self-determination. They fear becoming his objects. In retaliation, they would
perform an act of exorcism, "weave a circle" around him. This is not
merely an attempt at banishment. Exorcism, after all, seeks to include and place the formerly "possessed" among us once more, making him again recognizable as one of us "all." In "Kubla Khan" the
poet's audience seeks both to exclude the supernatural force radiat-
ing from his presence and to "contain" or reclaim its apparent victim, to bring him "to" his shared senses. But the poet will not be
neutralized in this manner. Having "drunk the milk of Paradise," he
has become part of something divine that cannot be reduced, objec-
tified, and defined by the minds of others. He will not return to his
"low self."

No other human relationship so closely resembles the tense confrontations between poet and auditor in Coleridge's poetry as that of
mesmerism. Again and again, the poet figure appears as a preternatural mesmerist, dominating, and resisting domination by, his subject
audience. This particular self-image has its empirical origins, as Lane
Cooper first pointed out some years ago, in Coleridge's keen and arcane early scientific interests in natural philosophy, where he expected to find, in the phenomenon of electromagnetism, a physical
basis for the workings of the "one Life within us and abroad."[26] Cooper suggests that eye imagery and themes of paralysis and stasis
in the poetry are specifically related to Coleridge's fascination with
current theories of mesmerism or "animal magnetism," and even
a cursory examination of Coleridge's three great poems of the

supernatural—"The Rime of the Ancient Mariner," "Christabel," and "Kubla Khan"—will convince us of this influence. In addition, Cooper provides an extensive list of references to eyes, looks, faces, and fixations in these and other poems to support his point.

But exposure alone cannot explain Coleridge's obsession with images of mesmeric control. It is true that the rage for mesmerism in London coincided with the impressionable period of Coleridge's adolescence and early manhood, 1782–1791. But more important than any evidence for the poet's direct acquaintance with Mesmer's theory or practice is the fact that, as Robert Darnton observes, mesmerism was culturally symptomatic of Western society's transition from the Enlightenment to what would later come to be known as Romanticism.[27] Mesmerism reflected a growing popular interest in the irrational and the enthusiastic, in "sensibility," sympathy, and empathic relations with others. It answered the metaphysical longings of the age for a sense of spiritual unity among individuals, and for an authoritative source of recognition, in the person of the mesmerist himself, for the increasingly fragmented public self.[28] The authority by which the mesmerist imposed his will rested on the assumption, shared by his initiates, that through his words, his eye, his touch, was conducted the universal, spiritual, healing "medium," the "electrical" or "magnetic" fluid animating all life—a crude, rather protomaterialistic version of Coleridge's "one Life." In the presence of the mesmerist, therefore, one could surrender the self, through a kind of ecstasy or hysteria, to that vital force which, according to Mesmer and his adherents, was ordinarily blocked or frustrated in its surreptitious animation of one's everyday personality. Momentarily, at least, the false self, the everyday or "low self," fell away and the magnetic and spontaneous inner being became manifest.[29] Mesmerism, like other current "enthusiasms," was good for the soul or, as Breuer and Freud were to recognize much later, for the psyche.[30]

There is not enough evidence to prove that Coleridge consciously employs mesmerism, per se, as a trope of the poet's imaginative dominance over his audience, for he evinced little interest in the phenomenon after his earliest enthusiasm. But the resemblance between the mesmeric relationship and the confrontations central to Coleridge's most important and suggestive works is striking, and that resemblance depends, I believe, on the cultural milieu common to both Mesmer and Coleridge. In using the word "mesmeric," therefore, and in drawing analogies between mesmeric theory and its associated images on the one hand, and Coleridge's poetic representations of human encounters on the other, I wish merely to stress the uncanny appropriateness of the mesmeric relationship as a paradigm of the interpersonal dynamics informing such encounters, and to suggest that this paradigm holds precisely because, as a popular scientific and cultural phenomenon, mesmerism and its accompanying *mythos* reflected the deepest fears and desires of the age, concerns that inform, for instance, Hegel's master-slave relationship, or Carlyle's hero worship, as well as Coleridge's poetry.

Coleridge's poet stands, like the mesmerist, in medial relation to the power, the "intellectual breeze," that animates all objects of consciousness in space and time, that "meets all motion and becomes its soul," that creates things out of chaos. In Coleridge's portraits of imaginative dominance and imposition, the poet's powers of evocation are exercised in a manner very similar to that of the mesmerist with a subject who is *en rapport*. In this familiar situation the subject completely surrenders his or her will and consciousness to the power of the hypnotist, inhabiting a dream that is shaped by another mind: he or she sees the self and the world entirely through the eyes of the medium. We now know that this is a false picture of hypnosis,[31] but for a very long time it gripped the popular imagination, and apparently Coleridge's as well: auditors in Coleridge's poems—the "all" of "Kubla Khan," the young Christabel, the Ancient Mariner's Wedding-Guest—often seem to be drawn into a waking dream of the world that is shaped or directed by the glittering eye and the incantatory words of the poet figure. And the pattern is not confined to the so-called poems of the supernatural but appears in modified form in the conversation poems as well.

As "Kubla Khan" demonstrates, what the mesmeric poet seeks to create are voice-directed dreams in the minds of his audience, dreams into which, apparently, he may even enter and be recognized in his visionary identity. But "Kubla Khan" is itself, according to Coleridge's account of the birth of the poem in its brief preface, a voice-directed dream of this sort. Here, the poet is represented as inhabiting a realm that takes shape at the word, or we might even say, pointing up the parallel with Kubla's own creative powers of imagination, the "decree" (2), of another. In his preface Coleridge says that he "continued for about three hours in a profound sleep, at least of the external senses, during which time he has the most vivid confidence, that he could not have composed less than from two to three hundred lines; if that indeed can be called composition in which all the images rose up before him as *things,* with a parallel production of the correspondent expressions, without any sensation or consciousness of effort."[32]

Although the preface was added to the poem some eighteen years or more after Coleridge's first draft, it appeared in a somewhat truncated form in an early manuscript version, and Wheeler has argued convincingly for considering it an integral part of the finished work.[33] Also, despite its obvious undependability as a guide to the actual process of the poem's composition, the preface can still, in Wheeler's words, lead us "to ponder why Coleridge chose to write a preface, and why he chose to include the details, facts or fancy, so minutely described."[34] What the preface describes, of course, is not the actual process by which the poem came into being, but an analogue of poetic creation as *logos,* a divine "decree" or fiat which transforms the Word into the world. "Images" and "things" manifest themselves simultaneously with "expressions," and this "without any sensation or consciousness of effort," impelled by a power independent of the dreamer's own volition. Like the Khan himself, who according to tradition had a vision of Xanadu in his slumber before undertaking to build it, the dreamer is in the presence of a disembodied will that speaks the world he dreams.[35] Everywhere and nowhere, this power is present only as the ground or essence of all things that can be held in mind: a divine mesmerist, so to speak.

The relationship of dreamer to dream-speaker in the preface is the same as that of auditor to poet in the final lines of "Kubla Khan," but depicted from a different perspective: in the preface the poet seems to play the role of mesmeric subject, and we perceive the process from within; in the "epilogue," he takes the role of mesmerist, and we observe the process from without. Both relationships represent attempts at a visionary appropriation of the world impinging on other minds, and both are to this extent "logoistic."[36] This conception of the mesmeric imagination as a reflection of divine *logos* informs the famous distinction Coleridge later drew, in chapter 13 of the *Biographia Literaria,* between the primary and the secondary imaginations. There the act of *poesis* is conceived as "an echo" of the "eternal act of creation in the infinite 'I AM' ":

> The IMAGINATION then I consider either as primary, or secondary. The primary IMAGINATION I hold to be the living Power and prime Agent of all human Perception, and as a repetition in the finite mind of the eternal act of creation in the infinite I AM. The secondary I consider as an echo of the former, co-existing with the conscious will, yet still as identical with the primary in the *kind* of its

agency, and differing only in *degree,* and in the *mode* of its operation. It dissolves, diffuses, dissipates, in order to re-create; or where this process is rendered impossible, yet still, at all events, it struggles to idealize and to unify. It is essentially *vital,* even as all objects (*as* objects) are essentially fixed and dead.[37]

The aural character of these operations of the imagination—expressed in the words "I AM" and "echo"—betrays the underlying concept of the *logos,* the Word that is both world and divine presence.[38] Because the "secondary imagination" employed in artistic creation is taken to be "identical with the primary in the *kind* of its agency," though not in scope or degree, it can be understood, like the primary, both to bring a world to light and, through this world, to manifest indirectly the presence of an unlocalized, illimitable creator. As Coleridge indicates elsewhere, the greatest poets are protean forces in this logoistic sense—Shakespeare's nature is "Nature Shakespeareanized,"[39] a dream, he suggests in a notebook entry, permeated with the presence of the creator who speaks it: "Poetry a rationalized dream dealing [?about] to manifold Forms our own Feelings, that never perhaps were attached by us consciously to our own personal Selves.—What is the Lear, the Othello, but a divine Dream / All Shakespere [*sic*], & nothing Shakespeare."[40] To the extent that the poet can imitate the "living Power and prime Agent of human Perception," Coleridge suggests, he wields a power similar to the Almighty's and manages to surmount his status as "object"— "essentially fixed and dead"—in the eyes of the world at large.

The secondary imagination, like the primary, is a form of self-referential speech that is not self-limiting or self-qualifying. It is, rather, the variform medium of the poet's amorphous, spiritual presence suffusing the world he creates for others. Indeed, like the mesmerist maintaining an *en rapport* relationship with his subject, the poet speaking in any given text tends to disappear from his audience's primary awareness. He has become a disembodied being manifested only in the "shapes and sounds" he utters. But maintaining the self in this mediated relationship cannot secure for the poet the proper recognition of this power as *his* power, as the higher soul that, by possessing him, confirms his unique status as possessor. Accordingly, in poems like "Kubla Khan" and "Rime of the Ancient Mariner," the poet's mesmeric power is directly represented from without, dramatized in its effects upon its auditors, and symbolized by striking images of the poet manqué's "glittering" or "flashing eyes."

In the first-person narratives of the conversation poems mesmeric power and its effects on others cannot be so objectively represented. But here, for this very reason—that the poet has, in effect, become a disembodied voice—the similarity between mesmerism and *logoism* as two forms of "voice-directed dream" is most pronounced. Recognition, moreover, is indirectly secured by means other than the depiction and registration of others' responses to the poet's self-embodiment. Particularly in "Frost at Midnight" and "This Lime-Tree Bower My Prison," recognition of the poet's power to transform the "inanimate, cold world" is, instead, implied by others' presumed assent to the "reality" of the transformations thus effected.

The Conversation Poems: Coming into the World as Word

Coleridge's conversation poems express two contradictory impulses or moments, the one self-removed and visionary, the other self-present and confirmatory: on the one hand, as the written record of the poet's formative speech or *logos*, the poems represent the poet's attempt to create, or re-create anew, the world his implied auditors are imagined as inhabiting. On the other hand, as semidramatic monologues apparently addressed *to* others, they reveal an impulse to enter the very world the poet himself has uttered, to reembody the self as a *recognized* sharer of perceptions that, as a mind removed and ruminating, it has just transformed. As artifacts arising from these two moments, "Frost and Midnight" and "This Lime-Tree Bower My Prison" end by placing the poet in a world whose ontological status is ambiguous because agreement between poet and auditor can be imaginatively presumed but not directly affirmed. The world made habitable by the poet's disembodied imagination and, finally, inhabited by the reembodied poet himself is neither dream nor reality, neither solipsistic nor wholly objective, but spectrally "affirmed" by the imagined responses of the absent Other whom the poet apostrophizes.

In nearly all of the most well-known conversation poems there are indications that something close to a mesmeric relationship obtains between poet and audience. In the opening lines of "The Nightingale," for instance, the poem whose subtitle has come to describe, for Coleridgeans, the genre he created,[41] the poet's auditors are encouraged to "rest," their attention directed to a shiny, glimmering, and silent object, and their thoughts directed as well (4–11):

Come, we will rest on this old mossy bridge!
You see the glimmer of the stream beneath,

But hear no murmuring: it flows silently,
O'er its soft bed of verdure. All is still,
A balmy night! and though the stars be dim,
Yet let us think upon the vernal showers
That gladden the green earth, and we shall find
A pleasure in the dimness of the stars.

The narrator, from the outset, assumes control over his audience. True, his address is in many ways indistinguishable from the typical address to the audience that is a standard part of eighteenth-century poetic diction, but it is used here to create a markedly *mesmeric* effect. In "The Nightingale" the speaker not only speaks to his audience— he stations them, soothes them, indicates what they are to see and hear—"you see ... but hear"—and plants the suggestion—"let us think ..."—not only that the dimness of the stars is pleasurable, contradicting what his listeners might ordinarily think, but that the nightingale's "melancholy" is purely fanciful. By means of something very close to mesmeric "suggestion," he attempts to influence, even upend, the conventional ways in which his listeners perceive the world around them, supplanting their fancies with his own (41–49):

... we may not thus profane
Nature's sweet voices, always full of love
And joyance! 'Tis the merry Nightingale
That crowds, and hurries, and precipitates
With fast thick warble his delicious notes,
As he were fearful that an April night
Would be too short for him to utter forth
His love-chant, and disburthen his full soul
Of all its music!

"We may not"—the proscription is gently phrased, but it is a proscription, nonetheless.

Though the subject of "The Nightingale" is the song of a bird and the associations it evokes, the poem formally enacts a mesmeric event, an audience's submission to the compelling presence and voice of the poet. When, finally, the poet bids farewell to the nightingale, and to his listeners, the effect is abrupt, exactly as though his friends, and we the readers, were being roused from a trance or a directed reverie. We are pointedly reminded that we have forgotten ourselves as well as the amount of time that has passed since we first rested on the bridge (87–90):

Farewell, O Warbler! till to-morrow eve,
And you, my friends! farewell, a short farewell!
We have been loitering long and pleasantly,
And now for our dear homes.

In "The Eolian Harp" Sara's darting eye is particularly devastating because it destroys this mood of gentle, dreamy persuasion. In the opening lines of the poem she appears in a submissive posture: "My pensive Sara! thy soft cheek reclined / Thus on mine arm." If we consider the issues of encirclement raised in "Kubla Khan," we should not be surprised to find that the poet begins, literally, with an act of counter-encirclement, embracing his auditor as he attempts to embrace her mind. We imagine Sara listening "pensively," yielding, as the poem unfolds, to a kind of reverie or half-dream in which the world is shaped and ordered, and the relative emotional value and allegorical significance of the things around her assigned, by the voice of her ruminating husband (1–12):

My pensive Sara! thy soft cheek reclined
Thus on mine arm, most soothing sweet it is
To sit beside our Cot, our Cot o'ergrown
With white-flower'd Jasmin, and the broad-leav'd Myrtle,
(Meet emblems they of Innocence and Love!)
And watch the clouds, that late were rich with light,
Slow saddening round, and mark the star of eve
Serenely brilliant (such should Wisdom be)
Shine opposite! How exquisite the scents
Snatch'd from yon bean-field! and the world *so* hush'd!
The stilly murmur of the distant Sea
Tells us of silence.
                    And that simplest Lute. . . .

Again we find the speaker drawing his listener's attention to a shining object, as well as a quiet, repetitive "murmur" that will leave her mind receptive to suggestion. The speaker's intent in these first lines is hermeneutical, albeit quite conventional: the flowers may be taken as "meet emblems" of emotions, and the "star of eve" as an image of "Wisdom." These are poetic commonplaces, but they are introduced sub rosa, in parentheses, just below the level of primary attention. "The way is now open," writes Geoffrey Yarlott, "for Coleridge, having lulled Sara into a state of acquiescence . . . to administer the metaphysical pill which he has been carefully sugar-ing."[42] The speaker's playful suggestions soon lead to more serious speculations, touching on the revealed truths of Christian religion: "And what if all of animated Nature / Be but organic harps, diversely framed?" By her darting look, Sara resists further complicity in this imaginative ordering, this reinterpretation, this "reading" of the world.

Coleridge was later to reflect on his tendencies to such "symbolical" scanning of Nature in a notebook entry of April 14, 1805:

> In looking at objects of Nature while I am thinking, as at yonder moon dim-glimmering thro' the dewy window-pane, I seem rather to be seeking, as it were *asking*, a symbolical language for something within me that already and forever exists, than observing any thing new. Even when that latter is the case, yet still I have always an obscure feeling as if that new phaenomenon were the dim Awaking of a forgotten or hidden Truth of my inner Nature / It is still interesting as a Word, a Symbol! It is [*logos*], the Creator! (and the Evolver!)[43]

In his emblematizing of Nature and characterization of the lute, the poet has spoken the words that are, in effect, the Word working through him, from "within him," like Wordsworth's "egotistical sublime," to transform the world it appropriates into something symbolically meaningful. Coleridge's yearning for such assurances of a divine presence mediated by the language of the senses appears as early as 1796, as Albert Gerard points out,[44] in "The Destiny of Nations" (18–23):

> For all that meets the bodily sense I deem
> Symbolical, one mighty alphabet
> For infant minds: and we in this low world
> Placed with our backs to bright Reality,
> That we may learn with young unwounded ken
> The substance from its shadow.

Coleridge's interest in nature as a divine text continued throughout his life and culminated in his making the concept of *logos* the capstone of his projected *Opus Maximum*, his "Logosophia."[45] In 1817, in the errata to *Sybilline Leaves*, he added to "The Eolian Harp" the famous lines (26–29),

O! the one Life within us and abroad,
Which meets all motion and becomes its soul,
A light in sound, a sound-like power in light,
Rhythm in all thought, and joyance every where— —

In the 1828 edition of his poems, when he was quite far into plans for the *Opus Maximum,* he made sure to include this passage, representing the vital power that shines forth in the *phaenomena* of the visible world as a something sounded, uttered, a pattern of speech that is the "rhythm" informing and organizing the perceived world ("all thought"). It is this divine speech, Coleridge suggests from the perspective of 1828, that orders the world as image and unfolds it "logically" in time.

As "Kubla Khan" and the opening lines of "The Nightingale" and "The Eolian Harp" suggest, *logos* is but a divine form of that power of speech by which any dream of the world can take form, and with which the poet can influence the relaxed or "pensive" mind of another. The parallels are further strengthened by Coleridge's own interpretation, in a notebook entry of 1802, of the image of moonlight glimmering on the water, as in the opening lines of "The Nightingale," where its soothing glow helps the poet lull his auditors into a submissive reverie: "Quiet stream, with all its eddies, & the moonlight playing on them, quiet as if they were Ideas in the divine mind anterior to the Creation."[46] Here is an example of the secondary imagination "seeking" or "asking" for a "symbolical language" by which to represent its own affinities with *logos.*

There is a further refinement to the manner in which Coleridge's later "logoism" is anticipated by the poet's mesmeric relationship to his audience, a refinement that is most pronounced in those conversation poems where the audience is not, in fact, present or aware of the poet: the world understood as breath or utterance is a world whose Speaker remains disembodied and unlocalized in his speech, in effect, actualizing his words *through* the mental agencies of the perceiving and interpreting subject, as a mesmerist would *en rapport.* Coleridge calls Sara's attention to the star, the scent, the sea; Sara calls Coleridge's attention back to himself.

If the "one Life" is *both* "within us and abroad," "*at once* the soul of each, and God of all," the real subject and final object of all thought, then the minds of particular beings are merely the instruments by which this fiat expresses itself and (to extend the central metaphor of "The Eolian Harp") "orchestrates" all "organic harps diversely framed" into our common experience of things. Similarly, the mesmerist who imitates or "echoes" the power of the "one Life" by speaking *en rapport* makes his subject's mind the projector of a hallucinatory cinema. The hypnotized subject remains receptive to, though not primarily conscious of, this suggestive voice, and through his half-conscious receptivity the world in which he must act and come to understand himself takes form. The mesmerist, meanwhile, like God, stands aloof from the subject's chief awareness, making his mind "tremble into thought" with the "intellectual breeze" of a commanding utterance.[47]

These parallels between God and poet as mesmeric "speakers" of the world are clearly drawn in a poem like "Frost at Midnight," where the poet's intended auditor, his sleeping infant son, is already in fact the inhabitant of a dream. Of course, neither here nor in "This Lime-Tree Bower My Prison" has Coleridge depicted a mesmeric event in the strict sense: Hartley is entirely unconscious of his father's presence and, even if he were awake, he could not possibly fall under his father's "spell." But the main features of the voice-directed dream appear in the poet's "strange power of speech," which proceeds by means of apostrophe and imperatives, revealing the mesmeric intention that informs the poet's rhetorical strategy and relationship to his "auditor": to direct the unfolding of a world into which the auditor is projected while the speaker remains, for most of the poem, absent. Here, and in "This Lime-Tree Bower," the poet speaks like one who would fashion, by saying it, a world with which to embrace the person he addresses.

"Frost at Midnight" is a supreme example of what Richard Haven calls the conversation poem's typical "pattern of consciousness,"[48] a pattern George Maclean Harper first identified as the "return," and which is now taken for granted in Coleridgean criticism. Max Schultz calls it a "centrifugal-centripetal action of the mind"; Albert Gerard, the "diastolic-systolic" rhythm; Humphry House, the repeated "movement of the thought" from "the Ego, the 'I'—the seeing, remembering, projecting mind" out to the world around it and back again.[49] It is an imaginative flight from quiet egocentrism to vital empathy with another and finally to a sense of the "one Life" expressed in the shapes and sounds of nature, "that eternal language, which . . . God / Utters, who from eternity doth teach / Himself in all, and all things in himself" (60–62). This movement, I wish to note, grows out of the poet's initial appropriation of the world around him as a dream, his breaking down of the boundary between "inside" and "outside." The silent world depicted in the opening lines displays all the hallmarks of a waking dream that we find associated with the boundary conditions of withdrawal, with that experiential solipsism which appears, for instance, in Wordsworth's initial encounter with the discharged soldier. Among these hallmarks are silence and stillness (1–13):

> The Frost performs its secret ministry,
> Unhelped by any wind. The owlet's cry
> Came loud—and hark, again! loud as before.
> The inmates of my cottage, all at rest,
> Have left me to that solitude, which suits
> Abstruser musings: save that at my side
> My cradled infant slumbers peacefully.
> 'Tis calm indeed! so calm, that it disturbs
> And vexes meditation with its strange
> And extreme silentness. Sea, hill, and wood,
> This populous village! Sea, and hill, and wood,
> With all the numberless goings-on of life,
> Inaudible as dreams!

In this dream of the world, objects become symbolically significant. They speak to the poet as "companionable forms" of his own mind (13–23):

> . . . the thin blue flame
> Lies on my low-burnt fire, and quivers not;
> Only that film, which fluttered on the grate,
> Still flutters there, the sole unquiet thing.
> Methinks, its motion in this hush of nature
> Gives it dim sympathies with me who live,
> Making it a companionable form,
> Whose puny flaps and freaks the idling Spirit
> By its own moods interprets, every where
> Echo or mirror seeking of itself,
> And makes a toy of Thought.

The world-turned-dream eventually surrenders itself to the projected power of the poet's "idling Spirit." Not surprisingly, this "Spirit" discovers a "companionable form" in the one object whose motion "gives it dim sympathies" with the living observer. The fire's "puny flaps and freaks" lend themselves to the poet's first tentative efforts at self-dispersion, which extend even to a sort of primitive animism: the flame is assumed to sympathize with the observer ("gives *it* dim sympathies with *me*") rather than the reverse. This assumption, furthermore, is quite in keeping with the folk associations of the flame as "the *stranger*" (26), a sign of the imminent arrival of an absent friend. Thus the first object fastened upon by the poet's wandering mind reflects his own restlessness and anxiety over his solitary condition, a condition of solipsistic withdrawal that, ironically, makes such symbolic appropriations of objects possible.

These reflections on and of his own solitude next lead the poet back in memory to his lonely childhood at Christ's hospital, when, "with most believing mind, / Presageful," he had "gazed upon the bars, / to watch that fluttering *stranger!*" (24–26), ever expecting a visit from home. From such memories of childhood abandonment and isolation, his thoughts turn effortlessly to the child asleep at his side. From this point on the movement from finite self to articulate universe proceeds by way of the poet's empathy with another "companionable form," his sleeping infant, Hartley. It is here that Coleridge assumes, in the words of Walter Jackson Bate, "his habitual role as usher—as benevolent and understanding usher":

> It was not he who could receive the "blessing" . . . the release, the happiness or confidence, the opportunity for insight, are either given or presumed to be possible only to another. What is involved here—at least we can say this when we think of his life as a whole— is an act of "blessing," and in the older meaning of that term: a surrender, a giving, which assumes sacrifice . . . Through surrender, Coleridge himself . . . can acquire his own vicarious release of heart, his own security and confidence in what he thinks and hopes.[50]

In this role as "usher," Coleridge rhetorically imitates the *logos* he invokes. Directed at molding and affirming a prophetic dream of his child's future life, his words are addressed as an apostrophe to his sleeping son, as though they were meant to enter Hartley's slumbering mind (44–64):

> Dear Babe, that sleepest cradled by my side,
> Whose gentle breathings, heard in this deep calm,
> Fill up the interspersed vacancies
> And momentary pauses of the thought!
> My babe so beautiful! it thrills my heart
> With tender gladness, thus to look at thee,

And think that thou shalt learn far other lore,
And in far other scenes! For I was reared
In the great city, pent 'mid cloisters dim,
And saw nought lovely but the sky and stars.
But *thou*, my babe! shalt wander like a breeze
By lakes and sandy shores, beneath the crags
Of ancient mountains, and beneath the clouds,
Which image in their bulk both lakes and shores
And mountain crags: so shalt thou see and hear
The lovely shapes and sounds intelligible
Of that eternal language, which thy God
Utters, who from eternity doth teach
Himself in all, and all things in himself.
Great universal Teacher! he shall mould
Thy spirit, and by giving make it ask.

Here the poet himself assumes the role of a shaping and speaking, "moulding" and prophetic power of creation, mediately addressing, through the world he utters, one who is in fact his own creature. It is he who speaks the "lovely shapes and sounds intelligible / Of that eternal language"—lakes, shores, crags, mountains, and clouds—which he assigns to God, and he speaks imperatively, like a demiurge: "But *thou . . . shalt wander,*" "so *shalt thou see and hear.*" We are reminded of the poet's expectation in "Kubla Khan" that "all who heard *should* see."

Although not literally "mesmeric," the poet's relationship to his son proceeds rhetorically as if it were, by way of imperatives and, more important, apostrophe: addressing the absent one as though he were present is, in a sense, to speak as a disembodied presence. As Bate and others agree, the movement of mind from self to a companionable cosmos proceeds vicariously, by the poet's envisioning a "presumed" childhood for his son quite different from his own.[51] But the fact that this presumption depends strictly on *the poet's* act of vision, and one in which he remains personally absent from the child's arena of perception, is exactly what reveals the signature of a mesmeric intent: Hartley's prospective childhood is a dream shaped, in the first instance, by the poet's own prophetic utterance. It is not, cannot be, a hope expressed by the boy and then entered into by the poet; it does not—obviously cannot—have its origins in Hartley's own mind. It results from an act of empathy, not sympathy, strictly defined.

The poet's mental distance from the person he addresses appears as well in other conversation poems, which, as a genre, are paradoxically named: only once—in "The Eolian Harp"—and with unsettling results does the poet's auditor demonstrate any awareness of his presence, let alone of what he says. Browning's dramatic monologues are more "conversational" in this respect. In "Frost at Midnight" we see why the transference of feeling from the poet to another must proceed at a mental distance. Only by keeping the finite self apart can Coleridge let his presumptive imagination go forward unchecked by the real presence of others.[52] Only thus can he take upon himself that divinely anticipatory power of articulation that informed his own daydreams of a happy infancy and early childhood, dreams recurring often when, as a schoolboy, "with most believing mind, / Presageful," he had "gazed upon the bars, / To watch that fluttering *stranger!*" (24–26). And (26–35)

> . . . as oft
> With unclosed lids, already had I dreamt
> Of my sweet birth-place, and the old church-tower,
> Whose bells, the poor man's only music, rang
> From morn to evening, all the hot Fair-day,
> So sweetly, that they stirred and haunted me
> With a wild pleasure, falling on mine ear
> Most like articulate sounds of things to come!
> So gazed I, till the soothing things, I dreamt,
> Lulled me to sleep, and sleep prolonged my dreams!

Here, at the heart of the poem, immediately after the speaker's fastening of attention on the fire-film and just before his turning to Hartley, we arrive at a dream within a dream, a dream that provides the fulcrum for the poet's shift of attention to his son. It is a dream infused with the presence of the Word. The church bells seem, to the inner ear of the schoolboy, "most like *articulate* sounds *of things to come*"—that is, "presageful" or prophetic—and the implication is that they are made so by the boy's own "believing mind" as, only a moment before, he had "gaz'd upon the bars" at "the *stranger.*" Thus does the boy's own "idling Spirit" become the *logos* of his dream of home, making of the church bells—a call to community—an "intelligible sound" expressive of his own most urgent anticipation of a "companionable form": "townsman, or aunt, or sister more beloved" (42).

The dream of home bears the same relation to the poet's apostrophe to his son as the dream described in the preface to "Kubla Khan" bears to the act of *poesis* represented in that poem's final stanza: first, the poet inhabits a universe made "intelligible" by a higher power working through his dreaming mind; next, he assumes the power to create such an imagined universe for another. In the same way that the schoolboy's believing mind became the *logos* of his dream of life—a "rationalized dream," like poetry itself, "dealing about to manifold Forms" his own feelings—so now, as an adult meditating in dreamlike silence, the isolated poet becomes, or would become, the *logos* of the companionable world he envisions for his son. The words addressed to his infant "articulate" the father's hopes for his child and "presage" the boy's future.

The final step in this process is the poet's reembodiment in the world he has uttered, his entering the very realm he has imagined, as he did when a schoolboy, dreaming of home. What conveys this sense of reembodiment is the gradual narrowing of attention to objects near in time (season) and space (just outside the window), as well as the reappearance of sounds—the song of the redbreast, the dripping of the icicles, the occasional blast of the wind (65–74):

> Therefore all seasons shall be sweeet to thee,
> Whether the summer clothe the general earth
> With greenness, or the redbreast sit and sing
> Betwixt the tufts of snow on the bare branch
> Of mossy apple-tree, while the night thatch
> Smokes in the sun-thaw; whether the eave-drops fall
> Heard only in the trances of the blast,
> Or if the secret ministry of frost
> Shall hang them up in silent icicles,
> Quietly shining to the quiet Moon.

The lovely image of the icicles glittering in the moonlight, it has often been observed, seems to symbolize the shaping powers of the poet's own visionary imagination, drawing their vitality from a transcendent source of "illumination."[53] The poem ends, then, with Nature itself offering, or "uttering" in the "eternal language" of its own forms, "a symbolical language for something within" the poet "that already and forever exists," "a forgotten or hidden Truth" of his *"inner* Nature" that has now become "outer" Nature: "a Word, a Symbol. It is [*logos*]."

But this world, though transformed by the self within, is no longer presumed to be exclusively a part of the self within. Recall that one important hallmark of the poet's initial solipsistic experience of the "populous village" and of the beings and forms around him was their inaudibility. The "owlet's cry" in the second line was the last sound to reach the poet from a world "out there." Silence signals distance and self-exclusion, leading to the mental incorporation of the world, but sounds come at us from without, like an address, often from sources not immediately attended to, not "kept in mind." Sounds embrace and include: here, they help bring the poet back to the world at hand.

The sounds that reappear at the end of "Frost at Midnight" reinforce the significant parallels between the schoolboy's dream of home and the poet's final vision of an "intelligible" universe: both are places to which *he* ultimately belongs, in which the embodied, finite self has a significant place. If sounds are spatially inclusive, then the sound of the church bells in the dream of home, like the sounds that reappear at the end of the poem, must be understood not only to reveal the imperative presence of *logos*, but to confirm the boy's "real"—and meaningful—existence in the very world his "idling Spirit" has created.

By the end of the poem the speaker has made his initially unreal world intelligible and "companionable," presumably to his child, in actuality to himself. It is now safe for him to reenter. I wish to emphasize, however, that the poet has not, as is so often suggested, undergone a simple change in attitude upon reawakening to reality. The "return" is complicated by the fact that this "reality" is itself strictly conditional. It still exists solely for *his* mind, though his presumptions otherwise give it a spectral validation. In a sense the poet is like a dreamer who no longer knows he dreams, like the absentminded schoolboy to whom his own absent mind reverts in the middle of the poem. He has dreamed himself a world in which he belongs. This is not to say that what the speaker perceives is merely an illusion. The world out there is no longer "inaudible as dreams," nor is it animated by the poet's personal anxieties—just "a toy of Thought." It is not a solipsistic vision, but a vision presumably shared: the individual mind, disembodied, becomes Mind, and then becomes reembodied in the very world it has imagined *for others*. But the presumption of sharing remains that, a presumption. There is not, as in Wordsworth's sobering encounters with others, a true confrontation in which the self and the world it has made for itself are challenged. The world transformed remains, in fact, unshared. Its "reality" depends on the exclusion of the real presence of others, who are addressed, throughout, from a distance.

This impression of a presumptive but unconfirmed "sharing" of the world to which the poet returns is even more pronounced in "This Lime-Tree Bower My Prison," where the poet again "speaks" the world that others are assumed to inhabit in order, finally, to enter the world that is his word (1–20):

> Well, they are gone, and here must I remain,
> This lime-tree bower my prison! I have lost
> Beauties and feelings, such as would have been
> Most sweet to my remembrance even when age
> Had dimm'd mine eyes to blindness! They, meanwhile,
> Friends, whom I never more may meet again,
> On springy heath, along the hill-top edge,
> Wander in gladness, and wind down, perchance,
> To that still roaring dell, of which I told:
> The roaring dell, o'erwooded, narrow, deep,
> And only speckled by the mid-day sun;
> Where its slim trunk the ash from rock to rock
> Flings arching like a bridge;—that branchless ash,
> Unsunn'd and damp, whose few poor yellow leaves
> Ne'er tremble in the gale, yet tremble still,
> Fann'd by the water-fall! and there my friends
> Behold the dark green file of long lank weeds,
> That all at once (a most fantastic sight!)
> Still nod and drip beneath the dripping edge
> Of the blue clay-stone.

The poem begins, like "Frost at Midnight," by emphasizing the narrator's physical isolation from his friends—"they are gone, and here must I remain." It is an isolation hyperbolically reinforced by the phrase, "Friends, whom I never more may meet again." We recognize something more than self-pity here. The poet is insisting on the radical discontinuity of his perceptual world, bounded by the bower, "my prison," and that of his friends. They are not simply separated by physical distance: there is assumed to be an impassable spiritual gulf fixed between them. The world in his mind and the world in theirs seem to exist "compossibly," like Leibnitz's hypothetical "monads," whose respective inhabitants can never meet, though they may coexist. The poet and his friends share no common objects of perception.

If physical meeting is now out of the question, then connections must be established by a sort of metempsychosis that is effected rhetorically. In addition to the devices of apostrophe and imperative used in "Frost at Midnight," the poet resorts to deixis. From statements about his own situation he passes, first, to a surmise about his friends: they are wandering and winding down "perchance, / To that still roaring dell, of which I told." "Perchance" is speculative, but "of which *I told*" is proprietary: we are being gently reminded that the dell and, later, the hill and the spectacular sunset, have no existence aside from their being "told." To draw on Bate's terminology, we, as well as the poet's friends, are being "ushered" into a realm that is, from the first, the property of the poet's mind, arising in response to the poet's word.

But even though the word "perchance" reminds us that the events to follow do take place only in the poet's mind, what does follow is so carefully and concretely depicted that we forget that its reality is ambiguous. The roaring dell arises in *our* minds, though at the *poet's* word and as conceived by him. Coleridge reinforces this point rhetorically. With all the alliterative and rhythmic skill at his command, and with shimmering fidelity, the poet concentrates our attention on the scene that his friends are assumed to be witnessing in the dell. The diction in these lines is markedly different from the breezy tone of the opening lines. We are drawn to the scene itself, not to the pouting personality of the speaker, and so compellingly that by the end of this description we are no longer invited to suppose a case. The presence of the poet's friends in the dell has become more than hypothetical: "And there my friends / *Behold* the dark green file of long lank weeds." The mood here is indicative, but even more interesting is the imperative note sounded by placing the verb at the beginning of the line. Our attention, too, is fixed on this "most fantastic sight," almost as though the phrase, "my friends," were addressed to us and we had been commanded to "behold."

The poet's apostrophic relationship to his friends is, like his relationship to his readers, "mesmeric." In the first paragraph of the poem he has advanced almost unnoticed from speculation to affirmation, even muted command. What was at first hypothesis—"perchance"—becomes apparent fact. In the second verse paragraph the mood shifts still further in the direction of the imperative, from fact to fiat. After describing his friends and the realm they traverse in his mind, the poet begins, in language reminiscent of his apostrophe to Hartley in "Frost at Midnight," to direct the unfolding of events (20–43).[54]

Now, my friends emerge
Beneath the wide wide Heaven—and view again
The many-steepled tract magnificent
Of hilly fields and meadows, and the sea,
With some fair bark, perhaps, whose sails light up
The slip of smooth clear blue betwixt two Isles
Of purple shadow! Yes! they wander on
In gladness all; but thou, methinks, most glad,
My gentle-hearted Charles! for thou hast pined
And hunger'd after Nature, many a year,
In the great City pent, winning thy way
With sad yet patient soul, through evil and pain
And strange calamity! Ah! slowly sink
Behind the western ridge, thou glorious Sun!
Shine in the slant beams of the sinking orb,
Ye purple heath-flowers! richlier burn, ye clouds!
Live in the yellow light, ye distant groves!
And kindle, thou blue Ocean! So my friend
Struck with deep joy may stand, as I have stood,
Silent with swimming sense; yea, gazing round
On the wide landscape, gaze till all doth seem
Less gross than bodily; and of such hues
As veil the Almighty Spirit, when yet he makes
Spirits perceive his presence.

"Now my friends emerge . . . and view again . . . Yes! They wander on / In gladness all." The interjection, "Yes!" signifies not only the approbative delight of the poetic imagination that, remaining distant, lifts the soul to "contemplate / With lively joy the joys" it "cannot share" (66–67), but the fulfillment of a wish, an intention: "Yes, that is how it should be, that is how it is to go." It is as though the poet were directing a movie or a play. This directorial intent becomes clearer following the apostrophe to "my gentle-hearted Charles," when the poet unleashes a series of imperatives or stage directions for the scenic display of Nature: "Ah! slowly sink . . . shine . . . richlier burn . . . live . . . and kindle." The poet's imagination strives to speak the world that others inhabit.

Charles stands where the poet has stood, but the poet, delighting in Charles's imagined gladness, now stands nowhere—and everywhere. The visionary world and the mind that envisions it have become one. In Richard Haven's words, "As the landscape is transformed, unified, and set on fire by the light of sunset, so it ceases to be a separate object of a collection of objects: it seems one, and one with the life of the consciousness which contemplates it."[55]

That this visionary consciousness has drastically suspended its sense of embodiment becomes clear only as the world at hand obtrudes on the poet's reverie. That process takes place as the poet "takes the place" of his friend (43–64):

> A delight
> Comes sudden on my heart, and I am glad
> As I myself were there! Nor in this bower,
> This little lime-tree bower, have I not mark'd
> Much that has sooth'd me. Pale beneath the blaze
> Hung the transparent foliage; and I watch'd
> Some broad and sunny leaf, and lov'd to see
> The shadow of the leaf and stem above
> Dappling its sunshine! And that walnut-tree
> Was richly ting'd, and a deep radiance lay
> Full on the ancient ivy, which usurps
> Those fronting elms, and now, with blackest mass
> Makes their dark branches gleam a lighter hue
> Through the late twilight: and though now the bat
> Wheels silent by, and not a swallow twitters,
> Yet still the solitary humble-bee
> Sings in the bean-flower! Henceforth I shall know
> That Nature ne'er deserts the wise and pure;
> No plot so narrow, be but Nature there,
> No waste so vacant, but may well employ
> Each faculty of sense, and keep the heart
> Awake to Love and Beauty!

The poet who would diffuse his presence throughout a world that germinates *in* his mind, awakens from his reveries of self-dispersion to find himself embowered by the very Nature he had enclosed. And, as in "Frost at Midnight," it is a sound that confirms the poet's return from solipsistic reverie to a sense of being in the world. The song of the bee vividly conveys the sense of awakening from a disembodied to a reembodied state of awareness, if only because nearly everything else in the poem—the description of the dell, of Charles's subsequent vision of sun, cloud, and ocean, and even of what the poet's "heart" has been "awake" to while his mind was elsewhere—is watched or envisioned silently, at a distance.

"The return to the bower is a return to the self," says Haven.[56] But as in "Frost at Midnight" there is no return to a self realized in the presence of others. In one sense, and as is generally assumed, the "lively joy" that the poet experiences upon his return to the bower, like the joy he experiences in the sights and sounds of Nature at the end of his apostrophe to Hartley, is drawn vicariously from the "contemplation" of his imagined friend or friends. But more is involved than simple identification. For the "soul" that is "lifted," disembodied and dispersed, in order to contemplate and appropriate these joys has already, by its very dispersion, become the Soul of the world that inspires them in Charles. Indeed, if, as the poet tells his lady in "Dejection: an Ode," "we receive but what we give, / And in our life alone does Nature live" (47–48), then Nature in "This Lime-Tree Bower" must be understood to live, first, in the imaginatively dilated life of the poet, not in the lives of his imagined friends.

The poet's "delight" is a vicarious delight, then, but it does not originate in the delight of Charles Lamb and the Wordsworths, any more than, in "Frost at Midnight," it arose from the hopes and dreams of Hartley. It is put there, as though embodied in fictional characters, and only then recalled and recognized by the poet himself. The friends' adventures, it cannot be overemphasized, are, within the narrative framework of the poem, fictitious—they *cannot* be "shared" in any real sense. Many critics speak of these absent events as though they were in fact taking place as the poet imagined them, one indication of the effectiveness of Coleridge's spell of words.[57] Most of us tend to forget that the dell, the hill, the sea are all "realities" conditioned by the speculative imagination of the solitary poet.

Moreover, so is the reality of the bower itself. The "return" here, as in "Frost at Midnight," is not a return to the shared world but to a world whose "reality" is maintained strictly within mental horizons that exclude the real presence of others. True, the bower is now suffused with the others' imagined joy: "I am glad / As I myself were *there*"—but at the moment he says this, the poet finds himself *here*, not with his friends, but back in a "prison" burning with appropriated fire. The pyrotechnic display of the setting sun, which Coleridge has made to "shine," "burn," and "kindle" in his own mind for the imagined pleasure of his friends, now manifests itself in the bower itself, symbol of that mind's solipsistic isolation. "Blaze," "sunny," "sunshine," "richly ting'd," "deep radiance," "gleam": the poet cut off from shared perception illumines his own perceptual prison with a light that, by "lifting" his "soul" Prometheus-like and freeing it from its sense of embodiment, he has just filched from heaven.[58]

Reincarnated in the bower of its own self-withdrawal, the "soul" of the poet finally enters *in propria persona* the very world it has dreamed. The sound of the bee, like the sound of the church bells or dripping icicles in "Frost at Midnight," seems to confirm the poet's real residence in this private world, a realm suffused with the presence of the "one Life" that, working from within, unites all sentient beings, however distant from each other. So, too, does the sound of the creeking rook flying overhead in the last lines (68–76):

> My gentle-hearted Charles! when the last rook
> Beat its straight path along the dusky air
> Homewards, I blest it! deeming its black wing
> (Now a dim speck, now vanishing in light)
> Had cross'd the mighty Orb's dilated glory,
> While thou stood'st gazing; or, when all was still,
> Flew creeking o'er thy head, and had a charm
> For thee, my gentle-hearted Charles, to whom
> No sound is dissonant which tells of Life.

The creeking rook *"tells* of life"; it is a word spoken by the "one Life," revealing the presence of *logos*. But it is also something whose audibility insures its existence outside the poet's mind and, by extension, reinforces our sense of the poet's finite embodiment. This sense of the bird's exteriority is enhanced by the poet's presumption that Charles too sees and hears the rook, that continuity of perception has been established between bower and hill, between the mind of the poet and the minds of others, a continuity that in the beginning of the poem had been despaired of.[59]

But the poet's relationship with Charles, even here, remains apostrophic, and Charles's perception of the rook, like all the rest of his whereabouts and activities, remains unconfirmed. The poet "deems" his experience of this object to have been shared, but the use of the disjunctive, "or" (73), hints at the tentativeness of that assumption. Thus, the final lines of the poem reaffirm the qualified nature of the poet's "return" to the world. The self-embodiment he assumes does not manifest itself in the real presence of others but in the presence of objects, like the bee or the rook, whose exteriority in turn requires the *presumed* presence of others: their agreement with the poet's view of life, and even with his characterization of them, can be taken for granted.[60]

"Frost at Midnight" and "This Lime-Tree Bower My Prison," then, reveal the poetic imagination in the act of privatizing the world ordinarily shared with others in order to make it conform to the contours of the self as Mind. In the process the world takes on the significance of *logos,* a "speaking" power working from within the poet to embrace the minds of his audience, while their real presence is kept distant, beyond the horizons of his own consciousness. The aim of the disembodied visionary imagination, the "lifted" soul, is to make the world "companionable," but it seems that such transformations can only take place in the absence of real companions, by imaginatively projecting the poet's vision on the passive minds of imagined others. The ultimate aim of such mesmerically intended utterances is, as in Wordsworth's poetry, to make the world safe for the return of the visionary self to embodied form.

In the end the poet can take his place in the world only in the spectral "presence" of imagined interlocutors, and as part of a "reality" he has imagined as confirmed in their eyes. In its mesmeric and logoistic rhetorical thrust, the conversation poem reveals a characteristically Coleridgean version of self-withdrawal and compensatory imaginative appropriation, the hallmarks of visionary solipsism. In its "return" to the embodied self, however, it reveals the poet's reaction to the self-dispersion that solipsistic withdrawal inevitably entails: the need to feel included in a world that accepts the poet as visionary, and accepts as well his extraordinary vision of things.

"The Rime of the Ancient Mariner": Solipsism and "Life-in-Death"

There is nothing particularly sinister about Coleridge's speculative flights or the appropriative nature of his imagination. Projective empathy and feelings of the "sublime" are common features of the Romantic lyric, going back to Gray's ruminations in the country churchyard and, probably, beyond. What is distinctive about the conversation poems, however, is the poet's use of apostrophe, imperative, and deixis to signify rhetorically the exertion of control or direction while maintaining physical distance. What we find here, as in many of Wordsworth's poems, are the phenomenological effects of a withdrawal or simple isolation or distancing of the self from the "goings-on" of life in the world and from the self "going on" as part of that life. It is a withdrawal that as often as not in Romantic poetry seems to presage or give rise to vivid imaginative and empathic experiences in which the world becomes unreal and dreamlike.

The real presence of others threatens the hermetic enclosure of consciousness that is characteristic of such experiences. As an independent mind or center of awareness, understood to be truly present in his embodiment, the Other can define himself in contradistinction to the poet's vision of him, and make the poet self-conscious, bringing him "to" his finite, phenomenal self. The independent, reflecting mind of the Other must therefore be denied if the visionary is to make his vision of things, and of others, prevail.

This visionary tendency to deny the independence of the Other can help explain one of the most puzzling events of "The Rime of the Ancient Mariner": why the crew must die for the old man's crime. The solution has only partially to do with notions of crime and punishment. The deaths of the crew, like their macabre reanimations, symbolically reflect the perceptual distortions effected by the Mariner's visionary solipsism: they have become his "objects . . . fixed and dead," their status as independent minds canceled as the Mariner moves toward an imaginative self-assimilation with the natural universe. This act of denial begins with the random and unpremeditated violence of the Mariner's crime, by which he first repudiates the self-determinative force of the judgments and expectations of the society to which he belongs. He removes his "self," in effect, from the world of others in which actions have meaning.

Though the Mariner's crime is often called "self-assertive," such a characterization must be qualified. As I have tried to show, what is sometimes called the "Romantic faith in the self" is in fact a faith in the asocial self-as-mind, the self abstracted from the real presence of others.[61] It is not "self-assertion," narrowly conceived, which leads to the Mariner's guilt and alienation, but self-withdrawal. By a crime that appears motiveless, the Mariner places himself outside that community where the actions by which the self is embodied as "real" are made meaningful in the eyes of others, reciprocally definitive of character, place, and role. This repudiation of a shared world, as in the opening lines of "This Lime-Tree Bower" and "Frost at Midnight," leads eventually to the boundary condition of visionary solipsism and a sense of assimilation with the "one Life." But the Mariner must first submit to the nightmare of insubstantiality, of "Life-in-Death," before he can assume that identity with a transcendent Mind which will change the derealized world into something visionary.

The Mariner's crime calls into question all conventional categories by which a self can be characterized as "assertive." If, as has often been remarked, this act is distinguished for its utter lack of personal malice, rationale, or motive, then killing the albatross is an affirmation of all that is "not-self," everything that will not fit into our predetermined notions of personality or character. "Ultimately, the cause is *himself:* 'I shot,' " writes Michael G. Cooke.[62] But this only begs the question of both self and cause, which remain equally indeterminate. The Mariner is an irreducible enigma. That we can assign no cause for the killing outside the Mariner "himself" makes his individuality so radical, his resistance to outside "interpretation" so complete, that he lacks a definite identity.

The complete impersonality, the "motiveless malignity," of the Mariner's act puts him at odds with the very idea of a person. Though nothing could be "sweeter" to the Mariner on returning from his horrendous voyage than "to walk together to the kirk / With a goodly company" (603–604), it is obvious that by the end of his ordeal he has become unfit to dwell among the living, represented more prominently by those carousing within doors at the wedding feast. The Mariner, observes Yarlott, "seeks the company of people solely for purposes of communal worship, not for a renewal of such intimate personal relationships as the wedding symbolizes."[63] Indeed, as Haven explains, "The world of the Wedding Guest . . . is a world in which selves are public objects defined by their social relationships as bride and groom or next of kin . . . [The Mariner] has returned to be in, though he can never again be entirely of, the social world."[64] Remaining throughout the narrative a shadowy presence, the Mariner is doomed to wander, but never settle, on the face of the earth—and doomed to unsettle as well those he meets (1–20):

It is an ancient Mariner,
And he stoppeth one of three.
"By thy long grey beard and glittering eye,
Now wherefore stopp'st thou me?

The Bridegroom's doors are opened wide,
And I am next of kin;
The guests are met, the feast is set:
May'st hear the merry din."

He holds him with his skinny hand,
"There was a ship," quoth he.
"Hold off! unhand me, grey-beard loon!"
Eftsoons his hand dropt he.

He holds him with his glittering eye—
The Wedding-Guest stood still,
And listens like a three years' child:
The Mariner hath his will.

The Wedding-Guest sat on a stone:
He cannot choose but hear;
And thus spake on that ancient man,
The bright-eyed Mariner.

The effect of the "bright-eyed" Mariner's initial exertion of mesmeric power over the Wedding-Guest is to petrify him, reduce him to a childlike dependency, and monopolize his senses so as to isolate him from the feast—the larger circle of friends, family, and relations in which he has a place and is expected—and to claim him for another world, a universe governed by the whims of the Mariner's imagination. At the end of the poem, the Wedding-Guest turns away from the gaity withindoors and returns home, awakening the next morning "a sadder and a wiser man" (624). Richard Harter Fogle, expressing the general view, has noted the Mariner's resemblance to "the ideal Romantic poet," the way he "fascinates an unwilling listener, overwhelms him with wonder, terror, and delight" and "awakens his imagination."[65] In mesmeric terms, the Mariner/poet encompasses his listener/reader with a new way of understanding himself and the world around him, much as the higher spirits and guardian saint eventually awaken in the Mariner a new imaginative power of apprehending the universe and his place in it.

The new world that arises at the word of the Mariner, and that causes the waking, shared world to fade away, lacks fully human relationships. In the Mariner's tale we behold the isolation of a social microcosm of mutually inimical minds from those institutional religious and familial conventions that insure proper self-recognition and acknowledgment of the spiritual being of others. It is these conventions of self-representation that bind otherwise private minds into a community of public, mutually embodied persons. The ship's crew is set adrift on the "wide, wide sea" of an inhuman netherworld,

"below the kirk, below the hill / Below the lighthouse top" (23–24).
Voyaging beyond the reach of any moral authority, any guiding
beacon to govern the relation of person to person, they descend
"below the hill"—into the realm of the dead, or living dead.[66] On the
sea there are no weddings, no feasts, and most importantly, no
God—"O Wedding-Guest! this soul hath been / Alone on a wide,
wide sea. / So lonely 'twas, that God himself / Scarce seemed there
to be" (597–600).

This missing "God" is conceived, here at the outset, as mediately
represented in His religious, specifically "Christian," institutions, for
example, the wedding feast and the "kirk," and not as an immediately felt presence. It is He who legitimates the social and moral
order, He who is the ultimate source and end of the purposive forms
of everyday intercourse. The "God" left behind with kirk and lighthouse gives the social—the conventional and ritualized—means of
self-expression moral weight, authority, meaning, uniting "inner"
and "outer" by making the behavior of the "real" self morally determinative of the self within. On the "wide, wide sea" of a godless universe, the Mariner's crime becomes, symbolically, a repudiation of
"Christian" respect for the "soul" in another (63–82):

"At length did cross an Albatross,
Thorough the fog it came;
As if it had been a Christian soul,
We hailed it in God's name.

It ate the food it ne'er had eat,
And round and round it flew.
The ice did split with a thunder-fit;
The helmsman steered us through!

And a good south wind sprung up behind;
The Albatross did follow,
And every day, for food or play,
Came to the mariners' hollo!

In mist or cloud, on mast or shroud,
It perched for vespers nine;
Whiles all the night, through fog-smoke white,
Glimmered the white Moon-shine."

"God save thee, ancient Mariner!
From the fiends, that plague thee thus!—

Why look'st thou so?"—With my cross-bow
I shot the ALBATROSS.

"As if it had been a *Christian soul,* / We hailed it *in God's name";* it
"came to the mariners' hollo!" The power of the act of recognition to
confirm the presence of a "soul" or consciousness within the bodily
form depends ultimately, as it did for Descartes, on the invocation of
a Supreme Being, for whom the existence of the soul is assumed to be
immediately manifest, not mediately inferred. But on the sea there is
no such being to invoke: there are only the rituals of invocation. As
Cooke notes, "The continual echo of a Christian vocabulary in the
early parts of the poem seems residual only, the survival of an idle
formula."[67] In this drifting community of souls conventions of self-
recognition and acknowledgment that otherwise exert a centripetal
force to counteract the pull of radical individualism and mental
withdrawal have become meaningless. No longer underwritten by an
omniscient and omnipotent spiritual power, no longer fastened down
by the moral and legal institutions that derive their authority from
that power, the "soul," which in John Lyons's phrase "belongs to
God," has become merely the "self," which belongs to the individual.[68] The individual, however, now belongs, phenomenally, to
others, and to the vagaries of their interpretation.

In "The Rime" conventional means of self-expression lose their
ultimate referent: substance is reduced to form, sign to signifier. Accordingly, the individual's ability to manifest the "soul" by means of
these conventions becomes more and more tenuous, more and more
dependent merely on the proper enactment of the rituals insuring
recognition. If those rituals are repudiated, the soul is, in effect,
snuffed out and the reality of other selves becomes questionable. The
Mariner, by his crime, has killed not just a bird but the self within. It
is in these terms that we come to understand the Mariner's crime as
indeed a crime against "hospitality," as the gloss terms it: the albatross, at first "received with great joy and hospitality" by the crew, is
"inhospitably" killed.[69] The murder of the albatross violates those
rites of "greeting" and welcoming that have become the only sup-
ports of the soul in a godless world. The self has become, for the Mariner at least, merely what others make of it.

Ironically, the Mariner himself now becomes the "fixed" object of
his mates' inhospitable attention. The gloss at this point suggests
that the crew themselves have become infected by the same spiritual
illness that has eventuated in the murder of the albatross: "His ship-
mates cry out against the ancient Mariner for killing the bird of good

luck. But when the fog cleared off, they justify the same and thus make themselves accomplices in the crime." The crew's verdicts are as arbitrary and irrational, as wanton and impulsive, as the Mariner's own act, and when the ship is becalmed in silence and drought, they again "in their distress . . . throw the whole guilt on the ancient Mariner."[70] In the Mariner's words (139–142),

> Ah! well a-day! what evil looks
> Had I from old and young!
> Instead of the cross, the Albatross
> About my neck was hung.

The cross is a symbol, not only of salvation but also of membership in a Christian community from which the Mariner is now excluded, and which seems, in any case, now merely a formulaic vestige of community. The crew's looks are "evil" not just because they "throw the whole guilt on the ancient Mariner," but because they rob him thereby of his autonomy, his freedom to identify himself as something, or someone, other than their object.

The albatross encircling the Mariner's neck recalls the circle with which the poet's audience in "Kubla Khan" would bind and exorcise the demonic power that emanates from the youth with "flashing eyes." Here, as there, it represents in one sense the subjection of the self to summary definition from without: the Mariner is a criminal and a sinner in the world's eyes. And yet it also betrays a supernatural horror, for placing the bird around the Mariner's neck is an act of exclusion, an admission that something in the Mariner must be defended against, banished. Having given in to the irrational and spontaneous impulses that put him beyond the limits of the communally definable, he can only be defined negatively, by exclusion, a fate that, although painful in its immediate consequences, will create opportunities for imaginative growth.

As his story continues to unfold, the Mariner, alienated from the self that the world has weighted down with an arbitrary guilt, responds to his condemnation and exclusion solipsistically, displaying all the "symptoms" associated in Wordsworth's poetry with visionary insight: a sense of detachment from the embodied self; appropriation of the world as an object in the single mind; identification of and with this single mind as an absolute, as Mind; the consequent depersonalization of others as embodied intelligences in their own right; and feelings of unease at, or even entrapment by, the gaze of others.

The principal symbol of this gradual ascendancy of the outcast Mariner's "glittering eye" over the crew, who would in turn burden him with their "evil looks," is the moon, and moonlight. Ever since Robert Penn Warren's pioneering study of the poem as a symbolic representation of the healing power of "sacramental vision" and the imagination, controversy has continued over the validity of his interpretation of the sun and moon as symbols, respectively, of common or "profane" and of imaginative or "sacramental" modes of perception. Certainly, Warren oversimplifies when he writes, "In the poem, the good events take place under the aegis of the moon, the bad events under that of the sun."[71] The mariners die under the aegis of the moon, for instance, and the "troop of angels blessed," which have taken the place of the crew's souls, cluster around the mast at dawn and sing sweetly at noon. Warren tries to argue away these inconsistencies (but not very convincingly) as resulting from the "vengeful" nature of the rejected and despised imagination. Referring to the deaths of the crew members, he writes: "The fact of these unhappy events under the aegis of the supposedly beneficient moon raises a question: Does this violate the symbolism of the moon? I do not feel that the poem is inconsistent here. First, if we accept the interpretation that the Pole Spirit belongs to the imagination cluster and yet exacts vengeance, then the fact that horror comes in the moonlight here is simply an extension of the same principle: violated and despised, the imagination yet persists and exacts vengeance."[72]

Later scholars, following the lead of Humphry House, have rightly dismissed this argument.[73] It is difficult to see why the imagination should seek vengeance on the crew in this way, as if it had somehow been personally wronged, let alone why it should seek vengeance on the crew and not on the Mariner himself. Further inconsistencies have been noted, some of them based on an overly fastidious reading, some attempting to deny any correlation at all. Abe Delson, for instance, believes that "there is a balance in the Mariner's voyage alternating between a 'sacramental' and a horrifying, autonomous view of nature," and that "more than any other of the natural forces, the sun and moon share in this polarity. The mistake symbolic commentators in the past have made is to insist on a favorable meaning for one and an unfavorable meaning for the other."[74]

Denying the ethical distinctions between sun and moon symbolism, however, does not mean that we should make no distinctions at all. The mistake of symbolic interpreters has, indeed, been to insist on characterizing the sun as wholly malevolent and the moon as wholly benign. Such ethical biases destroy a useful discrimination between daylight and moonlight as symbolic of altered states of mind: mundane, everyday perception on the one hand, and solipsistic perception—at times visionary or "sacramental," at times unreal, irrational, and horrifying—on the other. This kind of distinction would not prevent us from assigning positive and negative effects to either way of perceiving the world.

As John Beer has observed, in what is still perhaps the finest and most extended treatment to date of Coleridge's sun and moon imagery, "When [Coleridge] conceives of the visionary, the transmitter of divine light, it is normally not as a sun but as a moon."[75] And yet, as Warren himself points out, the Mariner's "blessed vision" is also "a curse."[76] This is certainly correct, but not because when the imagination is denied it wreaks "vengeance" (however that may be conceived), but because the exercise of the imagination involves the Ancient Mariner—like the poet, for that matter—in a dilemma. Uniting him spiritually with all things, all of nature, all the universe, imaginative vision tends at the same time to cut him off from other human beings as real presences:

> So we have here a peculiar and paradoxical situation: the poem is a poem in which the poetic imagination appears in a regenerative and healing capacity, but in the end the hero, who has, presumably, been healed, appears in one of his guises as the *poète maudit*. So we learn that the imagination does not only bless, for even as it blesses it lays on a curse. Though the Mariner brings the word which is salvation, he cannot quite save himself and taste the full joy of the fellowship he advertises. Society looks askance at him.[77]

The Mariner's word brings salvation, but only to him. It is inimical to any sense of fellowship in a shared society. We do look askance at the Mariner, and we try to stop our ears, because to look at his "glittering eyes" directly and to listen to his words with full attention is to lose our shared, waking senses and become swallowed up in a dream. The world drenched in moonlight is indeed the landscape of dream, of a mind-enclosed world. It offers the poet an analogue of the imaginative mind in the act of appropriating that which is otherwise alien to it. The moon, like the visionary mind, "brings to light," and thereby into existence, the world it attends to; and for Coleridge that attention is also intention—moonlit objects appear "like ideas in the divine mind anterior to creation." But at the same time, these objects remain private, only half real, *only* ideas "anterior" to full realization. The world that is brought into being by the moon verges on nonentity, and brings the mind to the edge of solipsism, self-enclosure. We contemplate the moon alone in the night, while the rest of the "populous" world, as in "Frost at Midnight," remains asleep.

These associations between moonlight, dream, and the solipsistic imagination become clearer if we consider our common associations of sunlight with the facticity of waking life. The world "by the light of day" is a world whose reality is assumed beyond doubt, not because it has been confirmed by a tactical maneuver of private imaginative appropriation, but because the sun shines for all waking things and makes the world—and our being in it—accessible to all eyes. The "reality" of the daylight world rests on our implicit deference to the power of others' perceptions to confirm, alter, or deny our own interpretation of events. And this deference or openness to the determinative power of others' views depends upon our understanding of the relativity of our position in the world and on our belief in the existence of other minds, a belief that commands a primary, and primitive, faith. Where this faith is missing or shaky, the world becomes dreamlike, and others become automata or walking corpses, like the ship's "ghastly crew" (340).

The rise of the moon is inimical to the lives of the crew members because it represents the ascendancy of a single, detached point of view in which they are reduced to mere phenomena, to what can be "seen" of them: their bodies. But this solipsisitic detachment is the prelude to the Mariner's experience of transcendence, his feeling of oneness with nature outside of community. There is some question here, then, as to whether the Mariner's "sacramental" feelings of conjunction with the "one Life" are not, in fact, delusory. For though his mesmeric power "echoes" the operations of the primary imagination, it remains withdrawn, and is fundamentally opposed to the universal operations of the Nous, or Reason, which, as Beer has convincingly demonstrated, is identified in Coleridge's work with the sun, whose light shines on all.[78] The Mariner, by contrast, passes "like night, from land to land" (586).

Thus, by the light of day, of that universal Reason which works through all minds to establish a reality of consensus, communal relations of a sort become reestablished—the choir of blessed spirits that sings at dawn, suggestive of a communal harmony, is one example (349–366). But the Mariner, significantly, remains an onlooker, and the sun at noon, a glaring, accusatory eye, symbolizes the paralyzing horror that he feels lurking in such public relationships, the fear of being fixed by another's "evil eye."[79] Similarly, the noonday sun that stares down on and paralyzes the "painted ship" in part II (118), just following the Mariner's crime against the spirit and the crew's ocular indictment of the Mariner, seems to represent, to the eyes of men who are now only atoms of awareness disjoined by the decomposition of the social organism, that "daytime," public relationship between self and others in which all self-representations subsist momentarily in suspension, in mutual paralysis and suspicion, as "painted" images merely (111–126):

> All in a hot and copper sky,
> The bloody Sun, at noon,
> Right up above the mast did stand,
> No bigger than the Moon.
>
> Day after day, day after day,
> We stuck, nor breath nor motion;
> As idle as a painted ship
> Upon a painted ocean.
>
> Water, water, every where,
> And all the boards did shrink;
> Water, water, every where,
> Nor any drop to drink.
>
> The very deep did rot: O Christ!
> That ever this should be!
> Yea, slimy things did crawl with legs
> Upon the slimy sea.

In these images of derealization, paralysis, drought, and rot, Coleridge depicts the plight of public men who can no longer reciprocate love, compassion, and acceptance. "And every tongue, through utter drought, / Was withered at the root; / We could not speak, no more than if / We had been choked with soot" (135–138). The loss of the spiritual sustenance that the water symbolizes results in a loss of speech, the vital medium of community. Silent and estranged, the crew can only recriminate with their "evil looks."

After "a weary time," the Mariner spots the approaching "skeleton ship," with her gruesome crew: Death and "the nightmare Life-in-Death," casting dice for the Mariner's soul (171–198). Life-in-Death wins the game, and no sooner has she claimed the Mariner as her prize than "the Sun's rim dips; the stars rush out: / At one stride comes the dark" (199–200), and the moon begins to rise (212–223):

One after one, by the star-dogged Moon,
Too quick for groan or sigh,
Each turned his face with a ghastly pang,
And cursed me with his eye.

Four times fifty living men,
(And I heard nor sigh nor groan)
With heavy thump, a lifeless lump,
They dropped down one by one.

The souls did from their bodies fly,—
They fled to bliss or woe!
And every soul, it passed me by,
Like the whizz of my cross-bow!

The crew's souls flee with the sound of the crossbow that killed the albatross, symbol of the "Christian soul."

The rising of the moon represents the ascendancy of the Mariner's sole self over all others, and their consequent depersonalization. As the world by moonlight becomes the private theater of an isolated mind, other human forms suddenly lose self-representative value. "Like the figures in a dream," observes Bostetter, "they have no identity apart from the dreamer. We have no awareness of them as living human beings."[80] The crew become things. The Mariner, on the other hand, begins to feel incorporeal, disembodied, like a ghost or spirit, much as we would expect to find in an experience of visionary solipsism. This occurs soon after what Warren identifies as the onset of the Mariner's "sacramental vision" (282–291), when he blesses the sea snakes and feels the albatross drop from his neck (305–308).

I moved, and could not feel my limbs:
I was so light—almost
I thought that I had died in sleep,
And was a blessed ghost.

Coleridge, in one version, even went so far as to insert the following lines into the account of the ship's navigation by the "blessed spirits" that descend to reanimate the crew's corpses:

The Mariners all 'gan pull the ropes,
But look at me they n'old:
Thought I, I am as thin as air—
They cannot me behold.[81]

Thus, we find operative in the poem a kind of fearful symmetry in an otherwise fortuitous and macabre series of Gothic horrors, a symmetry that becomes more and more definite as the Mariner's solipsism becomes visionary: the dreamlike derealization of the crew coincides with the Mariner's own impressions of a dreamlike disembodiment. But as the Mariner reassures the Wedding-Guest, who fears that the old man may indeed be a ghost, "This body dropt not down" (231). In contrast to the crew's being reduced to the level of the phenomenal, to heavy things, the Mariner's body becomes "light" and, as it seems to him, invisible. In one case the sundering of soul and body leaves only a cadaver, the self as mere object of perception; in the other, it leaves the mind or spirit bodiless, a subject that perceives, but feels itself removed from the world it perceives and the beings inhabiting it.

If the Mariner is condemned to "Life-in-Death"—a "life" passed outside the realm of the living—the mariners are condemned, like Frankenstein's "wretch," to what we might call "Death-in-Life." As a storm approaches (according to the gloss) "the bodies of the ship's crew are inspired [*inspirited,* in *Sybilline Leaves*] and the ship moves on."[82] "Inspirited" conveys more accurately what has literally taken place (327–344):

The loud wind never reached the ship,
Yet now the ship moved on!
Beneath the lightning and the Moon
The dead men gave a groan.

They groaned, they stirred, they all uprose,
Nor spake, nor moved their eyes;
It had been strange, even in a dream,
To have seen those dead men rise.

The helmsman steered, the ship moved on;
Yet never a breeze up-blew;
The mariners all 'gan work the ropes,
Where they were wont to do;

They raised their limbs like lifeless tools—
We were a ghastly crew.

The body of my brother's son
Stood by me, knee to knee:
The body and I pulled at one rope,
But he said nought to me.

The bodies of the crew are reanimated by "spirits" or powers not
their own, as though each were a puppet or a La Mettrian man-ma-
chine. Here the "lifeless tools" are attached to corporeal mechanisms
that go about playing their accustomed roles in the shipboard society: "The body and I pulled at one rope, / But he said nought to
me." That the mariners "nor spake nor moved their eyes," that the
body of his own nephew did not acknowledge his presence, reinforces
our feeling that the Mariner does not exist in their world. Unrecognized, he feels as if he were watching it from a place without.

Finally, that the "blessed troop of angelic spirits" which "inspirit"
the dead men is sent down by the invocation of the Mariner's
"guardian saint" to bring him, at last, back to his native country,
strengthens our understanding that the Mariner has succeeded in
making this world *his*. Like Wordsworth's solitaries, the crew has
surrendered their spiritual autonomy to a transcendent will that is,
in the end, the observer's own. They have become the passive "tools"
of the power that works through his imagination.

There is a certain tyranny characteristic of Coleridge's imagination, as of Wordsworth's, that comes to the fore in "The Rime of the
Ancient Mariner." Here and in "Kubla Khan" the imagination
threatens others. It is the poet's weapon against the crowd that
would make him theirs. Significantly, just preceding the moment of
the Mariner's "sacramental" vision, when he suddenly feels one with
a higher, omniscient power in whose gaze all things live, move, and
have their being, the narrative stresses the malevolent eyes of the
dead crew members lying on the deck (255–262):

The look with which they looked on me
Had never passed away.

An orphan's curse would drag to hell
A spirit from on high;
But oh! more horrible than that

Is the curse in a dead man's eye!
Seven days, seven nights, I saw that curse,
And yet I could not die.

As the moon makes its seventh ascent of the night sky, the Mariner
finally turns away from the accursed and accusatory gaze of the dead
men to seek relief in the sight of the "moving Moon" (263–271):

The moving Moon went up the sky,
And no where did abide:
Softly she was going up,
And a star or two beside—

Her beams bemocked the sultry main,
Like April hoar-frost spread;
But where the ship's huge shadow lay,
The charméd water burnt alway
A still and awful red.

There, in the shadow of the ship, the Mariner watches the water
snakes swimming in their "tracks of shining white" (274), their "rich
attire" (278) and "golden fire" (281), and undergoes the pivotal
transformation of the poem (282–291):

O happy living things! no tongue
Their beauty might declare:
A spring of love gushed from my heart,
And I blessed them unaware:
Sure my kind saint took pity on me,
And I blessed them unaware.

The self-same moment I could pray;
And from my neck so free
The Albatross fell off, and sank
Like lead into the sea.

From the accusatory stares of his dead companions the Mariner
turns to find a spiritual solidarity with nature's "happy living
things." The "spell" that, according to the gloss, begins to break,[83]
refers to the Mariner's encirclement and branding as a criminal: the
albatross, symbol of his alienated identity, falls away. The Ancient
Mariner's "sacramental" experience has at last freed him from the
burden of the false self. From this point on, the Mariner's imagina-

tion remains in the ascendant, and the universe mirrors the movements of his soul: as Beer points out, calling attention to the blending of internal and external images in the poem, "the 'spring' in the Mariner's heart is followed by the longed-for rain,"[84] symbol of spiritual renewal; the mariners are "inspirited" by the angels sent by the Mariner's guardian saint; the Mariner is returned to his own country, as he desires.

The Mariner's return is anticipated by his changed perception of the "moving Moon" that, up to this point, "no where did abide," an image that reflects the Mariner's own wandering and displaced existence. The gloss, in matchless prose, makes the identification more explicit: "In his loneliness and fixedness he yearneth towards the journeying Moon, and the stars that still sojourn, yet still move onward; and every where the blue sky belongs to them, and is their appointed rest, and their native country and their own natural homes, which they enter unannounced, as lords that are certainly expected and yet there is a silent joy at their arrival."[85]

Though homeless, the moon and attendant stars travel through the sky like a lord with his retainers in his own fiefdom. The image is another remarkable case of the "blending" of inner and outer, for it looks forward to the Mariner's own journey back to his native land, a homecoming that is, appropriately, dreamlike and unreal, unfolding as it does beneath the light of the moon (452–479):

> But soon there breathed a wind on me,
> Nor sound nor motion made:
> Its path was not upon the sea,
> In ripple or in shade.

> It raised my hair, it fanned my cheek
> Like a meadow-gale of spring—
> It mingled strangely with my fears,
> Yet it felt like a welcoming.

> Swiftly, swiftly flew the ship,
> Yet she sailed softly too:
> Sweetly, sweetly blew the breeze—
> On me alone it blew.

> Oh! dream of joy! is this indeed
> The light-house top I see?

Is this the hill? is this the kirk?
Is this my own countree?

We drifted o'er the harbour-bar,
And I with sobs did pray—
O let me be awake, my God!
Or let me sleep alway.

The harbour-bay was clear as glass,
So smoothly it was strewn!
And on the bay the moonlight lay,
And the shadow of the Moon.

The rock shone bright, the kirk no less,
That stands above the rock:
The moonlight steeped in silentness
The steady weathercock.

A number of features in this description of the Mariner's home-coming are noteworthy. He encounters a breeze, an offshore wind that blows only for him, suggesting that the land he nears exists, in some way, in his own mind but in no other's. This hint of solipsism is reinforced by moonlight, and by silence, which implies the poet's sense of distance and self-elision from the perceived world. Finally, in the Ancient Mariner's description of his "own countree" the ambiguous reality of his waking dream is emphasized. It is a "dream of joy," but he prays, "let me be awake, my God! / Or let me sleep alway."

The breeze feels like a "welcoming" because it blows from a land that is now firmly appropriated by the Mariner's own mind. This scene realizes the promise implicit in the earlier image of the lordly moon's procession across the sky: here is the Mariner's "appointed rest" and his "native countree" and his "own natural home," made wholly his, which he enters "unannounced . . . and yet there is a silent joy" at his arrival. Like the moon, which now floods the bay with light, he is sole "lord" over this dreamscape, for his is the sole Mind in which it appears to exist. The Mariner even has his own attendant "stars": the "inspirited" crew members who have "worked the ropes" for him have now become "all light" (480–495):

And the bay was white with silent light,
Till rising from the same,
Full many shapes, that shadows were,
In crimson colours came.

A little distance from the prow
Those crimson shadows were:

I turned my eyes upon the deck—
Oh, Christ! what saw I there!

Each corse lay flat, lifeless and flat,
And, by the holy rood!
A man all light, a seraph-man,
On every corse there stood.

This seraph-band, each waved his hand:
It was a heavenly sight!
They stood as signals to the land,
Each one a lovely light.

The silence of the Mariner's "welcoming" is broken by the dash of oars, the Pilot's cheer, the Hermit's voice, the nearing of a community that hails him (500–503). The ritual of greeting and recognition is again invoked, for the first time since the death of the albatross. But although the Ancient Mariner reenters the land of the living in part VII, it is as one who has died and only dreams himself awake. A dreadful sound rumbles under the water, smites sky and sea, and sinks the ship: "Stunned," says the Mariner, "Like one that hath been seven days drowned / My body lay afloat; / But swift as dreams, myself I found / Within the Pilot's boat" (550–555). "Swift as dreams," "like one that hath been seven days drowned": it is seven days since the Mainer began his ordeal, seven days of living death. Now, though he finds himself once again "within" the circle of the living, "the Pilot's boat," the others know he has no place there (560–581):

I moved my lips—the Pilot shrieked
And fell down in a fit;
The holy Hermit raised his eyes,
And prayed where he did sit.

I took the oars: the Pilot's boy,
Who now doth crazy go,
Laughed loud and long, and all the while
His eyes went to and fro.
"Ha! ha!" quoth he, "full plain I see,
The Devil knows how to row."

And now, all in my own countree,
I stood on the firm land!

The Hermit stepped forth from the boat,
And scarcely he could stand.

"O shrieve me, shrieve me, holy man!"
The Hermit crossed his brow.
"Say quick," quoth he, "I bid thee say—
What manner of man art thou?"

Forthwith this frame of mine was wrenched
With a woful agony,
Which forced me to begin my tale;
And then it left me free.

"What manner of man art thou?" It is a question of identity we
have been pursuing, and it is a question the Ancient Mariner cannot
answer except with the tale of his lonely and fantastic journey. This
is the "penance more" (409) the Mariner must do, what the gloss
calls, "the penance of life": to be among the living but not of them.[86]
When questioned as to who he is, the Ancient Mariner can only tell
the tale of himself, and to tell that tale he must define an entire world
that will draw his listener in, enwrap, mesmerize him, remove him
too from the land of the living. The ruling purposes and powers of
that dreamed universe are completely governed by the Mariner's
preternatural imagination. He cannot, after all, accept existence as
others understand it; he is no "manner of man" they have experience
of. Instead, with his "glittering eye," he performs a flanking maneuver, weaving a circle of his own around his hearer with his "strange
power of speech" (586–590):

I pass, like night, from land to land;
I have strange power of speech;
That moment that his face I see,
I know the man that must hear me:
To him my tale I teach.

The power of the Mariner's imagination is indeed like the power of
night: it can momentarily overcome the glaring facticity of a world
where things and people are conventionally defined by appeal to
others and by recourse to what is "commonly" understood. The
"merry din" of that land held in common—its "loud bassoon" (32),
"minstrelsy" (36), and "loud uproar" (591)—has punctuated the
mariner's tale of isolation and despair like a call from another

plane of existence. The world in which the finite self finds itself, stumbles upon itself, at times quite painfully, at times as upon a stranger, is not silent, nor is it amenable to appropriation by the single mind. The Mariner carefully skirts this world, creating his own charmed circle of awareness, and shutting out those public precincts where we are required to step forward and play our part, not linger in the shadows of existence.

Outside the Walls

There is an anecdote Coleridge once told his friend and physician, James Gillman, of his school years at Christ's Hospital. The tale appears in nearly all the biographies, principally on the strength of Gillman's account in his early *Life* (1838), where he quotes his friend thus:

> In my friendless wanderings on our *leave days* i.e. the Christ Hospital phrase, not for holidays altogether, but for those on which the boys are permitted to go beyond the precincts of the school (for I was an orphan, and had scarce any connexions in London), highly was I delighted, if any passenger, especially if he drest in black, would enter into conversation with me; for soon I found the means of directing it to my favorite subjects—
>
> > Of Providence, fore-knowledge, will, and fate,
> > Fix'd fate, free will, fore-knowledge absolute,
> > And found no end, in wandering mazes lost.[87]

Research by Norman Fruman and others into Coleridge's vexing autobiographical accounts has taught us to read such anecdotes as mythical rather than factual reconstructions of the poet's childhood. Whatever the case may be, Coleridge seems to have implied that, long before he set down the supernatural events related by his fictitious Mariner to the hapless Wedding-Guest, he himself had waylaid and engrossed the attention of guileless strangers with his own "strange power of speech." Here, perhaps, is a fictional self-portrait fleshed out on the armature of his own preternaturally mesmeric creation, an emblem, like the poems themselves, of Coleridge's "dream of power."

But it is an emblem of another "dream" as well, a counter-myth in which authority is invested in the adult figure of the scenario—the dream of finding, and being accepted by, one's lost parent. The "or-phan" boy's adventure beyond the walls of Christ's Hospital in search of solitary adults to impress with his precocious erudition speaks eloquently of his hunger for recognition and approval. In this respect the apocryphal incident recalls another, more Gothic account of an excursion beyond the stone walls and iron gate of childhood, and an encounter there with a visitant from "the upper sky" who, like the clergyman, is knowledgeable in those things ordinarily un-acknowledged by the waking mind, particularly matters of "free will" and compulsion. But Geraldine, the ambiguous femme fatale of "Christabel," poses a much more terrifying challenge to her young victim's sense of identity.

Written mostly during 1798–1799 and set aside during the next seventeen years except for minor revisions, "Christabel" reveals the pain of what Coleridge suspected to be an irreconcilable opposition between his inner and outer selves, an opposition represented in the character of Christabel as a personality split into asexual and sexual, conscious and unconscious, articulate and unspeakable identities. The story begins with Christabel, the young daughter of the aging and sickly Sir Leoline, leaving the safety of her father's castle walls to pray in the "midnight wood." There she meets Geraldine, a virgin abducted from *her* father's castle by five knights and left at the foot of a tree, where Christabel finds her. Just previous to this discovery, however, the narrator says (23–26),

> The lovely lady, Christabel,
> Whom her father loves so well,
> What makes her in the wood so late,
> A furlong from the castle gate?

If, encouraged by this apparently innocuous question, we reflect on the situation a bit, we soon realize that Christabel's reasons for visiting the woods are not very clear, and that her meeting with Geraldine, who seems in many respects a maturer alter ego or mirror image, is less than fortuitous. Christabel is there, we are told, because "She had dreams all yesternight / Of her own betrothe'd Knight; / And she in the midnight wood will pray / For the weal of her lover that's far away" (27–30). This explanation tells us nothing of why Christabel must do her praying at midnight and in the woods, though it does hint at a sexual restlessness more broadly al-luded to in the two lines immediately preceding this passage, lines appearing in the first edition of the poem and later erased in the corrected copy given to David Hivnes: "Dreams, that made her moan and leap, / As on her bed she lay in sleep."[88] Better than asking what she is doing out in the woods at night would be asking what she expects to find there. We suspect, for instance, that the howling of her father's "toothless mastiff bitch" (7) may indicate the presence of Christabel's dead mother—"Some say" the dog "sees my lady's shroud" (12). What Christabel discovers, however, is a "damsel bright / Drest in a silken robe of white, / That shadowy in the moonlight shone" (58–60), something very like a shroud, draping a woman who turns out to have macabre associations with Christabel's dead mother, and who will transform the girl's personality in a manner both horrifying and perversely irresistible.

Christabel takes Geraldine home and submits, with no show of resistance, to what the text strongly hints are sexual advances, after which Geraldine casts a spell of silence on the girl so that she cannot speak of what has happened. The next morning, after a restless night, Christabel remembers nothing until she confronts Geraldine in the presence of Sir Leoline and his court. At the sight of Geraldine's snakelike gaze, the girl is twice seized with violent, uncontrollable paroxysms of fear and loathing in which her personality alters drastically (584–592):

> A snake's small eye blinks dull and shy;
> And the lady's eyes they shrunk in her head,
> Each shrunk up to a serpent's eye,
> And with somewhat of malice, and more of dread,
> At Christabel she looked askance!—
> One moment—and the sight was fled!
> But Christabel in dizzy trance
> Stumbling on the unsteady ground
> Shuddered aloud, with a hissing sound.

To her father's questions of what ails her, she cannot reply, "O'ermastered" by Geraldine's "mighty spell" (620).

In such scenes Geraldine, the lamialike seductress of Coleridge's hapless ingenue, seems at first glance still another personification of mesmeric omnipotence, like the Ancient Mariner, playing a role in still another "dream of power": she is a preternatural, nocturnal creature from "a far countree" (225)—presumably, of the dead—and her eyes, "bright" and "glittering," make Christabel imagine things and behave in a fashion quite out of the ordinary. Geraldine leaves her struck dumb, as much "stunned" and "of sense forlorn" as is the Mariner's passive Wedding-Guest.

But if the poem is indeed another dream of power, then it is a dream in which the dreamer seems to have identified strongly with the apparent victim of that power. The narrator's point of view throughout the poem is almost entirely that of Christabel, except for those brief portions where Coleridge describes the court minstrel's premonitory nightmares, or the thoughts of Christabel's father, Sir Leoline. Geraldine's inner life remains an enigma: compared to the Mariner she has little to say about herself, and her sinister actions and appearance are reported exclusively through Christabel's eyes, as part of the girl's "vision of fear" (453). For this reason her effects on Christabel's behavior and perception seem as much rooted in the child's own psyche and "forced unconscious sympathy" as in Coleridge's Gothic machinery. In fact, long before we read of Geraldine's snakelike appearance, we find Christabel drawing "in her breath with a hissing sound" (459) when she first sees Geraldine at court the next morning. Later, Coleridge appears to emphasize the psychological origins of Christabel's obsession (597–606):

> The maid, alas! her thoughts are gone,
> She nothing sees—no thought but one!
> The maid, devoid of guile and sin,
> I know not how, in fearful wise,
> So deeply had she drunken in
> That look, those shrunken serpent eyes,
> That all her features were resigned
> To this sole image in her mind:
> And passively did imitate
> That look of dull and treacherous hate!

Read literally, these lines say that what Christabel "sees" *is* a "thought," that this image *does* reside solely in Christabel's mind, as a part of her most intimate self.

If the inimical Geraldine is in large measure the product of Christabel's preternaturally active imagination, then the question naturally arises: Why should Christabel's mind project such an image on another, and why this particular other? This is simply another way of asking: Who, or what, is Christabel seeking in Geraldine? And since, to judge from the narrative point of view, Coleridge seems to have identified closely with Christabel, this question gives rise to another: Who, or what, was *Coleridge* seeking in Geraldine?

To begin with, the authority Geraldine exerts over the girl is, quite clearly, and as critics generally have agreed, a mother's.[89] The moaning of the mastiff bitch, supposedly at "my lady's shroud," for instance, is repeated when Christabel escorts Geraldine into the castle (145–153); the old oak under which Geraldine and Christabel meet is described as "broad-breasted" (421); Christabel offers Geraldine her mother's wildflower wine (190–194), whereupon the woman, until now weak and faint, becomes suddenly reinvigorated and formally takes on the dead mother's role and aura by driving away her rival's lingering ghost (205–213). Geraldine then disrobes, lies down next to Christabel, and casts her spell of silence by "the touch of this bosom" (267), a phrase whose maternal associations are highlighted later by Coleridge's description of Christabel as an infant (318) and by a portrait of Geraldine slumbering beside her "still and mild, / As a mother with her child" (300–301).

Let us assume, then, that Geraldine's powers to transform and to silence Christabel are somehow associated with Christabel's dead mother. Why should Geraldine exercise those powers in a sexually sinister way? Many critics have seen the "lofty lady" as a projection of Christabel's deepest desires and fears about approaching sexual maturity, and the, literally, unspeakable but ambiguous seduction as a rite of sexual initiation.[90] But if this is a poem about sexual initiation, why shouldn't Christabel's mentor be male, like her betrothed knight? Even leaving aside the question of sexual preference, how are we to relate Geraldine's specifically *maternal* features to her disturbing, sexually perverse associations and effects on Christabel?

First, I believe the idea of "initiation" as a physical act of seduction is not really helpful here. Whatever happened in Christabel's bedchamber is, to say the least, ambiguous: Geraldine disrobes, revealing "a sight to dream of, not to tell!" (253)—presumably the later "vision of fear" that Christabel cannot "tell." Then she pauses a moment, collects herself, and lies down next to the girl, enjoining her silence. There the scene ends. What is important is that the next morning Christabel *believes* that she acted shamefully—"Sure I have sinn'd!" she exclaims—even though her exact "sins" remain "unknown" to her (380–390). Anxiety and guilt over an unknown—literally "unthinkable"—act would suggest that some form of repression is at work, but whether of a factual or fantasized event is unclear. Furthermore, judging from her behavior the next morning, Christabel is convinced that Geraldine has the power to elicit such "un-thinkable" acts and sights by her very presence, her very gaze. In-stead of considering Geraldine as a conjugal partner, I suggest that she be thought of as a person whose presence enables Christabel un-consciously to embody, and thus make real for another, desires that her waking mind cannot accept.

If indeed we grant that the image of the malevolent and maternal Geraldine lies "in her mind," then by her behavior Christabel seems to be unknowingly manifesting, or making "real" *for that imagined Other* a predatory, sexually aware self that lies buried within her, a side of her personality that she cannot *consciously* bring herself to express. In Christabel we have a perfect illustration of Paul Ricoeur's contention that "it is only for someone other that I even possess an unconscious." Clinically, Christabel exhibits all the symptoms of transference commonly observed in cases of dissociative hysteria: in her confrontations with Geraldine she attributes final authority over her self-interpretation, like a patient in analysis or a subject in hyp-nosis, to an accepting "parent figure,"[91] for whom her repressed drives and desires can be unconsciously expressed without fear of re-prisal and without her assuming responsibility for them. Christabel's hidden self, then, seems to move almost irresistibly toward expres-sion in response to the parentally authoritative eye of another like it, but very unlike the conscious, public self that is compelled to repudi-ate this manifestation of the self within.

Here lies Geraldine's significance as a sexually mature mother fig-ure, a stand-in for Christabel's dead mother. Geraldine provides an authoritative role model and real source of recognition for the girl's newly emerging, sexually mature, but repressed self. She is the pas-sive catalyst for Christabel's reenactment, as an adolescent, of that process of parental interiorization or "introjection" by which, in in-fancy, the child comes to see, reflect on, and finally accept herself as a person separate from the real parent.[92] But in Christabel this process is rejected and repressed with horror by the waking self. The person evoked by Geraldine's look must be submerged in the night world of dreams. Should it erupt into waking life, it will be disavowed by a silence the girl must assume is imposed by the very authority figure who calls this behavior forth. Not she but the Other "makes" her into this person, or makes this person "real" through her.

Without going too far into the mechanisms of transference or re-pression, one can provide a plausible etiology for Christabel's sub-conscious horror of sexual maturity, consummation, and its aftermath, as well as her need to find a mother substitute whom the waking mind will not recognize as such: the child's real mother died in giving birth to her (194–197). Should Christabel grow up, dream logic would dictate, she too must die, unless she takes as her model of maturity and source of self-confirmation someone who can play the mother's role without being consciously recognized as doing so.

My purpose here is not to "psychoanalyze" Christabel, but to relate her dreams, desires, fears, and inhibitions to those of the poet she personifies, and ultimately to the situation of the Romantic poet seeking self-definition in a society whose expectations of him he considers a stifling imposition on the true self. Who was Coleridge seeking—and in the person of Christabel recoiling from—when he created Geraldine? Quite aside from what it might tell us of the girl's obscure motivations for befriending Geraldine, the mother's death reflects Coleridge's own problematic relation to his mother. Geraldine resembles other sexually inimical, maternal figures in Coleridge's notebooks and other writings, which critics like Bostetter, Yarlott, and Fruman have related to the poet's subconscious feelings of guilt, shame, unworthiness, and even latent homoeroticism, all connected in some way with his mother's de facto abandonment of him as a child.[93] For the writer of "Christabel," subconscious feelings of responsibility for the early absence of his mother would not only be consonant with his deeply rooted sense of insecurity and self-disesteem—maternal neglect would naturally lead to such feelings of unworthiness—but also with an unacknowledged desire for revenge, expressed symbolically in Christabel's passive responsibility for the mother's "death." This repressed rage could only intensify the torments of Coleridge's self-hatred. His inability to accept his own strong sexual feelings, his sense that they somehow defiled his scrupulously chaste self-image,[94] can also be attributed to a strong desire to remain the "dead" mother's well-behaved boy, just as Christabel wishes to remain "So fair, so innocent, so mild" (624) in the eyes of her surviving parent for the sake of her mother's dying prayer "that the babe for whom she died, / Might prove her dear lord's joy and pride" (629–630). But in Coleridge's dreams and waking nightmares another mother—loathed and feared—encouraged the most hideous expression of the sexual self.

Whatever the exact relation of the mother's "death" to Christabel's (or Coleridge's) visions of fear, one thing is clear: the attempt to embody the hidden self in response to certain sympathetic expectations attributed to its parentally authoritative audience is, in "Christabel," opposed by consciousness itself, which in reaction splits off and denies the undesirable impulse toward sexual expression and self-recognition, and recoils from the Other who elicits such behavior. Consciousness clings instead to the false self that appears in response to authoritative expectations that are dyspathic to the true self, expectations also parental in origin but identified with society at large. In the eyes of her father, Sir Leoline, and his court, Christabel always assumes the appearance of his "gentle daughter." Each time she succumbs to her "vision of fear" in the presence of Geraldine, for instance, she returns to her ordinary self when her father turns his eyes on her: when "the Knight turned wildly round" at the sound of Christabel's hissing breath, he "nothing saw, but his own sweet maid / With eyes upraised, as one that prayed" (460–462). Whether true or false, the "real" self, the "apparent" self, is always composed in the eye of another.

In "Christabel" we find the logical obverse of Coleridge's dream of power: it is the dream of submission to and acceptance by the parental Other. It arises from the same needs, the same fears and anxieties, as the dream of power, but it represents a different way of responding to these. Both dreams presume that the inner or true self is inchoate, evanescent, unstable, and liable to be rejected or misunderstood should it be embodied. In the first scenario this inability to be recognized and included among others allows the poet to dilate the self as mind, stand outside the "all," incorporate the world and its inhabitants in himself, and finally presume the acquiescence of other minds in the "reality" of what his imagination alone has created. But the second scenario reveals the basic insecurity underlying such attempts to appropriate as part of the self the world outside, and thus neutralize the others in it. Ultimately, what the true self must do is not dominate and direct the minds of others, but feel itself confirmed as real in its own embodied being.

The "confirmation" accorded Christabel, however, is no more real than that accorded the poet at the end of "This Lime-Tree Bower," when he assumes the sharing of his vision by "gentle-hearted Charles." Confirmation of Christabel's true self is *attributed* to Geraldine but not ratified by a single incontrovertible sign or word that anyone else, in the court scene in part II, at any rate, can recognize. In fact, not only do we see things only through Christabel's eyes, but it is she who takes the active role throughout part I, up to the moment of Geraldine's struggle with and victory over the mother's ghost: it was Christabel who entered the woods, "raised up" Geraldine (373)—the words suggest a conjuration—beneath the oak, led her home, carried her, "a weary weight" (131), across the threshold, and offered her the potent wildflower wine. And it is Christabel, not the mesmeric Geraldine, who comes closest to visionary solipsism, transforming the world around her into something unreal, a part of the self that has been repressed and withdrawn from embodiment. While Christabel does not reach the boundary condition of with-drawal—a mystical sense of oneness with the perceived world—the dreamlike transformations of her surroundings and of Geraldine verge very closely on complete mental enclosure and self-annihila-tion: "her thoughts are gone, / She nothing sees—no thought but one" (597–598).

Thus, the dream of submission and acceptance turns out to be a dream of power after all, the power to transform another so as to en-able the self to feel transformed *by* the other. But the power to trans-form the self is projected and disowned in this way precisely because the dreamer is helpless to transform herself. Lacking her own inter-nal mirror of self-certainty, Christabel depends utterly on the expec-tations she attributes to authority figures outside her. She becomes what she assumes they want her to be. The ghost of the "wandering mother" (205) has left behind a void within the psyche—symbolized by the fortified castle itself—which her daughter seeks to fill by in-troducing surrogates that can never be assimilated by consciousness.

For this reason the dream of acceptance, at least as Coleridge rep-resents it in "Christabel," cannot progress to self-acceptance. The predatory, sexually knowledgeable Christabel realized in the eye of Geraldine is never, in Erikson's words, "successfully reintegrated in an ensemble of roles that also receive recognition" by the world at large. The transformed self lives only in nightmares where its loathe-some desires can be disguised as the malevolent impositions of the mother who shapes it. Such is the burden, also, of Coleridge's own nightmares in the years that followed his leaving off "Christabel." Indeed, if Geraldine is a dream disowned by the dreamer, a vision that repulses the visionary, the same might be said for the poem it-self, which was never finished.

For the mother, it turns out, is not only the ultimate arbiter of sex-ual identity but also, figuratively, the ultimate arbiter of a "poetic" identity closely associated with the sexual self—an identity expressed in speech. Geraldine is the Muse turned mute, and Christabel's aphasia represents Coleridge's own failure of speech. It was a failure caused, as many have suggested, by his realization that the chthonic source of creative inspiration and imaginative power within him was becoming, in its sexually lurid suggestiveness, a threat to his conscious self-image, if not indeed to his sanity.[95] Geraldine, the predatory mother, ruled that underworld, nurtured and tormented the dream self that inhabited there, and finally enjoined silence.

Keats's "Muse," the Titan goddess Moneta, another divinely authoritative mother figure, looks quite different, principally, as I shall argue in the next chapter, because by the time Keats wrote *The Fall of Hyperion* he had come to distinguish clearly between his sexual and his poetic identities. These two self-images had been closely allied in earlier poems like *Endymion* and "The Eve of St. Agnes," where the poet figure was also a lover, and the imagination was highly colored by erotic fantasies. This is not to say that earlier versions of the Muse—like, say, Cynthia—at all resembled Geraldine (though "La Belle Dame sans Merci" might qualify as an outstanding exception). Keats, after all, was hardly squeamish about identifying the power of *poesis* with the power of love, and his sexual impulses, to judge from the evidence of the letters, were more consciously restrained by the social self than subconsciously repressed.

What led Keats to create his austere mother of memory was not a fear of the sexual self, but his need to disentangle his poetic identity from the appetitive self in general: not to deny or repress desire, but to free his poetry from the impulse toward imaginative self-indulgence, and thus to free the poet in him to shape the visions of desire with a godlike control and deliberation. In the gaze of Moneta he quite intentionally embodies an image of his poetic self that will directly challenge his audience's image of him as an indolent dreamer and sensualist, replacing it with that of a visionary and friend to man. In contrast to Coleridge's alter ego Christabel, who cannot bring herself to acknowledge for society at large the true self that Geraldine evokes, Keats's scenario of recognition in *The Fall,* where he confronts and wins the acceptance of Moneta, is a dream of self-affirmation consciously *intended* for the eyes of the world. Coleridge, like his creation, could not interiorize a parental presence that would allow him, consciously and wholly, to accept himself. Moneta confirms Keats's sense of worthiness, his "high reason," his new powers to "see as a god sees"; Geraldine inspires a "vision of fear" from which Christabel, and apparently her creator, recoils in a hatred that is self-hatred.

Most significant, Keats is enabled to "tell [his] dreams, / With the fine spell of words ... save / Imagination from the sable charm / And dumb enchantment" (I, 8–11). "Well nurtured" by his spiritual mother "in his mother tongue" (15), he can "rehearse" the tale of his recognition by this superior being and thus vindicate in the eyes of the wide world his visionary identity. Geraldine locks up Christabel's tongue by the touch of her bosom—the primal, maternal source of self-nourishment—keeping the girl's emerging identity a secret from others, and thereby excluding from the realm of conscious, public discourse both her vision of maturity and herself as its visionary.

It is significant that all three of the poets I have chosen as subjects of this book were orphaned by the age of ten. Keats alone seems to have overcome, without excessive dependence on external surrogates, the resulting, recurring feelings of self-dispersion that both exhilarated and frustrated him, inspired and limited his poetic ambitions. It can plausibly be argued that Wordsworth, like his friend Coleridge, failed to internalize a strong self-affirming presence during his childhood and young manhood, and that this lack of an assured source of maternal love, recognition, and affection within the psyche, this "abyss of idealism," encouraged in Wordsworth the displacement of desire through projections of maternal care and solicitude onto the natural world, as well as feelings of self-dispersion. Indeed, his dreamlike confusions between the self and perceived reality seem characteristic of that simple, undifferentiated form of consciousness which precedes the earliest stages of "introjection" and embodied self-awareness.

Wordsworth, however, successfully filled the place within him left empty after the death of his mother by turning to a surrogate—his sister. Dorothy's presence, far from reinforcing the nightmarish withdrawal and suppression of the true self, helped to lead Wordsworth back into the world of others, where he could lay claim to his "office upon earth." Coleridge was unable to find a woman as confident, solicitous, and understanding of his poetic gifts as was Dorothy of her brother's, although Sara Hutchinson, the beloved object of the "Asra" poems, came close. That love, however, was illicit as long as Coleridge's marriage lasted, and his feelings for Sara exacerbated his own repressed feelings of sexual guilt and shame, with their accompanying psychological and somatic torments, to the point where by 1806, when the Coleridges had agreed to a formal separation, it was too late: Coleridge, as Yarlott observes, "was now the husk of the man Asra had once loved" and Asra herself had changed toward him.[96]

The two parts of "Christabel" were not published until 1817. As the intervening years passed and he sank further and further into his bondage to opium, Coleridge began to suffer night-sweats and waking nightmares, hallucinations and psychosomatic ailments, that heightened his terror of what lay within him. The true self was the repository of dark desires and darker fears: "Christabel" was evidence of how dangerous it had become to tap that source. The spring had to be capped, and in it was sealed Coleridge's poetic identity. He now turned to what he called, in "Dejection: an Ode," the more "abstruse research" of philosophy.

The Eye Extinguished

From *logos* to silence, from conversation to confrontation to secret sharing, Coleridge's poetry evolves toward the isolation of imaginative vision, the sense that, although the powers of the secondary imagination may indeed "echo" those of the primary, that echo may be but a sad mimicry of the Divine fiat. It may in fact be the surest symptom not of transcendent identification with the "infinite I AM," but of an all-too-finite and corrupting self-enclosure that keeps the poet from participating fully in a community of perception and mutual self-affirmation. In "Dejection: an Ode," Coleridge's last conversation poem, he chooses a motto from "The Ballad of Sir Patrick Spence"—"Late, late yestreen I saw the new Moon, / With the old Moon in her arms"—which tells us that the moon, supreme symbol of visionary power in previous poems, has gone out. With it has vanished all conviction in the ability of the imagination to fashion forth symbolic images that bespeak a Divine Presence working in and through the mind of the poet (1–8):

> Well! If the Bard was weather-wise, who made
>   The grand old ballad of Sir Patrick Spence,
>   This night, so tranquil now, will not go hence
> Unroused by winds, that ply a busier trade
> Than those which mould yon cloud in lazy flakes,
> Or the dull sobbing draft, that moans and rakes
> Upon the strings of this Aeolian lute,
>   Which better far were mute.

The poet is sarcastic, and his sarcasm infects his perceptions. The wind-shaped cloud and the Aeolian lute, grist for the esemplastic powers of the imagination in previous conversation poems, have here lost their radiance. "Lazy flakes," "dull sobbing draft," "moans and rakes": the poet's choice of words secularizes and demystifies from the outset. Once-magical things have become the unconvincing props of an enfeebled imagination. The image of the moon immediately following these lines reveals the transformation that has taken place (9–13):

> For lo! The New-moon winter-bright!
> And overspread with phantom light,
> (With swimming phantom light o'erspread
> But rimmed and circled by a silver thread)
> I see the old moon in her lap.

The new moon is dark, illuminated only by the feeble "phantom light" reflected from the earth, which is ordinarily understood to be subject to the moon's influence and which the moon itself should have brought to light. "Dejection," accordingly, describes an inverted relationship between the poet's once-visionary mind and the darkling earth it would transfigure: no longer illuminated by the primary imagination, the secondary esemplastic powers of the finite mind disappear, giving way to the false light of sense reflected, quite literally in this symbolic representation of empirical perception, from a world outside the mind, what Coleridge a few lines later calls "reality's dark dream" (95).

Disconnected from any source of transcendent power, the poet's imagination is defeated by his own cynicism: "we receive but what we give, / And in our life alone does Nature live" (47–48): "our life," not "the one Life," and "alone." In "Dejection" the poet achieves no visionary, dreamlike communion with world, God, or others. There is no escape from this "inanimate cold world" (51) into a world made rich and strange and, finally, companionable—no escape from the imaginary into the imaginative. In such a state "passion" and "life" are no longer "within us *and* abroad"—their "fountains are within" (46), solely. The phrase "we receive *but* what we give" reduces the joyful excess of God's imminence in perceived nature to a mere will-o'-the-wisp.

Just before the last stanza, with its characteristic gesture of hope for the poet's absent interlocutor, Sara Hutchinson, Coleridge turns to the roaring of the wind in search of that "wonted impulse" for vivid images that will "startle this dull pain, and make it move and

live" (19–20). It is one index of his despair that he must make the
mind so dependent on a physical stimulus for its imaginative im-
petus, as though consciousness were a physical mechanism itself. The
last image prodded forth in this manner is (121–125)

> ... of a little child
> Upon a lonesome wild,
> Not far from home, but she hath lost her way:
> And now moans low in bitter grief and fear,
> And now screams loud, and hopes to make her mother hear.

It is an image of Coleridge's final sense of isolation and abandonment beyond the walls of community, cut off from family and
friends, orphaned by his now self-enclosed imagination. It is another
version of the poet as Christabel, but with no moon to see by and not
even a ghostly parent at hand—only his undirected dreams, raving
in his ears like the wind itself, a "Mad Lutanist!" making "Devils'
Yule" (104–106).

Keats:
Watcher and Witness

O my friends you loose [lose] the action—
and attitude is everything.
—Letter to the George Keatses, September 17–27, 1819

IN HIS ATTITUDES toward self, world, and others, Keats bears some resemblance to each of his first-generation predecessors. Like Coleridge, he at first sought to create an intimately "real" dream context, vis-à-vis imagined others, for the incarnation of the spectral inner self. This context, in poems like *Lamia* and "The Eve of St. Agnes," took the form of a fantasized world of artifice, confirmed in its apparent substantiality by the assenting gaze of the Beloved, herself a "theatrical" illusion. Like Wordsworth, however, Keats understood his destiny as a poet to lie elsewhere, and the course of his work, like that of Wordsworth, appears as a continuing experiment in making places for the self in a world of others. He was highly conscious, at the outset of his career, of the physical impression he made as a prospective lover and as a poet, and he was initially drawn to the imagination as a vehicle of escape and to poetry as, in part, a vehicle of his own ambitious self-display. But Keats came, in the poems of his maturity like *The Fall of Hyperion* and "To Autumn," to embrace the realm of history, process, and mortality, and to transform his self-withdrawn voyeurism of life into the highest form of moral witness: a vision of the human condition on which the poet stakes his real existence. In Keats we find the poet seeking to transform himself from a character or persona represented in the theater of his own work into an artist who takes his responsibilities as seer and "Stager," as beholder and presenter of his vision, with deadly seriousness.

The Poet as Spectator

For the early Keats, as for Coleridge, the "poetical Character" or self of the poet aspired to the condition of an intelligence or mind that, by shedding its proper identity, could vicariously assume any shape or form of embodiment. In this respect—again, like Coleridge—Keats differed a great deal, in his early career at least, from Wordsworth. Keats and Coleridge wished to exploit the volatility of the poetical self in the service of a protean self-dispersion, while Wordsworth feared the spurious "idealism" of his disembodied self, its unmoored condition, ever anxious to make overt claim to that detached, impersonal consciousness which found a diffuse presence in Nature mirroring its own solipsistic appropriation of the world. Wordsworth strove to identify as his this "gift," this peculiar power of disembodied vision, to find a place for it in the epical unfolding of the growth of his mind, and to draw conclusions that bear on the conduct of human life.

From this "Wordsworthian or egotistical sublime; which is a thing per se and stands alone" (I, 387)[1] and which stubbornly attempts, by retrospective glimpses, to maintain a proprietory claim on its most self-diffusive moments, Keats in mid-career distinguishes his "poetical Character" as a "camelion" that "has no self," but is "every thing and nothing." "It has no character," he writes Richard Woodhouse on October 27, 1818, "it enjoys light and shade; it lives in gusto, be it foul or fair, high or low, rich or poor, mean or elevated—It has as much delight in conceiving an Iago as an Imogen . . . A Poet is the most unpoetical of any thing in existence; because he has no Identity—he is continually in for—and filling some other Body" (I, 387). Keats draws on his own experience for an example of what he means: "When I am in a room with People if I ever am free from speculating on creations of my own brain, then not myself goes home to myself: but the identity of every one in the room begins to [*for* so] to press upon me that, I am in a very little time an[ni]hilated" (I, 387).

Looking over Keats's letters, we soon realize that there are different gradations and types of "pressure" that others' identities can exert. Of his younger sister, Fanny, the poet could write his sister-in-law, Georgiana, "her character is not formed; her identity does not press upon me as yours does" (I, 392). By this Keats means that Fanny, a comparative child, has not gained enough depth of experience or complexity of understanding to engage the prehensile imagination of the poet.

But how are we to take this added depth of "character"? In what way is it apprehended by the mind of the poet? How can it be said to "press" upon him? We might at first assume that by "character" Keats means something abstract, but this cannot be strictly true. As he makes clear in another journal-letter to George and Georgiana Keats spanning the months from December 1818 to January 1819, the "characters" of people must be apprehended from their actions, their mode of dress, gesture, and speech. It is these embodied, tangible expressions of personality that "impress" their owners' identities on the "camelion poet":

> Suppose Brown or Haslam or any one whom I understand in the nether degee to which I do you, were in America [as Georgiana is], they would be so much the farther from me in proportion as their identity was less impressed upon me. Now the reason why I do not feel at the present moment so far from you is that I remember your Ways and Manners and actions; I [have] known you[r] manner of thinking, you[r] manner of feeling: I know what shape your joy or your sorrow would take, I know the manner of you[r] walking, standing, sauntering, sitting down, laughing, punning, and eve[r]y action so truly that you seem near to me.   (II, 5)

Here Keats demonstrates his acute dramatic sense, his responsiveness to the "pressure" of the self as embodied in manner, gesture, and speech. There is a close connection in Keats's mind between the intellectual or emotional life of the person whose identity is impressed upon him—the "manner of thinking," the "manner of feeling"—and the "Ways and Manners and actions" of that person; more specifically, between the "shape" Georgiana's joy or sorrow would take and the "manner" of her "walking, standing, sauntering, sitting down, laughing." For Keats, the intangible identity of a person is inextricable from his or her physically representable "character." People who lend themselves to being vividly imagined or remembered possess physical features and manners that "press" upon the poet's chameleon mind, even in memory, when these people are absent. Thus, consistent with the poet's tendency toward empathic self-annihilation and vicarious identification with others is his appreciation of vividly embodied "characters."

Again and again in the letters we find instances of Keats's sensitivity to the dramatic effects of personality, quite in keeping with his well-documented enthusiasm for the theater.[2] This theatrical sense, however, can at times degenerate into a skeptical disengagement, impeding rather than encouraging vicarious participation. Contrast the "camelion" excitement of the letter to Woodhouse with the following, written to J.H. Reynolds the next summer, in which Keats acknowledges without a trace of grief the passing of his former unreflective "flights" (I use the word advisedly) of imaginative empathy: "I make use of my Judgment more deliberately than I yet have done . . . [and] look upon the affairs of the world with a healthy deliberation. I have of late been moulting: not for fresh feathers & wings: they are gone, and in their stead I hope to have a pair of patient sublunary legs. I have altered not from a Chrysalis into a butterfly, but the Contrary. having two little loopholes, whence I may look out into the stage of the world" (II, 128).

The poet feels his body to be a thing apart from but enclosing him, like a cocoon with eyeholes. His mind or psyche (classically represented by a butterfly) is hidden from view by the embodied self, making Keats feel cut off from rather than engaged by the "stage of the world" on which others perform. By the end of the summer this kind of retreat has almost reached the extremes of a schizoid withdrawal: "My own being which I know to be becomes of more consequence to me than the crowds of Shadows in the shape of Man and women that inhabit a kingdom" (II, 146).

Keats has begun to project his own sense of bodily disengagement onto others. As the world becomes a stage, life becomes a play of phantoms. Others are derealized. We have encountered such experiences in the work of Wordsworth and Coleridge both, and we have seen that they usually entail a conviction that the true self—"My own being which I know to be"—is to be found at a remove from the world, completely integrated and its own only when it is so. By the end of the year, Keats can write to George and Georgiana "I am tired of the Theatres. Almost all the parties I may chance to fall into I know by heart—I know the different Styles of talk in different places: what subjects will be started how it will proceed, like an acted play, from the first to the last Act" (II, 244).

At first glance, the early "camelion" attitudes and the later, more detached view of the world stage from within the "Chrysalis" seem to contradict each other. But in fact both attitudes result from an essentially theatrical, which is to say, self-distancing, point of view. The earlier is simply a more naive, the later a more cynical, view of *theatrum mundi*. Consider, for instance, the implied analogy in the earlier letter to Woodhouse between "creations of my own brain" and "the identity of every one in the room": far from being dissimilar, as we might assume from a first reading, both objects of Keats's attention apparently demand the same imaginative mode of apprehension. If the passage on self-annihilation is meant to illustrate the impressionable nature of Keats's own "poetical Character," then we must understand the poet's proper self to be "annihilated" from its own awareness by the pressure of others' identities in much the same manner as the "camelion" poet's when he apprehends dramatic characters, for example, "an Iago" or "an Imogen." Other people in the room are in fact apprehended by a mind that had but a moment before been preoccupied with *imaginary* characters like these, "creations of my own brain." Already "others in the room" are halfway to becoming "Shadows in the Shape of Man and women," inhabitants of a world that momentarily appears as a sort of walking daydream or stage play.

The main difference between Keats's earlier and later experiences of public life is that the later Keats cannot maintain that "willing suspension of disbelief" necessary for dramatic realization of the scene and a complementary "speculative" self-annihilation. He is too cynical and, as we shall see, his cynicism stems in large part from an increasing discomfort with the principal task facing him as a young man, the task of fashioning and finding acceptance for an adult identity among adults, in the role *he* is expected to play on the stage of the world. Keats, in short, loses his ability to forget himself as he becomes more and more uncomfortably self-conscious in the company of others, and less and less sure that the self they perceive is really his. In consequence, the spark of his chameleon imagination is dampened. Feeling trapped in and yet alienated from his own body, he cannot be "filling other Bodies."

Keats begins to experience a radically different kind of "pressure" exerted by others, a pressure that demands not aesthetic disinterestedness or imaginative empathy but a self-conscious and overt response: either acquiescence or argument, but not "relish." Before considering this second, more self-conscious type of "pressure," however, I would like to take a moment of trace the conditions and consequences of the first type, which so often appears as part of a self-destroying spectatorship in Keats's early and middle work.

For the chameleon poet to cultivate a theatrical, self-annihilating empathy, his attention must be distracted entirely from his embodied self, as it is when he is "speculating" on his own "creations," or when he is engaged in imagining, remembering, or calling to mind the "characters" of those who are absent, like Georgiana Keats, or as it is when he in fact views an Iago or an Imogen in a play. The "speculative" poet is the poet as onlooker, free to stand "in for" others to the extent that he is freed from accountability for a particular role or self-image to be maintained for those on whom he speculates. Others can "press" imaginatively upon the mind provided they pose no threat of confronting the poet *in propria persona*. It would be hard to imagine Keats maintaining this kind of introverted reverie in a "room with People" if he were approached and invited to join in a conversation, to pay attention to his own part in the "acted play."

The connection between remaining a removed spectator and retaining one's self-annihilating powers of empathic projection is reflected in the poet's tendency to station himself outside yet near the scenes he describes in his poetry. The technique is evident quite early in Keats's writing, where the poet or speaker is generally conceived as an unobserved watcher or listener. Christopher Ricks, alluding to this strain of voyeurism in Keats's work, writes, "The sense not just that something is happening but that something is being watched is an important giver of depth."[3] It is also important as an indication of the disembodied nature of chameleon speculation, the poetical character's need to escape self-consciousness. Characteristically, the poet partakes in the existence of inanimate objects[4]—for example, the urn, a landscape, or as Woodhouse has reported a billiard ball[5]—or of unreflective, unself-conscious forms of life from which his presence is effectively screened, like the nightingale in the ode. "If a Sparrow come before my Window," he writes Benjamin Bailey in November of 1817, "I take part in its existince [*sic*] and pick about the Gravel" (I, 186).

The poet of "no self" approaches his subjects stealthily or imagines them or stumbles on them, surprised at his find, like the narrator of "Sleep and Poetry," who (unwatched) gazes at the nameless charioteer conjuring, with "wond'rous gesture," "Shapes of delight, of mystery, and fear" (136, 138).[6] As the poet observes (151-154),

> . . . Most awfully intent,
> The driver of those steeds is forward bent,
> And seems to listen: O that I might know
> All that he writes with such a hurrying glow.

The charioteer, personification of the ideal poet, remains unapproachable by the aspirant but at the same time is caught in a candid moment, unself-consciously intent on his business, open to chameleon speculation—"O that I might know." Likewise, in the "Ode to Psyche," when the narrator chances on the hiding place of Cupid and Psyche, they remain blissfully unaware of his presence (7-15):

I wander'd in a forest thoughtlessly,
  And, on the sudden, fainting with surprise,
Saw two fair creatures, couched side by side
  In deepest grass, beneath the whispering roof
  Of leaves and trembled blossoms, where there ran
     A brooklet, scarce espied:
'Mid hush'd cool-rooted flowers, fragrant-eyed,
  Blue, silver-white and budded Tyrian,
They lay calm-breathing on the bedded grass.

Here the "brooklet scarce espied" reinforces the impression of secretiveness, and the "fragrant-eyed" flowers remind us that the scene is being watched.

One great advantage of hidden watching is that the poet can catch the object of speculation unawares. In "I Stood Tip-Toe upon a Little Hill" standing tip-toe implies an effort at furtive observation: "There was wide wand'ring for the *greediest eye*, / To *peer* about upon variety" (15–16; my emphasis). The poet would "linger awhile upon some bending planks / That lean against a streamlet's rushy banks / And *watch* intently Nature's gentle doings" (61–63; my emphasis). But should his presence be revealed, nature will retreat, her candor will vanish. Thus, while "swarms of minnows . . . ever wrestle / With their own sweet delight, and ever nestle / Their silver bellies on the pebbly sand," one need only "scantily hold out the hand" and "That very instant not one will remain; / But turn your eye and they are there again" (72–80). The whole effort of the imagination is directed here at capturing a candid, unself-conscious nature, the world as it goes on when no one is present to disturb it. At such moments Nature does not reflect back to the perceiver a sense of his physical presence, of his proper embodied self. It is as though he had vanished.

It is but a small step from watching the "gentle doings" of Nature in "I Stood Tip-Toe" to listening to the song of an unself-conscious nightingale or to watching the arrested, candid display of human passions in a "leaf-fring'd legend . . . of deities or mortals" on a Grecian urn. "Leaf-fring'd" suggests the arboreal enclosure central to so many of Keats's discovered scenes, like the "whispering roof / Of leaves and trembled blossoms" that hides Cupid and Psyche from prying eyes. In the "Ode on a Grecian Urn" the pastoral screen is in effect pulled gently aside while the poet peers in on "men or gods" in "mad pursuit," in "wild ecstasy."

Those whom the chameleon poet observes are, ideally, unconscious of his attention, which is to say, unself-conscious, sincere, even
instinctive in their actions and pursuits. They are true to their inner
selves—"creatures of impulse," Keats calls them in the letter on the
"poetical Character," and goes on to say that such creatures alone
can be said to have a proper identity. In a letter to George and Georgiana in 1819, Keats makes clear the connection between the display
of such instinctive behavior in animals and unself-conscious, spontaneous behavior in human beings, both proper subjects of "Amusement . . . to a speculative Mind. I go among the Feilds [*sic*] and catch
a glimpse of a stoat or a fieldmouse peeping out of the withered
grass—the creature hath a purpose and its eyes are bright with it—I
go amongst the buildings of a city and I see a Man hurrying along—
to what? The Creature has a purpose and his eyes are bright with it"
(II, 79–80). "The Creature has a purpose," and his eyes attend to
that, unaware of the poet who is as inaccessible to the attentions of
the man in the street as he is to those of the fieldmouse.

To watch the doings of another in spontaneous, candid moments
while remaining aloof and unself-conscious is close to seeing as a god
sees. It is to watch unwatched as the true self emerges—perhaps even
to become, for a moment, that person, animal, or thing observed.
And yet Keats, unlike Wordsworth or Coleridge, saves his speculative mind from thoughts of self-deification by his awareness of the
relativity of all mental vantage points. He is constantly calling attention to the conditions of the possibility of imaginative transcendence; he is constantly outflanking his own absorbed point of view.
He is not like Coleridge a transcendental metaphysician, nor quite a
prophet of the imagination, like Wordsworth. Keats's waking dreams
hardly ever result in a "sense sublime / Of something far more
deeply interfused" throughout the landscape; rather they result in an
intense identification with some particular object or other. His disembodied eye seeks, usually, not so much to revitalize the old world
as to substitute new dream-worlds for the old, dream worlds that co-
alesce around the particular datum of intense experience—nightingale, urn, or Beloved. Keats is thus vulnerable to ruder awakenings
than Wordsworth and, as a result, more skeptical of the permanent
significance of visionary solipsism.

With respect to those purposive "creatures" that provide the speculative mind with so much amusement, Keats writes,

> I myself am pursueing [*sic*] the same instinctive course as the veriest
> human animal you can think of—I am however young writing at

random—straining at particles of light in the midst of a great darkness . . . Yet may I not in this be free from sin? May there not be
superior beings amused with any graceful, though instinctive attitude my mind m[a]y fall into, as I am entertained with the alertness
of a Stoat or the anxiety of a Deer? Though a quarrel in the streets
is a thing to be hated, the energies displayed in it are fine; the commonest Man shows a grace in his quarrel—By a superior being our
reasoning[s] may take the same tone—though erroneous they may be
fine—This is the very thing in which consists poetry.   (II, 80–81)

There is always, for Keats, the possibility of a "superior," more
encompassing prospect that will reveal the poet's own point of view
to be as limited and "instinctive" as those of the very creatures he
most enjoys watching. For that reason, his point of view cannot, finally, be absolute, however absorbed in it he may momentarily become. Indeed, from a "superior" vantage point, the identity of the
poet, momentarily "annihilated" in his own eyes, is revealed from
without in its truest form: not as "nothing," not as a "camelion," but
as an unself-conscious, unpremeditated, and completely self-expres-
sive *act*—here, "writing at random"—that embodies a spontaneous
"attitude" of mind. This is what poetry is to the poet *in propria persona:* headlong expression that runs the risk of an error in reasoning
for the sake of displaying something "fine." "If Poetry comes not as
naturally as the Leaves to a tree," writes Keats in a letter to John
Taylor, dated February 27, 1818, "it had better not come at all" (I,
238–239).

As in the case of Wordsworth, such sentiments must be taken with
severe qualifications. Poetry is rarely the product of automatic
writing, and Keats, superb and meticulous artist that he was, understood that the fever of spontaneous composition was not always salu-
tary. But what I believe he found attractive in the notion of creative
spontaneity was the same thing that attracted Wordsworth: its implication that the ideal poet, like the ideal poetic subject, should show
his "energies" without attention to how others might judge their effect. He should, like the speaker of the "Ode to Maia," sing "unheard, / Save of the quiet primrose, and the span / Of heaven, and
few ears"; his "song should die away, / Content . . . rich in the simple
worship of a day" (9–14). Such is the situation of choice for the Romantic poet, singing alone or for the "fit . . . though few" ears of a
select—and sympathetic—audience. It is a situation conceived as
ideal by one who contended he "never wrote one single Line of Poetry with the least Shadow of public thought" (I, 267), and for whom

"the Public" is "a thing [he] cannot help looking upon as an Enemy," "cannot address without feelings of Hostility" (I, 266). The poet, to sing *as* the poet he truly is, must sing first for himself.

The "Ode to a Nightingale" is an excellent example of Keats's attention to theatrical perspectives and concentric frames of perception, as well as of his ambivalence toward that "Public" he professes to despise. The poet, like the object of his rhapsody, is ideally overheard from hiding as he enacts, like the charioteer of "Sleep and Poetry," those "wond'rous gestures"—here, aural "gestures" toward a dark world—which bring that world imaginatively to life for his reader. Much of the poem's enduring appeal lies in the way it epitomizes the ideal situation of the Romantic poet. The ode implicitly analogizes the nightingale who sings "in shadows numberless," in the "forest dim," to the poet, Shelley's lyric "nightingale," who sings "unseen" by the world, and blind to it, in "embalmed darkness."[7] The situation is very like the one surrounding the "speculative Mind" that finds amusement in the activities of a stoat, a deer, or a fieldmouse, and who provides, in turn, "Amusement" for the speculative minds of others outside his situation. The written poem itself represents the poet's "instinctive attitude" toward a creature of Nature, and his unself-conscious, unpremeditated responses to the bird's song become, in turn, the subject both of admiration and of identification for his readers. They are in the most real sense—as words on the page—the poet's truest expression of his identity as a poet.

Of course, poetic effects must be distinguished from the facts of composition. The speaker's "song," though it gives the typically odal impression of spontaneity and instinctiveness, is in fact premediatated and totally under Keats's control. But by shrouding the poet in darkness, like Gray's elegist, Keats has contrived to enhance the apparent sincerity of the speaker's utterance: it cannot possibly be addressed to us, "the Public," or even with us in mind. The poet is apparently free of "the least Shadow of public thought." Like the bird, he appears to be caught in a candid moment, in an "instinctive attitude" that, we are encouraged to assume, truly reveals his inmost self, the "soul" which he too is "pouring forth . . . in such an ecstasy" while he sings (57–58).

As in Gray's elegy, the disappearance of the world for the poet is merely the obverse of the poet's desire to disappear from the world: not simply to escape embodiment and the physical encumbrances of embodiment but to escape awareness of the mind's limitation by embodiment, to "leave the world unseen" (19), to "Fade far away, dissolve, and ... forget ... / The weariness, the fever, and the fret / Here, where men sit and hear each other groan" (21–24).[8] "Unseen" is ambiguous. It can mean that the poet wishes the world were invisible to him, as in fact it is "here," where "there is no light" (38), but it can also refer to the speaker. He would "fade away" and *be* "unseen"—a disembodied presence, like the nightingale he overhears. Thus defended against self-awareness, the poet can shed his particular character or identity and merge with something universal, a Bardic consciousness that transcends all "hungry generations," singing, like the bird, in a voice that "was heard / In ancient days by emperor and clown" (62–64).[9]

In darkness, then, the poet's identity as an individual situated among mortal men who "sit and hear each other groan," men painfully aware of each other's presence, is made obscure, as invisible to himself as to those who listen. The "soul" that the poet pours abroad has become, from his point of view, undifferentiated Mind, an ahistorical, impersonal consciousness that the poet would project into another being, another situation, standing "in for—and filling some other Body." This body could belong to the nightingale (although stanza 4 suggests that that attempt has ended in failure)[10] or more to the point, other *listeners* of the nightingale, like those in stanza 7: "emperor and clown," or "Ruth, when, sick for home, / She stood in tears amid the alien corn" (66–67).[11]

On such moments of intense experience is Keats's poetry founded: the loss of all sense of self in his absorbed attention to a beautiful object or being, preparatory to an exhilarating projection of self in the embodied being of another. This is one way of understanding Keats's famous lines in *Endymion:* "Wherein lies happiness? In that which becks / Our ready minds to fellowship divine, / A fellowship with essence; till we shine, / Full alchemiz'd, and free of space" (I, 777–780). This moment is "free of space"—infinite in duration and in extent—because it does not appear against any background of objectively lived space and time. In an instant the subject and object of perception are fused and eternized. There are for the mind no "last" nor "next," no past nor future moments of consciousness in which the awareness of the present moment can inhere and be recognized as a part of the "self" that is aware. That "self" has already faded from its own view, until all that exists is the pure percept, outside of time, unlocalized.[12]

Thus the mortal nightingale becomes an "immortal bird" as the self of the subject undergoes a living death: "Now more than ever seems it rich to die" (55). The self, losing in the focused intensity of its "rich" perception of beauty all sense of its finitude in a circumambient world, "passes away" while the timeless moment persists. A similar experience is described in book III of *Hyperion,* where the intensity of death clearly represents a dying of the mortal, finite self into the timeless life of a god. Apollo becomes "celestial" (124–130):

> Soon wild commotions shook him, and made flush
> All the immortal fairness of his limbs;
> Most like the struggle at the gate of death;
> Or liker still to one who should take leave
> Of pale immortal death, and with a pang
> As hot as death's is chill, with fierce convulse
> Die into life . . .

Six lines later the fragment ends. Beyond this point, Keats could not go. In the manuscript he penciled in: "Glory dawned: he was a God—."

Mortals are deified through the intensity of their perception of physical beauty, an intensity that makes such beauty "true." In these experiences there is no second-guessing, no doubts about the reality of what is apprehended, because in the moment apprehension occurs there is no embodied "self" for consciousness to interpose between it and its object, and thus, no room to doubt the existence and the immutability of what is experienced. In his famous letter to Benjamin Bailey, of November 22, 1817, still early in his short career, Keats writes about the "authenticity of the Imagination" as follows:

> I am certain of nothing but of the holiness of the Heart's affections and the truth of Imagination—What the imagination seizes as Beauty must be truth—whether it existed before or not . . . The Imagination may be compared to Adam's dream—he awoke and found it truth. I am the more zealous in this affair, because I have never yet been able to perceive how any thing can be known for truth by consequitive reasoning—and yet it must be—Can it be that even the greatest Philosopher ever arrived at his goal without putting aside numerous objections—However it may be, O for a Life of Sensations rather than of Thoughts! (I, 184–185)

It is these pure sensations themselves, the "atoms of perception" as Keats calls them in his "Soul-making" letter of February-May 1819, those anonymous "sparks of the divinity" that "know" and "see" and "are pure, in short they are God" (II, 102). These, he goes on, cannot but be "truth." Keats's premise has its roots, ironically enough, in Locke and Descartes: *that* something is being perceived cannot be doubted. But the poet here turns the philosophers inside out. The simple reality of sensation does not point to the necessary existence of a perceiving self, a reflective "ego cogitans"; rather, it presumes just the opposite, the "annihilation" of the self that is assumed to perceive. Consciousness per se is impersonal, as Hume believed. And because the bare sensation, this "atom of perception" or "intelligence," fills a moment that is utterly isolated from the continuum of time that human consciousness ordinarily inhabits as a "self"—extended into the future with personal desire and expectation, and into the past by personal memories, by congratulation and regret—this sensation cannot be "disagreeable": "The excellence of every Art is its intensity, capable of making all disagreeables evaporate, from their being in close relationship with Beauty & Truth" (I, 192). The "disagreeable" can be found only in what the "self" perceives in relation to itself. "Disagreeables evaporate" in the "intensity" of sensations only as the self evaporates, for the disagreeable is a category of apprehension inapplicable to the disinterested, self-less experience of imaginative perception.

Thus Keats could write in December of 1817, in the letter to George and Tom Keats describing the "intensity" of excellent art, and even as late as May 1819, he could end the "Ode on a Grecian Urn" with the cryptic aphorism, " 'Beauty is Truth, Truth Beauty'—that is all / Ye know on earth, and all ye need to know" (49–50). But Keats was , characteristically, torn by the issue. What remains of the fusion of Beauty and Truth when the moment of self-annihilating vision has passed? "A sense of real things comes doubly strong" ("Sleep and Poetry," 157). The truth-beauty equation at the end of the "Ode on a Grecian Urn" offers solace but is finally no more convincing than the experience it describes is durable. This is *"all"* mortal men "know *on earth"*—which means that mortal knowledge is limited to this—and all they *"need* to know"—which implies that "on earth" such experiences raise as many doubts as they allay, and incite us to *want* to know more than we "need" to. The urn's aphorism would seem pat if it came at the end of the "Ode to a Nightingale," in answer to such questions as "Was it a vision, or a waking dream?" and "Do I wake or sleep?" These questions arise in the act of reflecting on experience, on the self that perceives, the world it perceives, and its own existence there. They are self-conscious questions.

Morris Dickstein has pointed out that the Nightingale ode marks a turning point in Keats's poetic evolution from a chameleon poet in search of pleasurable, self-annihilating sensations to a mature artist who has come to accept the world and his being in it. At the end of the poem, writes Dickstein, "Keats at last takes up residence as he has repeatedly promised, in the difficult domain of the 'sole self.' "[13] If "but to think is to be full of sorrow" (27), there might be some value in contemplating a "silent form" like the urn that "doth tease us out of thought / As doth eternity" (44–45), and the urn's aphorism prolongs this cold comfort by teasing. The lines offered us are meant to preempt questions, not answer them. Only the "sole self" (72) to which the poet awakens at the end of the Nightingale ode can question the reality of such visions in all seriousness, for only the poet who is aware of his finitude and separateness can be made to feel answerable—as though to another—for the decisions he must make and act on in the world, decisions which are embodied nowhere else but in the poem itself, the sole objective index of the poet's shadowy subjectivity. The "sole self" is the self of the philosopher: not the passive chameleon poet, nor his persona, the ostensibly spontaneous, unself-conscious singer of "instinctive attitudes," but the poet *in propria persona,* back in the world—John Keats.

The Poet as Pet-Lamb

What can it mean, after all, to awaken to one's "sole self"? At the end of the Nightingale ode, the hidden listener "comes to" in a physical space whose contours are traced by the fading anthem of the nightingale, which is now moving as a separate thing (71–80):

> Forlorn! the very word is like a bell
>   To toll me back from thee to my sole self!
> Adieu! the fancy cannot cheat so well
>   As she is fam'd to do, deceiving elf.
> Adieu! adieu! thy plaintive anthem fades
>   Past the near meadows, over the still stream,
>   Up the hill-side; and now 'tis buried deep
>   In the next valley-glades:
> Was it a vision, or a waking dream?
>   Fled is that music:—Do I wake or sleep?

Suddenly awake, self-conscious, the listener doubts the truth of the beauty that something not identified as his "self " has perceived, and the beauty of truth, of the real world to which the embodied "self" must return. He awakens from the empathic voyeurism of imaginative self-annihilation to the burden of proper self-embodiment in a realm where beauty is lacking, or ever passing.

He awakens, more importantly, to "pressures" completely different from those relished by the "camelion Poet": the stifling pressures of "men who sit and hear each other groan," men who endure "the weariness, the fever, and the fret" of life, men like Tom Keats: "I wish I could say Tom was any better. His identity presses upon me so all day that I am obliged to go out" (I, 368–369). The pressure Keats feels from his dying brother, unlike that he feels from real or imaginary "characters," or people apprehended like "creations of my own brain," occasions anxiety, uneasiness. Tom's identity does not "press" upon the chameleon imagination in the way a roomful of people might, or as the thought of Georgiana Keats might. Tom's identity is not *im*pressive, but *op*pressive, and not simply because it is disagreeable or in pain: Keats, after all, had written that the "poetical character" "enjoys light *and* shade; it lives in gusto, *be it foul or fair* . . . It does no harm from *its relish of the dark side of things* any more than from its taste for the bright one, because they both end in speculation."

"Speculation": a word used frequently in Keats's letters, and integral to his aesthetic. Tom's illness is not "speculative," in its etymologically pertinent sense: it is not something that can be simply observed, as in a distant mirror, by a spectator removed from the scene of suffering. Here in his brother's agony, certainly, is the "intensity" that Keats felt was "the excellence of every Art," "capable of making all disagreeables evaporate." But in this "intensity" no "disagreeables evaporate." Tom, unlike Iago or Imogen, Lear or Cordelia, can excite no "momentous depth of speculation" in his suffering because it is not, like theirs, distanced, as it would be in a theater. It "presses" for a response, for comfort, for relief or release, and thus confronts Keats with his own helpless presence in the room. The "pressure" of Tom's identity does not "annihilate" Keats's proper self, but rather, makes that self all too unbearably present and burdensome, all too conscious of its "response-ability."

Keats felt this burdensome sort of "pressure" on more than one occasion. In a long journal-letter to George and Georgiana Keats, written in the summer of 1819, he distinguishes two kinds of indolence: that in which one is alone, and that in which one is with others.

> I cannot bare [*sic*] a day an[ni]hilated in that manner—there is a great difference between an easy and an uneasy indolence—An indolent day—*fill'd with speculations even of an unpleasant colour—is bearable and even pleasant alone*—when one's thoughts cannot find out any th[i]ng better in the world; and experience has told us that locomotion is no change: but to have nothing to do, and *to be surrounded with unpleasant human identities; who press upon one just enough to prevent one getting into a lazy position; and not enough to interest or rouse one;* is a capital punishment of a capital crime. (II, 77; italics added)

The difference between easy and uneasy indolence has nothing to do with the relative disagreeableness of the objects of contemplation. Other people's identities observed too close up can be oppressive in a way that disagreeable persons seen from a distance or only imagined cannot. The pressure of unpleasant people's identities can in some instances demand a response, "prevent one getting into a lazy position," and responses restrict one's attention to the immediate situation and one's role in it. In the presence of others we become too aware of what Wordsworth called "the burthen of the unnatural self," which inhibits empathic identification.

Keats's aspiration to be sublime spectator of, rather than participant in, the theater of life complements his growing dissatisfaction during the "Great Year" of 1819—when he wrote the odes, his major romances, and *Otho the Great*—with the role he feels assigned him in that theater, at those parties, for instance, that proceeded "like an acted Play." Irritated and frustrated by the discrepancy he perceives between his true talents, genius, and passions and the figure he cuts in society, Keats becomes quite sensitive to what his acquaintances make of him in two roles especially, as lover and as poet. Considering his youth, we should not be surprised that his sexual and professional identities particularly should have concerned him, nor that the poet should so often appear *as* a lover, in search of affection and acceptance, in his work. Yet Keats feels ambivalent: his hostility and impatience are a measure of his irksome dependence on others' approval of him, much like his animadversions on "the Public." This too is understandable, for only by the right recognition of his claims as lover and artist could the poet just emerging into manhood find the legitimation of his proper place in the adult world.

Keats was especially sensitive about his height. Among female company, he writes Bailey, he "cannot speak or be silent":

I am full of Suspicions and therefore listen to no thing—I am in a hurry to be gone—You must be charitable and put all this perversity to my being disappointed since Boyhood—Yet with such feelings I am happier alone among Crowds of men, by myself or with a friend or two . . . I could say a good deal about this but I will leave it . . . content that I am wronging no one, for after all I do think better of Womankind than to suppose they care whether Mister John Keats five feet hight [*sic*] likes them or not.   (I, 341–342)

Given the source of Keats's discomfort, it seems quite obvious that he cares very much whether women care that he likes them. As Christopher Ricks observes, "There can be no doubt that [Keats's height] mattered most to him, and was an embarrassment more than superficial, because of love and desire."[14] "When I am among Women," Keats writes in the same letter to Bailey, "I have evil thoughts" (I, 341); he is anxious to leave. He would rather be "*alone* among Crowds of men," ignored, a cipher, if you will, "in a room with People" whose identities, at a proper remove, can monopolize his preternaturally active imagination. Thus unnoticed, unapproached, left to himself or to "no self," he is free to fantasize: "When I was a Schoolboy I though[t] a fair Woman a pure Goddess, my mind was a soft nest in which some one of them slept though she knew it not" (I, 341).

Keats's height also mattered to him as an aspiring poet. In a letter to George and Georgiana, written during the time he was working on "The Eve of St. Agnes," Keats mentions a remark made about him that he learned of secondhand: "Says he 'O, he is quite the little Poet' now this is abominable—you might as well say Buonaparte is quite the little Soldier—You see what it is to be under six foot and not a lord" (II, 61). Keats was coming to realize that "conversation is not a search after knowledge, but an endeavor at effect," and beginning to feel the exasperations of being among "that most vulgar of all crowds the literary" (II, 43). As early as October of 1818, soon after returning from a walking tour of Scotland with Charles Brown, Keats writes George and Georgiana protesting his indifference to "Society," perhaps too much: "It does me not the least harm in Society to make me appear little and rediculous [*sic*] . . . I feel that I make an impression upon them which insures me personal respect

while I am in sight whatever they may say when my back is turned"
(I, 394).

The last sentence, like his remarks on what women think of him, or
on his "Public," sounds like whistling in the dark. His effect upon the
literati was evidently on his mind.[15] Two weeks later he writes again:

> Th[i]nk of my Pleasure in Solitude, in comparision of my commerce
> with the world—there I am a child—there they do not know me not
> even my most intimate acquaintance—I give into their feelings as
> though I were refraining from irritating [a] little child—Some think
> me middling, others silly, others foolish—every one thinks he sees
> my weak side against my will; when in truth it is with my will—I
> am content to be thought all this because I have in my own breast
> so great a resource. This is one great reason why they like me so;
> because they can all show to advantage in a room, and eclipese [*sic*]
> from a certain tact one who is reckoned to be a good Poet.   (I, 404)

Keats's confidence in his "resource" is here as much a function of
what others think of him, of being "reckoned" a good poet, as it is a
sign of his own inner certainty. And that confidence is not enough to
overcome his doubts about his presence, his "effect": compared to
him, everyone else "show[s] to advantage in a room."

By early 1819 Keats has become even more bitter over his role in
"Saciety" (II, 244) and upset at the discrepancies he sees between his
potential as a "miserable and mighty Poet of the human Heart" and
the constraints he feels on his behavior in company. "One of the
great reasons that the english have produced the finest writers in the
world; is, that the English world has ill-treated them during their
lives and foster'd them after their deaths. They have in general been
trampled aside into the bye paths of life and seen the festerings of
Society . . . [Boyardo] was a noble Poet of Romance; not a miserable
and mighty Poet of the human Heart" (II, 115). The great poet, unlike Boyardo, stands outside society and looks on. He does not play
along. This passage, from a letter to Mary-Ann Jeffery,[16] appears in
the same paragraph in which Keats, with his medical training at
Guy's Hospital, toys with the idea of signing aboard a merchant ship
as a doctor: "You are a little in the wrong concerning its destroying
the energies of Mind: on the contrary it would be the finest thing in
the world to strengthen them—To be thrown among people who care
not for you, with whom you have no sympathies forces the Mind
upon its own resources, and leaves it free to make its speculations of

the differences of human character and to class them with the calmness of a Botanist" (II, 115).

The "calmness of a Botanist" is a far cry from that intensity in which "all disagreeables evaporate," the experience that is at the heart of Keats's earlier poetic theorizing.[17] These two attitudes, however, are related—both presume theatrical distancing, but leavened with a greater or lesser degree of skepticism and reflection. In any case Keats seems again to be saying that the mind feels "free to make its speculations" when the true identity of the person speculating is, as it were, inaccessible to outside scrutiny: he would prefer to be anonymous or so new on the scene as to have no familiar history to make him susceptible to others' expectations of him as "the little Poet."

However he might disdain the notice of the public (and he came to contemn it more and more), Keats was never entirely free of caring about it. Though he found his literary persona increasingly inhibiting, his "love of fame" was an important spur to his work, as he himself realized. In the same letter to Mary-Ann Jeffery[18] he attributes his late idleness and aversion to writing to "the overpowering idea of our dead poets and . . . abatement of my love of fame. I hope I am a little more of a Philosopher than I was, consequently a little less of a versifying Pet-lamb" (II, 116). Dwindling love of fame leads to idleness, but idleness with some degree of integrity, perhaps: philosopher figures in Keats's poetry, like Appollonius and Otho, are admired for their detachment and self-possession, though faulted for their lack of imagination. In the "Ode on Idolence" Keats sheds light on the image of poet as "Pet-lamb" when he bids the "three Ghosts" portrayed on the visionary urn—Love, Ambition, and Poesy—"adieu" (51–54):

> . . . Ye cannot raise
> My head cool-bedded on the flowery grass;
> For I would not be dieted with praise,
> A pet-lamb in a sentimental farce!

Helen Vendler has called attention to the self-accusatory mien of the three figures when, passing before the poet for the third time, they turn from profile to full face (22), as though to rebuke Keats for his passivity and languor and to incite him to the task of artistic creation. The ghosts, she writes, represent "different internalized objects of the self. Love represents the erotic object, Ambition the social object, and Poesy the creative object."[19] But Keats resists their rebukes, obscurely feeling the need for a longer period of internal creative gestation before undertaking the sequence of his great odes, of which one, the "Grecian Urn," is here foreshadowed in the "dreamy urn" (56) itself. He understands that to respond prematurely to the urge to create is to respond to the wrong motives. "The 'moral' argument of the [Indolence] ode," continues Vendler, "pretends to see poetic ambition as a temptation toward praise, love as a temptation to sentimentality."[20] True, but at this precise moment the moral argument is not a pretense: until Keats feels he is ready to write what is in him and not what others expect of him, he will not write, and the temptation to do so will be taken, correctly, as a temptation to compromise his integrity as a poet.

A passage in the journal-letter to George and Georgiana, of February-May 1819, casts further light on the associations of "Pet-lamb" for Keats: "A Parson is a Lamb in a drawng room and a lion in a Vestry—The notions of Society will not permit a Parson to give way to his temper in any shape—so he festers in himself . . . He is continually acting—His mind is against every Man and every Mans mind is against him—He is an Hippocrite to the Believer and a Coward to the unbeliever" (II, 63). Keats's sensitivity to the parson's hypocritical self-restraint can only stem from his awareness of his own situation in parlor society: "I am full of Suspicions"; "I have evil thoughts, malice spleen." And yet the amorous—or ambitious— young man so distracted in thought must behave himself, must be docile, obedient, decorous: "I suffer greatly by going into parties where from the rules of society and a natural pride I am obliged to smother my Spirit and look like an Idiot—because I feel my impulses given way to would too much amaze them—I live under an everlasting restraint—Never relieved except when I am composing" (II, 12). Keats finds relief when he can turn his attention to the *activity* of writing, the real embodiment of the true "Spirit" he is obliged to smother in an insupportable public role. Although hope of notice, "love of fame," could help fan the fever of composition, it could also confine Keats in a stifling and demeaning pose. To Charles Wentworth Dilke he writes, "If I think of fame of poetry it seems a crime to me, and yet I must do so or suffer" (I, 369). Bothered by his dependence on "fame," the poet who purports to have "no self" comes to resent the audience whose recognition he needs. Because he does not yet feel securely in control of the image he would present, he cannot simply ignore it.

This heightened concern with recognition spilled over into Keats's work in the "Great Year." There we find much the same tense preoccupation with confrontations and with "anti-self-consciousness," much the same sense of the burdensomeness of the self-for-others as we find in the poetry of Wordsworth and Coleridge. Yet Keats did not, like Coleridge, seem overborne by doubts as to his inner resources, his talents, his "own being," though they might for the moment go unrecognized in the wide world. Nor did his poetry offer as great a challenge, even affront, to the tastes of his age as Wordsworth's: he is, of all the major Romantic poets, the most enthusiastically and originally imitative in style. He was not afraid of adopting models from the past—Shakespeare, Jonson, Spenser, Milton, even Dryden!—and making them his own.

Keats impresses us with a great deal of self-confidence in his destiny, and talents, as a poet. What he seemed to need, at least at this stage of his brief career, was assurance that his destiny and talents were recognized by others, that he was, quite simply, loved and admired for the poet he was. This view is supported by the fact that he repeatedly tested his image of himself as poet or artificer vicariously, in the projected self-portraits of lovers seeking love—Porphyro, Ludolph, and Lycius. All three of these protagonists strive to gain recognition for, to reinforce and make prevail in the eyes of their lovers or their audiences, not only an ideal vision of beauty, but an ideal personality or character—with varying degrees of success. The works in which they appear represent an extended thought experiment in the science of self-realization, probing to what extent the ideal image of the embodied self that wins acceptance in an exclusive love relationship can win, or do without, a similar acceptance in the world at large. As he sought answers to this question, Keats discovered that the true self of a poet cannot be validated merely as a passive object of his audiences's affection and approval, but only as an active, highly self-conscious witness and scribe of human history, responsible, in the end, only to the "Superior being" within him.

The Poet as Lover: The Theatrical Self

It is noteworthy that the single image of the performing pet-lamb in "Ode on Indolence" should do triple duty, representing the poet's active engagement with love, ambition, and poesy: all three temptations are there associated with being "dieted with praise," selling out in exchange for public notice and a condescending affection. Significantly, the roles of poet and lover are linked: Ambition and Poesy, "love of fame" and of poetic composition, go hand in hand with *eros*—all three pass before him, literally, "with . . . joined hands" (2).

From early on the search for an ideal self-realization within the restricted limits of an exclusive love relationship informs many of Keats's descriptions of poetic or imaginative experiences. Here lies that "chief intensity" which Endymion seeks *beyond* "fellowship with essence": the intensity of life as it is lived for and in the company of the Beloved. Even when we have stepped "Into a sort of oneness, and our state / Is like a floating spirit's" (I, 796–797), he tells his sister Peona, there still remain (I, 798–807)

> Richer entanglements, enthralments far
> More self-destroying, leading, by degrees,
> To the chief intensity: the crown of these
> Is made of love and friendship, and sits high
> Upon the forehead of humanity.
> All its more ponderous and bulky worth
> Is friendship, whence there ever issues forth
> A steady splendour; but at the tip-top,
> There hangs by unseen film, an orbed drop
> Of light, and that is love . . .

Clearly, a relationship in which the poet-lover is directly engaged with another represents the ideal end point of "fellowship with essence," or initial self-annihilation.[21] But how can the self be said to be destroyed to an even *greater* degree than in its initial "alchemized" state if, as Keats's language suggests, the richer entanglements of friendship and love are merely extrapolations of that state? Keats, after all, seems to conceive of such a love beyond self-annihilation still in terms of melting and commingling—"Melting into its radiance, we blend, / Mingle, and so become a part of it,— / Nor with aught else can our souls interknit / So wingedly" (I, 810–813).

But "it" here is "love" (I, 807), the power that governs the relationship, not the object of intense passion, Diana, to whom Endymion would be related in love. It is important to distinguish between empathic self-annihilation and the richer entanglements it can give rise to: the two states differ in kind as well as in degree. In the one the poet identifies with the object of perception or imagination; in the other the poet goes beyond the annihilation of the "sole self" to identify with a new self entirely, as reflected in the eyes of the Be-loved. Keats would completely put from mind the everyday social self in order to become immersed, like his hero, Endymion, in the "richer entanglements" of reciprocated desire and esteem. From this perspective Keats's famous description, in a letter to John Taylor, dated January 30, 1818, of the entire Endymion passage as a "step-ping of the Imagination towards a Truth," a depiction of the grada-tions of pleasure as if inscribed on a "Pleasure Thermometer" (I, 218), seems to imply that these gradations move from the finite plea-sures appropriate to the finite self, *through* "fellowship with essence," and thence to the ultimate pleasures and gratifications of mutual and perfect friendship and love.

It is no accident, in any case, that in countless passages in the poems and letters, Keats should eroticize the workings of the Imagi-nation,[22] that in his letter to Bailey on the "authenticity" of the Imagination, for instance, he should compare its truth to that of "Adam's dream" in *Paradise Lost*—"He awoke and found it truth" (I, 185). Adam awoke to find Eve, whom Milton calls Adam's "other self."[23]

As demonstrated at the end of "Ode to a Nightingale," awakening is usually, for Keats's protagonists, "forlorn" or painful, unless they awake in the loving presence of another. After his vision of Diana's wedding, Endymion's "first touch of the earth went nigh to kill" (IV, 614); the knight of "La Belle Dame sans Merci" awakes alone "on the cold hill side" (44); and Madeline's awakening from dreams of her future lover in "The Eve of St. Agnes" is, at first, "a painful change" (300), but only until Porphyro's "stratagem," his elaborate staging of her dream in the real world, takes hold of her imagination. The wak-ing dream of beauty can be prolonged, intensified, made as "real" as "the dreams of Gods" (*Lamia* I, 127), if the dreamer can find a real source of acknowledgment outside his own mind, a lover who cor-roborates both the dreamer's dream and his ideal self-representation therein. In "Ode to Psyche," for instance, the speaker discovers Cupid and Psyche maintaining just such an *égoisme à deux* (15–20):

> They lay calm-breathing on the bedded grass;
>   Their arms embraced, and their pinions too;
>   Their lips touch'd not, but had not bade adieu,
> As if disjoined by soft-handed slumber,
> And ready still past kisses to outnumber
>   At tender eye-dawn of aurorean love.

We find a similar scene in *Lamia,* where the lovers "reposed, / Where use had made it sweet, with eyelids closed, / Saving a tythe which love still open kept, / That they might see each other while they almost slept" (II, 22–25).

In Keats's sonnet, "To ———" (also known as "Time's Sea"), addressed to a woman he had glimpsed for a moment at Vauxhall some five years before, the poet's desire for an imaginary acknowledgment of his ideal self is clearly linked to the distancing of his proper self from the woman he addresses, freeing him from the restrictions of ordinary self-consciousness. The sonnet is a convenient work by which to mark the logical transition from the covert, self-annihilating impulse of the "poetical Character" to the more overt self-reciprocating tendencies that we find in *Lamia,* "The Eve of St. Agnes," and *Otho the Great.*

> Time's sea hath been five years at its slow ebb;
>   Long hours have to and fro let creep the sand,
> Since I was tangled in thy beauty's web,
>   And snared by the ungloving of thine hand:
> And yet I never look on midnight sky,
>   But I behold thine eyes' well-memoried light;
> I cannot look upon the rose's dye,
>   But to thy cheek my soul doth take its flight:
> I cannot look on any budding flower,
>   But my fond ear, in fancy at thy lips,
> And hearkening for a love-sound, doth devour
>   Its sweets in the wrong sense.—Thou dost eclipse
> Every delight with sweet remembering,
> And grief unto my darling joys dost bring.

First of all, the sonnet is spoken to one who is "well-memoried," closely observed and vividly imagined, but never approached; recall Keats's letter to Bailey—"my mind was a soft nest in which some one of them slept though she knew it not." Second, the poet's rich entanglement in "beauty's web" is the result of one simple gesture: "the ungloving of thine hand." An action such as removing an item of clothing can mean any number of things depending on the social context, and some meanings are obviously more flattering to one's fancy than others. Keats's speculative interpretation posits a fictitious identity, one which, he hopes or fancies, will *speak* that "love sound" which his "fond ear" strains at the Beloved's lips to hear.

"John Keats five feet hight" wants the lady to acknowledge him, but in the way he wishes to be acknowledged—as her lover. He wants her picture to speak, to ratify that impression of her own desire for him that he has "read" into the gesture of ungloving.

It is singularly appropriate that this sonnet, which describes one of those "richer entanglements" Endymion envisioned beyond "fellowship with essence," should be addressed to a lady Keats saw at Vauxhall. The relationship it assumes is nothing if not "theatrical," a thing of willful faith in surfaces. If life as theater can be an oppressive burden to the diminutive poet who is powerless over the script and unsure of his ability to act convincingly in the role assigned him, it can also, if "staged" correctly, provide him with an opportunity to act out his most cherished fantasies of himself. What resolves the poet's ambivalence is the sort of recognition, or at least understanding of his role, he can assume in another. In a letter to his brother and sister-in-law Keats describes a cousin of the Misses Reynolds, Jane Cox, whom he classifies as "a fine thing speaking in a worldly way: for there are two distinct tempers of mind in which we judge of things—the worldly, theatrical, and pantomimical; and the unearthly, spiritual and etherial" (I, 395). Miss Cox, along with Bonaparte and Lord Byron, appeals to the first "temper":

> She is not a Cleopatra; but she is at least a Charmian. She has a rich eastern look; she has fine eyes and fine manners. When she comes into a room she makes an impression the same as the Beauty of a Leopardess. She is too fine and too conscious of her Self to repulse any Man who may address her—from habit she thinks that nothing *particular.* I always find myself more at ease with such a woman: the picture before me always gives me a life and animation which I cannot possibly feel with anything inferiour [*sic*]—I am at such times too much occupied in admiring to be awkward or on a tremble. I forget myself entirely because I live in her.   (I, 395)

No talk here of the uncomfortable "pressure" of Charmian's identity, and no "Suspicions" about his own appearance. Keats forgets himself and "is at ease with such a woman" when one would expect just the opposite.

Keats's last sentence suggests that the "camelion Poet" is once again "filling some other Body." But I think an interpretation more appropriate than any that pertains to a vicarious or empathic chameleon experience might be drawn from *Lamia,* at the point where

Lamia's spell shortens the distance to Corinth. It is a trick "not at all surmised / By blinded Lycius, so *in her* comprized" (I, 346–347; italics added). Keats "lives in" Charmian's "fine eyes and fine manners" in the same way that Lycius is "comprized" in Lamia: he finds his ideal self-image recognized and accepted in the presence of a beautiful woman. In this way he forgets his ordinary self ("I forget myself entirely") in assuming an identity that is transformed by such tacit recognition into a "theatrical" type: the amoroso.

That Charmian is a "picture" scarcely aware of Keats as an individual only reinforces his feeling of safety in assuming the anonymity of a type. He finds this mutual playacting a relief: "I like her and her like because one has no *sensations*—what we both are is taken for granted" (I, 395). The statement suggests, again, that Keats is not describing another example of chameleon self-effacement and empathic participation in the intense "sensation" of a beautiful object, but something else. Recalling how often, in the letters and the poems, "sensations" depend on surprise, one realizes that what appeals to Keats in this kind of relationship is its *lack* of surprises. There is nothing in it to rouse him from his absorption in the social fiction. Charmian's lack of discrimination (she will not "repulse any Man who may address her") allows Keats to enjoy the role of a stereotypically romantic gallant—along with every other man in the room. In the "theatrical" relationship what each of us "is" is what we pretend to be, unarticulated but understood. That is the only way such a fiction can become "real": by its being enacted without being referred to. Life becomes a stage for the playing out of fantasies that receive confirmation in a reciprocal voyeurism that shuts out the rest of the world.

The "theatrical" self, then, results from a conspiracy to cut fantasies out of the stuff of public reality. It is an attempt to realize a waking dream that the eye of any third party might instantly destroy. Thus the Charmian figure is susceptible to "smoking" by others: "There are the Miss Reynoldses on the look out . . . They call her a flirt to me—What a want of knowledge?" "They hate her; and from what I hear she is not without faults—of a real kind" (I, 395). Keats tries to ignore this unsympathetic third-person gaze. Personalities with "real faults" are not an issue in the waking dream; what counts is effect, and its immediate credibility. For either of the participants to return the gaze of an outside observer would be to see his or her self there, in the world at large.

Keats's distinctions among "Things real—things semireal—and

no things" in a letter to Benjamin Bailey can help shed some light on the degree of "reality" to be assigned to the theatrical personality. Three levels of "reality" can be distinguished in the class of "ethereal"—or beautiful—things (not to be confused with "etherial" personalities): "Ethereal thing[s] may at least be thus real, divided under three heads—Things real—things semireal—and no things— Things real—such as existences of Sun Moon & Stars and passages of Shakespeare—Things semireal such as Love, the Clouds &c which require a greeting of the Spirit to make them wholly exist—and Nothings which are made Great and dignified by an ardent pursuit" (I, 242-243). Charmian's faults are "real," a part of her "real" personality; her effect is "semireal," requiring the assent of her audience to "wholly exist," just as the vague, suggestive shapes of clouds require imaginative reconstitution by a human subject. But to the extent that real faults or real personalities evident to uninvolved observers like the Misses Reynolds obtrude on the semireal, theatrical effect, it becomes a "Nothing . . . made Great and dignified by an ardent pursuit." The stage machinery shows to one looking on.

From the "inside" the experience of the theatrical effect "wholly exists"; from the "outside" the theatrical effect is seen as make-believe and delusion. In "The Eve of St. Agnes," *Otho the Great,* and *Lamia,* Keats tries to determine the extent to which the theatrical self, the self as "picture," artifice, or effect, can be made to prevail in the eyes of the world and become a part of public, consensual reality. In all this posing, however, there remains the true self, what Keats calls "my own being, which I know to be." Struggling for a sense of reality independent of all that others make of it, the true self feels betrayed both by the "sentimental farce" of society and, when the romance has faded, by the "theatrical" relationship as well. This is the self Keats contrasts with Charmian's: it appeals to the "unearthly, spiritual, and etherial" temperament, in which, Keats writes Georgiana, "John Howard, Bishop Hooker rocking his child's cradle and you my dear Sister are the conquering feelings" (I, 395-396).

"Unearthly, spiritual and etherial" suggest that the self which appeals to this "temper" of mind somehow transcends the social and material conditions of its appearance. It is unaffected by the exigencies of convention, fashion, or opinion and thus always consistent, regardless of context. The "etherial" self gives little or no thought to its own embodiment, or to how others might judge it. Furthermore, as the examples of Howard, the prison reformer, and Hooker, the church reformer, attest, the "etherial" self appears in good actions, not in good acting. Although Charmian's attention to others arises from her concern for "her self," a Howard's or a Hooker's or Georgiana Keats's concern for others is disinterested and unself-conscious: the great scholar of the *Ecclesiastical Polity* stoops to rock his child's cradle without stopping to think of its "effect."

In short, the "etherial" self plays to no audience but itself, whoever else may be looking on. It is wholly self-contained, answerable to nothing but that ideal mirror of conscientious self-scrutiny which is so intimately a part of its interior life as to be almost taken for granted. There is no place for such a being in the theatrical reciprocity that Keats achieves with Charmian, nor, for that matter, is there any possibility of winning the direct, personal acknowledgment the poet longed for from the lady at Vauxhall. He is not an individualized lover in such situations, only an accepted admirer among many, and the self he embodies is as ephemeral as a mist. The Charmian relationship is impersonal, but Keats is willing in this case to settle for less if only to be relieved of the responsibility for having to prove himself more.

Keats did receive such acceptance as a lover once in his life, or at least he believed he did, from Fanny Brawne, whom he describes in terms appropriate to Charmian. She is "elegant, graceful" (II, 8), "with a fine style of countenance . . . Her shape is very graceful and so are her movements." She has a "penchant . . . for acting stylishly." "I am however tired of such style," he adds, "and shall decline any more of it" (II, 13).

This resolve was never acted upon, but it does indicate an awareness of the fragile foundations of such a relationship. The tête à tête of mutual objectification is always threatening to shatter from the surfacing of real personalities with real demands, or to degenerate in time into another wearisome farce, a "known play," like those literary evenings at the Hunts'. As Keats undertakes the longer romances and only play of his mature career, he finds himself coming to grips with a nagging question: In this conspiratorial realization of the ideal, what will insure the reality of the "etherial" self, which eschews all "effects"? Keats's response takes the form of the two *Hyperions* and a new concept of the poet, not as lover or beloved, but as an "ethereal" witness, recognized in the eyes of a superior, internalized, and severe divinity—and embodied, finally, in the written record of his visions.

Miraculous Stratagems

Banquets, feasts, and palaces are important in Keats's later work in the same way the wedding feast is important to "The Rime of the Ancient Mariner."[24] All such gatherings define an arena of public life, the scene of publicly witnessed performances. Palaces, especially, are stages for self-display as well as for habitation, and are generally designed to accommodate audiences of one sort or another. It is in opposition to the "acted play" of such palace life, a banquet thronged with guests "numerous as shadows" (39), that Porphyro— the Romeo figure of "The Eve of St. Agnes" who braves the perils of her family's enmity to visit his "Juliet," Madeline—arranges his own closet performance, carefully placing his props in and about the bed-room stage prepared for his Beloved's awakening (253–261):

> Then by the bed-side, where the faded moon
> Made a dim, silver twilight, soft he set
> A table, and, half anguish'd, threw thereon
> A cloth of woven crimson, gold, and jet:—
> O for some drowsy Morphean amulet!
> The boisterous, midnight, festive clarion,
> The kettle-drum, and far-heard clarionet,
> Affray his ears, though but in dying tone:—
> The hall door shuts again, and all the noise is gone.

Destruction of the private waking dream threatens from without, like the Misses Reynolds, a profane, cynical gaze intruding from beyond the fragilely maintained theatrical horizon. That the scene of the banquet *is* a profane realm Keats suggest by words like "hyena-foemen" and "hot-blooded lords" (86), his choice of such emblematic instruments as the boisterous "clarion," "kettle-drum," and "clarionet," or the "snarling trumpets" of an earlier stanza (31). The impression of profanity or sacrilege is further heightened by the "carved angels" (34) who look on the banquet with "wings put cross-wise on their breasts" as if to ward off contamination (36). What is essential to the ambiguous realization of the ideal in "The Eve of St. Agnes," and of these lovers' ideal self-images therein, is the avoidance of hostile public attention, of the guests carousing at the banquet, "the whole blood-thirsty race" (99).

These are Madeline's kinsmen, her "race," and the banquet at which they gorge themselves is the forum in which she initially appears both as something to be virtually devoured and as her father's daughter, part of a network of familial or "racial" ties. By the phrase "blood-thirsty," Keats seems to be suggesting in this context that appetite, whether gluttonous *or* lustful, binds our identities to the physical world and places us firmly in the generative continuum of time, where we consume the "blood" of others—seek to dominate, to seduce, to subjugate—in order to perpetuate our own lives, and are ourselves consumed in the process. At the banquet, suitors approach and retire, "many a tiptoe, amorous cavalier" (60). Madeline is one man's daughter; she will become another man's wife. These roles are predetermined. The banquet, the larger play of "shadows" we call life, is where Madeline has her "proper" place, another finite consumable, another object of desire, and she must bear all the attentions that go with the life of an object.

Bear them, but not necessarily return them. Early on, in the midst of the evening's merriment, she is distracted by thoughts of the coming night, when according to the superstitions concerning St. Agnes' Eve the image of her future husband will appear to her in a dream. She must, however, observe all the "rules," which means, among other things, looking at no other man all evening (55–62; italics added):

Full of this whim was thoughtful Madeline:
The music, yearning like a God in pain,
She scarcely heard: *her maiden eyes divine,*
Fix'd on the floor, saw many a sweeping train
Pass by—*she heeded not at all:* in vain
Came many a tiptoe, amorous cavalier,
And back retir'd, not cool'd by high disdain;
But she saw not . . .

Madeline will not acknowledge an amorous advance: she is not a Charmian. Far from being wrapped up in her effect, her expected role, she is wholly unconscious of it. She seeks only the eyes of her "future lord" (rejected stanza 7),[25] whose image she is intent on conjuring up. So entranced with this beau ideal is Madeline that even before she falls asleep "pensive awhile she dreams awake" (232), and "in a sort of wakeful swoon, perplex'd she lay" (236). It is in this unreal image alone that her waking dream of herself will find its proper reflection. She must "nor look behind, nor sideways, but require / Of heaven with upward eyes" (53–54) what she desires. Preoccupied in this manner, Madeline is indeed "hoodwink'd," "all amort," dead to the world (64–70; italics added):

She danc'd along with *vague, regardless eyes,*
Anxious her lips, her breathing quick and short:
The hallow'd hour was near at hand: she sighs
Amid the timbrels, and the throng'd resort
Of whisperers in anger, or in sport;
'Mid looks of love, defiance, hate, and scorn,
Hoodwink'd with faery fancy; *all amort.*

Madeline seeks escape from the profane yet passionate world that impinges on her inwardness, demanding her attention and imposing its own. Indeed, in her private, solipsistic devotion to the beautiful, Madeline vaguely resembles the Beadsman of the first stanza at his prayers in the crypt, before "the sweet Virgin's picture" (9) and among the "sculptur'd dead" (14). He, too, is a solitary image-worshipper who is not recognized by the image he adores, and whose fancied addresses cannot, for this reason, take him beyond a longed-for "fellowship with essence" to the "richer entanglements" of reciprocated love. The Beadsman's thoughts, the "prayers he saith" (9), may indeed, like his "frosted breath"(6), seem "taking flight for heaven, without a death" (8), but at the end of the poem he is consigned to the realm of time and change: "The Beadsman, after thousand aves told, / For aye unsought for slept among his ashes cold" (377–378).

"Unsought for" points to the Beadsman's problem. In the last analysis the wholly private fancy indeed "cannot cheat so well as she is fam'd to do." The Beadsman resembles the speaker of the "Ode to a Nightingale" whose soul would fly away: in both cases, the sole self inevitably makes its final claim. More precisely, and in a more vulgar sense, he resembles the speaker of "Time's Sea," adoring at a distance that beautiful image which cannot speak and acknowledge his adoration. The world staged and enacted by Porphyro and assented to by Madeline lies somewhere between the Beadsman's private, idealized "heaven" and the vulgar precincts of the "hyena foemen," this side of abstract apotheosis, but beyond conventional social definitions of the self. Porphyro's theatrical design makes the beautiful prevail as "objective" truth, that is, mutually confirmed fact, and makes what is factually confirmed beautiful.

Though Madeline resembles the Beadsman in her longing, she

even more strongly resembles, in her unresponsiveness to those who adore her, the "sweet Virgin's picture" that he worships. She is virtually represented as an image of beauty blind and deaf to the public that surrounds her and that, as it were, tries to bring her to life by evoking a response from her. Not yet a Charmian, she comes to assume, in the course of the poem, an artificial and, in the end, "theatrical" persona like her more feline counterpart: she becomes a human image elaborated as a work of art. Like the figures on the Grecian urn,[26] which require a "greeting of the Spirit," an act of faith, to "wholly exist," Keats's most focused image of Madeline turns out to be highly ornamented, carefully staged, and surrounded by props.

This carefully detailed image, with its "theatrical" qualities, is not elaborated until the moment Madeline enters her bedchamber, that is, the moment she becomes an object solely for Porphyro's furtive gaze. Now, not only she but Porphyro too, safely stowed in Madeline's bedchamber by her aged nurse, Angela, resembles the Beadsman in his solitary worship of an iconic, artificial, and unresponsive image of the divine. At her prayers Madeline wears a silver cross, in her hair "a glory, like a saint" (222), recalling "the sweet Virgin's picture" before which the Beadsman prays. And this divine object of Porphyro's devotion is portrayed before a casement "garlanded with carven imag'ries . . . and diamonded with panes of quaint device" (209–211). She is bathed in dyed lights from stained glass windows decorated with "twilight saints, and dim emblazonings, / A shielded scutcheon blush'd with blood of queens and kings" (215–216), all of which remind us of the "sculptur'd dead" that surround the Beadsman as he leaves the chapel after his prayers (14–18; italics added):

> The sculptur'd dead, on each side, seem to freeze,
> Emprison'd in black, purgatorial rails:
> Knights, *ladies, praying in dumb orat'ries,*
> He passeth by; and his weak spirit fails
> *To think how they may ache in icy hoods and mails.*

The "ladies, praying in dumb orat'ries," of course, foreshadow Madeline herself as she kneels to pray silently in her chamber (217–222), and the image is reinforced when she is described lying in bed, "trembling in her soft and chilly nest" (235) much as the stone effigies in the chapel had ached in their icy armor.

On beholding her in the act of prayer, Porphyro, her "famish'd pilgrim" (339), begins to swoon (223–225):

She seem'd a splendid angel, newly drest,
Save wings, for heaven:—Porphyro grew faint:
She knelt, so pure a thing, so free from mortal taint.

Here is that characteristically Keatsian moment of intense sensation that verges on waking sleep or living death. In the same way that the mortal nightingale overheard becomes an "immortal bird" for its listener, so Madeline suddenly becomes, in Porphyro's eyes, an immortal image of beauty.

But Madeline is an object of flesh and blood desire as well. Keats's aesthetic is highly erotic: he is careful to emphasize and maintain the tensions between Madeline's artificiality and her living presence, much as in the "Ode on a Grecian Urn" he maintains the tensions between the urn as a "Cold Pastoral" and as embodying the very "breathing human passion" that it remains "far above" (45, 28). In "St. Agnes" this tension between artifice and life dissipates as Porphyro recovers (226–228):

Anon his heart revives: her vespers done,
Of all its wreathed pearls her hair she frees;
Unclasps her warmed jewels one by one.

The tactile contrasts between the hard pearls and the soft hair, the cold gems and Madeline's warm breast, are striking, and it is appropriate that Porphyro should revive from his faint and resume mortal life at the instant that Madeline removes her jewelry and "rich attire" (230) and reverts to human form: an object of sexual desire, not religious adoration; a real human presence that invites approach, and not a frozen and distant icon.

As the object of Porphyro's waking dream, Madeline is a mortal goddess, like Diana in *Endymion;* she is an ontological oxymoron, mortal immortality, temporal eternity, both the promise of carnal fulfillment in time and of eternal virginity in "slow time." She is a "still unravish'd bride," to draw on the language of the "Ode on a Grecian Urn" (2), that offers a love "for ever warm and still to be enjoy'd, / For ever panting and for ever young" (26–27), and at the same time she is a "theatrical" object, a "Cold Pastoral" (45), a "fair attitude" (41) like the carved images around her and the "sculptur'd dead" in the chapel.

In "The Eve of St. Agnes," then, Keats is careful to distinguish not one, but two private and discontinuous waking dreams that are both beautiful, even "true" in the severely qualified mode of intense self-absorption, but not yet real: that in which Madeline is fascinated by the image of her "future lord," and that in which Porphyro is fascinated by an image of Madeline. Both fantasies are patterned on the Beadsman's devotion to "the sweet Virgin's picture," and in neither of them can the acknowledgment necessary to the realization of the observer's ideal self-image take place. Porphyo's intention is to make his dream and Madeline's coincide in the waking world, to present himself, in the starring role of her "future lord," as just such an artificial and theatrical object of Madeline's gaze as she has become of his, and to gain her assent to the reality of the role he plays.[27]

Porphyro's elaborate preparations consist of a table covered with a gorgeously woven cloth, bearing preserved fruits and jellies, "creamy curd, / And lucent syrops, tinct with cinnamon" (266–267), all "heap'd with glowing hand / On golden dishes and in baskets bright / Of wreathed silver" (271–273). Each of these items, even the once perishable fruit, is an object wrought by human art or preserved or distilled by human skill. They are as artificial as the scene they ornament, or as the roles to be played out in it. Thus Porphyro sets a stage full of props in which he can appear as the erotic fantasy object of Madeline's waking dream, much as Madeline, in her jewels, silver cross, and rich attire, surrounded by carved images and colored lights, appeared to his hidden, worshipful gaze as a carnal goddess. Porphyro's "stratagem" (139)—Keats's word to describe the lover's plan—is not, strictly speaking, to "hoodwink" Madeline, but to open her eyes in the most radical way possible: to become the sole object of her vision, to fascinate her by his presence as she has fascinated him. He will so fill up her awareness that no public horizon can appear beyond that within which the two lovers respond to each other.

When his stage is set, Porphyro bids Madeline awake. But " 'twas a midnight charm / Impossible to melt as iced stream . . . It seem'd he never, never could redeem / From such a stedfast spell his lady's eyes" (282–287). Eyes in Keats's work are important indices of self-entanglement. Porphyro cannot "redeem" Madeline's "eyes," he cannot bring them to their proper object, for no "spell" can be broken except by a formal, measured sort of speech, like an incantation, or a song (289–292):

Awakening up, he took her hollow lute,—
Tumultuous,—and, in chords that tenderest be,

He play'd an ancient ditty, long since mute,
In Provence call'd, "La belle dame sans mercy."

Even the form of address by which Porphyro gains access to Madeline's dream is artificial.

In contrast to Porphyro's lyricism, Madeline is described earlier as a "tongueless nightingale" who must "swell / Her throat in vain, and die, heart-stifled, in her dell" (206–207). The lines recall the monkish Beadsman: his mute, self-enclosed form of devotion and the "ladies, praying in dumb orat'ries" surrounding him. But "to her heart, her heart was voluble"—that is, she is absorbed in seeking recognition, not from a real person in the world, but from her dream object, her "future lord." Her "voluble" address is imaginary, internal, like Keats's to the woman at Vauxhall, and the response from the beloved object is in turn unreal, illusory. "Heart-stifled," Madeline will share the fate of those "fanatics" in the opening lines of *The Fall of Hyperion* who, lacking "melodious utterance" (6), can only "live, dream, and die" (7). She refuses to address and thus admit to consciousness the world outside her mind, and in doing so she foregoes the possibility of affirming herself and her vision in the eyes of another.

Porphyro's song "La belle dame sans mercy" tells of unrequited love and, as Keats rendered it later in his famous poem, of a lover who for the most part receives ambiguous responses to his earnest caresses. His "fairy's child" ("La Belle Dame," 14)—her genealogy is not of this world—has "wild" eyes (16)—a frenzied and unfocussed glance—and the knight shuts her eyes with "kisses four" (32), so that the very moment of erotic address is expressed by a blinding of the object of desire. The fairy's child becomes, then, like her counterpart Madeline, merely a picture of that desire. While the knight saw "nothing else . . . all day long" (22) but the lady, she looks at the knight "*as* she did love, / And made sweet moan" (19–20, emphasis added), an inarticulate and ambiguous requital. Her only articulate utterance is uncannily distorted in the knight's mind: "In *language strange* she said— / I love thee true" (27–28; italics mine). All these interpretations of the lady's behavior are the knight's and none of them reflect a clear recognition of him as her lover. In the words of Gerald Enscoe, "What the knight does, what he sees, and what he makes of the encounter are more important than the activities of the enchantress . . . She is essentially passive."[28]

Porphyro's lyrical outpouring and Madeline's silent, "heart-stifled" self-enclosure point up what is at issue in the two lovers' encounter—ideal self-representation and its proper requital. When Porphyro finishes his song, Madeline awakes (294–297):

> Wherewith disturb'd, she utter'd a soft moan:
> He ceased—she panted quick—and suddenly
> Her blue affrayed eyes wide open shone:
> Upon his knees he sank, pale as smooth-sculptured stone.

The lines suggest that Madeline has been listening to Porphyro's song in her sleep. Her "soft moan" is uttered before she awakes, before she is aware of the real presence of Porphyro. When he ceases his song, Madeline begins to pant as she did on entering her chamber (201), an indication not only of sexual longing but also of her anxiety at losing the dream lover she heard singing. That lover is now accessible to her only if she awakes. In a way Porphyro has melted into her dream from the moment he began his song; when he stops singing, he fades out of it, drawing her after him.

When Madeline's eyes open, Porphyro becomes "pale as smooth-sculptured stone," a graven image. Now it is he who resembles the "sculptur'd dead," a man of marble like the figures on the Grecian urn. Fixed as an image wrought by his own art, he surrenders himself to Madeline's verdict. At this point the lovers' waking dreams begin to coincide, but the coincidence is not yet complete (298–306; emphasis added):

> Her eyes were open, but *she still beheld,*
> *Now wide awake, the vision of her sleep:*
> There was a painful change, that nigh expell'd
> The blisses of her dream so pure and deep:
> At which fair Madeline began to weep,
> And moan forth witless words with many a sigh;
> While still her gaze on Porphyro would keep;
> Who knelt, with joined hands and piteous eye,
> Fearing to move or speak, she looked so dreamingly.

Madeline is no longer described as if she *were* a dream, but rather as if she were doing the dreaming—"she looked so dream*ing*ly—and what she is dreaming, but now "wide awake," is Porphyro. We should take Keats literally here—"she *still* beheld . . . the vision of her sleep." Porphyro had already, in his song, begun to assimilate himself with the object of her dream, to play the role she wants him to play. On her awakening, he is suddenly fixed in that role, in a pose of supplication as petrified and lifeless as a work of art, as silent, motionless, and unresponsive an object of undying love as the cold "marble men and maidens" on an urn.

Porphyro's "painful change" has provided ammunition for skeptical critics of the poem who insist on the cynicism of the lover's "stratagem" while ignoring the "miracle" (339), as Porphyro himself calls it, of its success. Thus, Jack Stillinger writes, "For one thing, when the imaginative vision of beauty turns out to be a truth—when Madeline awakens to find Porphyro in her bed—she is not really so pleased as Adam was when he awakened and discovered Eve."[29] Not, of course, at first, not *until* Porphyro—like the living, breathing Eve and not some "picture" of a sweet virgin—responds. For what, more precisely, is the nature of this "painful change"? Is it a result of Porphyro's turning out at this moment to be a "real" lover, or rather the opposite? The poem continues (307–315; emphasis added),

> "Ah, Porphyro!" said she, "but even now
> Thy voice was at sweet tremble in mine ear,
> Made tuneable with every sweetest vow;
> And those sad eyes were spiritual and clear:
> How chang'd thou art! how pallid, chill, and drear!
> *Give me that voice again,* my Porphyro,
> Those looks immortal, those complainings dear!
> Oh leave me not in this eternal woe,
> For if thou diest, my love, I know not where to go."

Madeline's words reinforce the suggestion that Porphyro has already mingled with her dream—"even now / Thy voice," "Give me that voice again"—and, since we know she is still "dreaming" (or sleep "waking") it cannot be merely the "reality" of his presence that disturbs her. In fact, it is the inhumanity of Porphyro's presence that makes a "painful change," his transformation into an inanimate, artificial object, as "pallid, chill, and drear" as "smooth-sculptured stone." It is this unresponsiveness that distresses Madeline, not the ugliness of Porphyro in the flesh as opposed to her dream lover. He has stopped responding. His eyes, which before were imagined "spiritual and clear," revealing a "spirit" or an "immortal" soul within ("those looks immortal") now appear dead to her ("if thou diest, my love . . ."), like those of a sightless statue. To stop singing is to be made immortal indeed, but lifeless. Porphyro is momentarily paralyzed into a "silent form" like the "melodist, unwearied" (23) depicted on the urn, playing his "ditties of no tone" (14). He cannot be reanimated in time until he, in turn, receives a proper "greeting of the Spirit."

But Madeline's plaint is already a sympathetic response to Porphyro's theatrical presence, an articulation of her desire that confirms the self-image he has so elaborately, so skillfully presented to her and thus brings it to life. Recall that in the Vauxhall sonnet only the woman's direct affirmation of her love could ratify the image the poet would present. In "The Eve of St. Agnes" Madeline addresses Porphyro not in his fancy but in the reality of a mutually affirmed waking dream. In her response she acknowledges him as her "future lord," and in that response he sees the realization of his theatrical self (316–322):

Beyond a mortal man impassion'd far
At these voluptuous accents, he arose,
Ethereal, flush'd, and like a throbbing star
Seen mid the sapphire heaven's deep repose;
Into her dream he melted, as the rose
Blendeth its odour with the violet,—
Solution sweet . . .

With the transfixing of Porphyro's presented self as the sole object of Madeline's gaze and the acceptance of this theatrical image in her profession of love, the reciprocal confirmation of the lovers' dreams is complete. Porphyro has greeted Madeline as she would be greeted, and vice versa. Each is now content to subsist wholly in the eyes of the other; each ratifies the other in a charmed circle of dramatization that is both dream and reality, personal fantasy and interchanged truth.

But what of the outcome, which remains ambiguous despite, or rather because of, the lovers' fortunate avoidance of the drowsy eye of profane, public factuality? The lovers flee Porphyro's lavish stage set, but whither do they flee? Not into the world, certainly, but into the mists, the "elfin-storm" (343) of Romance, the fourth dimension of fiction. "They glide, like phantoms, into the wide hall; / Like phantoms, to the iron porch, they glide . . . And they are gone: ay, ages long ago / These lovers fled away into the storm" (361–371). Porphyro and Madeline achieve their apotheosis, but only as ghosts.

The ambiguity of the poem's conclusion, like Madeline's initial disappointment on awakening, has been exploited by skeptics in their attack on the "metaphysical" school of Keats criticism represented by scholars such as Earl Wasserman. The tête à tête Porphyro stages is beautiful, but is it "true"? Will it stand the test of worldly, waking eyes, or is it merely a self-indulgent, cynical charade? The answer depends on one's idea of what Keats understood by "truth" at this stage of his intellectual development. "Truth," at least in the romances, seems to be what most unreflective people can be brought to agree on. Thus the moral ambiguities of Porphyro's position and the skeptical allusions in much of the verse must make a rather damning case against the lovers—on reflection. To a philosopher's (or a critic's) eye, Madeline and Porphyro seem something less than divine, and fall somewhat short of that "fellowship . . . with essence" to which Wasserman elevates them in *The Finer Tone*.[30]

Skeptics like Stillinger, however, go too far in asserting that Keats uncategorically "condemned his hoodwinked dreamers who shut out the world."[31] Keats was simply and hopelessly ambivalent about the possibility of realizing "Adam's dream." He was uncertain of the truth-value of Beauty, especially in art, and of the beauty of Truth, especially philosophical truth, which is to say, any truth capable of withstanding public scrutiny and requiring the acquiescence of an objective mind. But a merely cynical interpretation of Porphyro's ploy and Madeline's ambiguous motivations in playing along contributes as little, and as much, to a complete understanding of what happens in the poem as does Wasserman's contention that the image of the "pleasure thermometer" that Keats used to explain "fellowship with essence" should constitute the ground zero of one's interpretations of the rest of the poetry.

The truth about Porphyro's and Madeline's waking dream lies somewhere between earth and heaven. "The Eve of St. Agnes" is no more a bedroom satire or sentimental moral tale like *Clarissa* (to which at one point Stillinger compares it)[32] than it is a metaphysical tract. Nor is it the mere fairy romance Victorians conceived it to be. For all of our attempts to interpret (or to debunk) the poem as an allegory of the transfiguring imagination or the tale of an artist who would unite truth with beauty, the real tensions of the poems are erotic and psycho-social. It may provide a figurative comment on the proper relation of art to reality or to society, but Keats's immediate preoccupation throughout is with the theatrical nature of the embodied personality and the degree of credibility it can achieve in another's eyes.

Can one *make* one's dream of oneself real? Only, perhaps, by making the reality of others one's dream. The issue in "The Eve of St. Agnes," as in much of the poetry of Wordsworth and Coleridge, can best be stated as the problem of defining, selecting, or controlling one's audience, and the social context of one's art and artistic self-representation, so as to make the image of the poet (or poet-lover) prevail as an objective, agreed-upon reality. The apotheosis that the lovers achieve is ambiguous because the poem obtrudes its characters' artifices (and its own) while ignoring them, invites us to question as we assent, thus reminding us that we do assent despite our questions. We, like Madeline and Porphyro themselves, must actively conspire to make real the "semireal" spectacle of this waking dream and of its participants.

Lover and Philosopher: The Claims of the Ethereal Self

The social tensions of the great romances written in 1819 are what distinguish them from Keats's other poetical explorations of the relationship between the factually true and the ideally beautiful. They depict not only the process by which the aesthetic or erotic object of desire can be made "real," and in what manner that "reality" is finally called into question, but also the extent to which the identity of the lover of beauty can be manifested objectively, and in what manner that tenuous manifestation is finally compromised. Porphyro lives forever and Lycius and Ludolph (the young heroes, respectively, of *Lamia* and *Otho the Great*) expire, depending on whether or not the objects of beauty in which their identities have become so richly "entangled" escape or succumb to the skeptical gaze of outside audiences.

Looking at the three great romances in order of composition, we can see that, to the extent that it invites skepticism, even while it "teases us out of thought" with its ravishing (and at times cloying) beauties, "The Eve of St. Agnes" stands as the first of a series of philosophical reflections on the consensual nature of reality: it teaches us more about the precariousness of identity, its limitations, its dependence on others, and the conditions of our self-consciousness, than either of the more ponderously allegorical *Hyperions*. Later in the "Great Year," as Keats's disillusionment with the "acted play" of life becomes more pronounced, so does his theatrical skepticism, until in *Otho the Great* and *Lamia* he comes face to face with the realization that the theatrical self, like the beauty it embraces and surrenders to, cannot become "etherial," cannot achieve independence, spontaneity, and frankness of expression, simply by enlisting another's assent to its fantasies.

It can, in fact, become endangered by its radical contingency on such assent. The examples of Lycius and Ludolph demonstrate that making the self dependent on another's acknowledgment ultimately drains the substance of one's identity. It takes but one frank disbeliever, like Apollonius, to destroy the fiction of the "theatrical" self. Ludolph and Lycius bring to mind Kierkegaard's knight of "infinite passion," enmeshed in a love relationship that so shapes, colors, and gives meaning to his world that to step out of it would be impossible, would contradict the very terms of his being, leading to a radical disjunction in the continuity of the self. Kierkegaard, in *Fear and Trembling,* describes his young lover in language reminiscent of Keats's "richer entanglements": "He is not afraid of letting love creep into his most secret, his most hidden thoughts, to let it twine in innumerable coils about every ligament of his consciousness—if the love becomes unhappy love, he will never be able to tear himself loose from it. He feels a blissful rapture in letting love tingle through every nerve, and yet his soul is as solemn as that of the man who has drained the poisoned goblet and feels how the juice permeates every drop of blood—for this instant is life and death."[33] To revert to an old romantic term, the beloved is the "infinite" lover's *idée fixe.*

But should his idol turn out to have feet of clay, the lover suddenly becomes life's fool, his very identity an empty mask. He becomes Keats's "Pet-lamb," and his "infinite" relationship just another "sentimental farce." This is why, for Kierkegaard, the self cannot survive as an integral whole if it is related to itself only through its erotic attachment to another person. The self can be related to itself "infinitely" and imperishably only through its relation to an "infinite," unchanging, and omniscient Other: God. That Other, internalized, removed from the vagaries of social intercourse, theologians may recognize as "conscience," Freudians as the "superego," and phenomenologists as the "transcendental ego." Whatever its appellation, its function in the structure of self-individuation is the same. It is the authoritative, sometimes parental, glass of self-consciousness, absolute, uncompromising, omniscient with respect to the claims of the self, and the final magistrate of identity. For Keats, this authority is embodied, but in externalized form, in paternal philosopher figures like Otho, Ludolph's father in *Otho the Great,* and Apollonius, Lycius' mentor in *Lamia.* It will become, finally, interiorized as the maternal goddess, Moneta, in Keats's vision in a dream, *The Fall of Hyperion.*

As fictional characters, Apollonius and Otho exemplify the "etherial" self that challenges the "theatrical" fantasies of Lycius and Ludolph. Rather than seek unqualified endorsements of their identities from others, such personalities, like Keats's "etherial" heroes Howard or Hooker, defy or refute public opinion and, by their intransigence, destroy those agreed-upon fictions that would compromise, would "trammel up and snare," the true self. They are touchstones of objective reality in the prevailing social play, and they do not hesitate to point up the fictitious basis of the ephemera in which they participate. The sources of their own self-certainty lie within.

Otho the Great, Keats's only play, is contemporaneous with *Lamia* and the two works bear some striking resemblances in theme and characterization. *Otho,* however, has been all but ignored by Keatsians. Admittedly, it is static, bombastic, and badly paced, even for a first play.[34] But it contains remarkable vignettes illustrating the poet's speculations on personal identity, specifically, the notion that changing social circumstances can change one's sense of identity, and that only a strong inner sense of self can withstand such impositions. By direct reference to theatrical types and ironic undercutting of the conventional high tragedy's extravagant tropes and diction, Keats, particularly in those scenes which are relatively free of Charles Brown's collaboration, attempts to unmask the "acted play" of society so as to make his audience aware of the "theatrical" nature of everyday life: the fact that we are nearly always "playing" a role in a public performance for one audience or another. *Otho* tests the limits to which others' beliefs and expectations can "typecast" the social self.

Throughout the play Keats qualifies and even overturns theatrical conventions governing speech, behavior, and character type in English tragedy so as to comment on corresponding conventions that govern public self-expression. This theatrical self-consciousness cannot be entirely attributed to Keats's social philosophy. *Otho* displays a sense of dramatic irony and self-reference very much in vogue in the playhouses of the Regency period. As Joseph W. Donohue, Jr., has pointed out in *Dramatic Character in the English Romantic Age,* audiences and critics were beginning to place a high premium on a player's ability to convey a feeling of tension between art and life, between the constraint of form and the spontaneous passions of the moment, by playing well-known theatrical types and conventionally stylized gestures in a "natural," even casual and offhand manner.[35]

Edmund Kean, the most popular actor on the English stage during Keats's poetic maturity, stunned playgoers and critics alike from the moment of his London debut at Drury Lane by playing off against his audience's heightened consciousness of long-standing theatrical conventions and stereotyped roles an infinitely varied and wholly unpredictable range of emotional expressions. As Donohue notes in his book on Kean, "Abrupt transitions, unexpected pauses, lightning descents from the grand to the colloquial . . . the spasmodic nature of Kean's gesture and utterance would always draw attention, especially because, to many commentators, it called into question the whole relationship between artistic convention and life."[36]

Like his early mentor, Leigh Hunt, Keats was an ardent admirer of Kean. Commenting on *Otho* in a letter to Bailey, dated August 14, 1819, Keats expresses his ambition "to make as great a revolution in modern dramatic writing as Kean has done in acting" (II, 139). However qualified his success, Keats did manage formally to incorporate the "Keansian" style of acting and characterization into his text, the "dramatic writing" of the play. By this means *Otho* encourages its audience to consider not only the relation of theater to the life it represents, but the notion of life itself as fundamentally, and almost inescapably, "theatrical."

Otho was written in the summer of 1819, in collaboration with Keats's friend Charles Brown, who was largely responsible for the plot, as the poet admitted to his publisher, Taylor, in September: "Brown likes the Tragedy very much: but he is not a fit judge, as I have only acted Midwife to his plot, and of course he will be fond of his child" (II, 157). Evidence in the letters suggest that Keats, having discussed the play with Brown earlier in Hampstead, had completed act I and a good portion of act II before his friend joined him at Shanklin, on the Isle of Wight, in late July. Though Keats wrote the next two acts pretty much as Brown dictated them, Brown's testimony states that the young poet "wrote the fifth act in accordance with his own view."[37] We would expect Keats's hand to show itself, then, more in the first and last acts than in the others, and we are not disappointed. Keats's preoccupation with the play of life and the extent to which personal identity is comprised in public roles appears principally in act I, while Ludolph, the most Keatsian character in the play and the one most committed to his "role" as Auranthe's lover, begins to monopolize our attention in act V.

Otho is from the start self-conscious, even tongue-in-cheek theater. It opens with the Machiavellian Conrad, brother to the anti-heroine, Auranthe, musing on the course of the recent rebellion against Otho, Emperor of Germany, a rebellion Conrad has fomented. He ends his soliloquy by asking, "But why do I stand babbling to myself?" (I, i, 14). The very questioning of the convention of soliloquy immediately calls attention to the artificialities of the play, and at the same time to the artifice of the conventions by which life is rendered in the context of a play. The life on stage, we are reminded, goes on as a dramatic fiction, and personality is expressed within the limits of dramatic convention.

Only a few lines later, Auranthe warns Conrad not to "overact / The hyprocrite" (I, i, 30–31). "Overact" gains added force from its end-line position. What can it mean, to "*over*act the hypocrite," especially when the phrase is spoken by one character in a play to another? Does it mean that "the" hypocrite (the definite article already classifies him as a theatrical "type") is in this instance too obviously insincere? Or rather that this actor is so exaggerating his character as *not* to appear hypocritical after all, but only playing at hypocrisy? In the latter case Conrad would prove to be the ultimate "actor" in the theater of life, duplicitous even in his professions of duplicity. However we resolve the matter, we cannot escape the impression that even the most cynical denizens of this society are expected to play their parts respectably. "The hypocrite," after all, is just another such role.

Other characters besides Conrad seem similarly conscious of themselves as playing one role or another for varying audiences. Auranthe, Ludolph's intended, shows a remarkable flexibility in her self-understanding. Informed by Conrad that Otho has granted his consent to her marriage with Ludolph, Auranthe throws over both her former lover, the knight Albert, and her former self, the "Auranthe" who loved him: "This is to wake in Paradise! farewell / Thou clod of yesterday—*'twas not myself!*" (I, i, 90–91; italics mine). Auranthe's new identity is conceived in relation to a new public image, that of crown princess. That her new image seems the product more of creative marketing techniques than of anything else becomes apparent when she thanks her brother for arranging the marriage: "Thou, Jove-like, struck'dst thy forehead, / and from the teeming marrow of thy brain / I spring complete Minerva!" (I, i, 95–97).

Gersa, the rebel leader, undergoes a similar transformation of identity when he is led into Otho's presence in chains. Much like his literary prototype, Marlowe's Bajazeth in *Tambourlaine the Great,* Gersa expects (and we expect to witness) scorn and humiliation at the hands of his conqueror. Proud and defiant, Gersa steels himself for it (I, ii, 93–108):

Gersa.   Not a word of greeting,
   No welcome to a princely visitor,
   Most mighty Otho? Will not my great host
   Vouchsafe a syllable, before he bids
   His gentlemen conduct me with all care
   To some securest lodging—cold perhaps!
Otho.   What mood is this? Hath fortune touch'd thy brain?
Gersa.   O kings and princes of this fevrous world,
   What abject things, what mockeries must ye be,
   What nerveless minions of safe palaces!
   When here, a monarch, whose proud foot is used
   To fallen princes' necks, as to his stirrup,
   Must needs exclaim that I am mad forsooth,
   Because I cannot flatter with bent knees
   My conqueror!
Otho.   Gersa, I think you wrong me:
   I think I have a better fame abroad.

But Gersa insists on misinterpreting Otho's words, completely wrapped up in his stage role: "I pr'ythee mock me not with gentle speech," he tells Otho, "But, as a favour, bid me from thy presence; / Let me no longer be the wondering food / Of all these eyes; pr'ythee command me hence!" (109–112). Gersa is well aware of what the public "script" (and Marlowe's) demands—sullen defiance. When Otho tells Auranthe to unbind him, the rebel is caught completely offguard: "I am wound up in deep astonishment! / Thank you, fair lady—Otho!—Emperor! / *You rob me of myself;* my dignity / Is now your infant;—I am a weak child" (I, ii, 117–120; italics mine). Gersa's very identity, built on a certain reading of the social physiognomy, is shattered when that reading is contradicted by his being freed. He must project himself into a new role, adopt a new identity.

Otho, by contrast, appears as one of those "etherial" personalities that remain unaffected by the expectations of the world at large. His self-reliance shows when he cautions the astonished Gersa, "I do not personate / The stage-play emperor to entrap applause, / To set the silly sort o' the world agape, / And make the politic smile" (I, ii, 143-146). The rigidity of a conventional theatrical type is broken by Otho's refusal to play along with the other characters to satisfy the audience's expectations: he will not "personate" someone like Tambourlaine, a "stage-play emperor," because he will not follow another's script. He knows himself to be, in fact, the Emperor, however unconventional his behavior. Thus secure in his identity, Otho feels free later on to "play" the tyrant as a practical joke on his son (II, i, 60-95), and at one point Keats even envisioned him, according to a letter Brown wrote to Dilke, "threatening cold pig to the newly married couple."[38] "Cold pig" means waking someone up by dousing him with cold water, impulsive, unrestrained, and ludicrous behavior hardly befitting a "stage-play emperor."

Such behavior was not only quite consistent with emerging standards for acting technique in Regency theater, expectations of more "life" and less "art," but also a comment on the rigid restrictions and expectations that Keats felt limited, even determined, one's sense of identity in Regency society. While Conrad, Auranthe, and Gersa must cope with the various "identities" expected of them in changing social circumstances, Otho can dispense with such role playing altogether. He hates posing and speechifying: "Pray, do not prose, good Ethelbert," he tells the loquacious monk, "but speak / What is your purpose" (I, ii, 180-190). In the second scene of act III Keats drives the point home with forty-two lines of Ethelbert's windy procrastination, until Otho is forced to command him to state his purpose: "Confess, or by the wheel—" (160). As drama, this is tiresome, but Keats is poking fun at stage-play speeches as well as kings. In Otho's scene with Gersa, the rebel gets all the "prose," even a description of Otho (103-105) more apt as the *conqueror's* boast, while Otho reveals himself in fine, and consequential, actions: he frees Gersa.

Ludolph lacks both his father's independence and the other characters' facility in adjusting their roles to changing expectations. Instead, he commits himself utterly and irrevocably to his vision of the false Auranthe, rejecting the true love of Erminia, the princess to whom he was at first betrothed. Ludolph's devotion thus seems more a species of infatuation than of love, and as the outcome of the play makes clear, such an entanglement, intoxicating as it may be, depends entirely on Auranthe's (and Ludolph's) maintaining the fiction of her innocence, even when the reality is in question.

Ludolph's tragedy is the loss of his true self in the mazes of an essentially narcissistic relationship, the gradual surrender of the self to a "theatrical" *égoisme à deux* that the acknowledged fact of Auranthe's infidelity must eventually destroy. Ludolph becomes obsessed with maintaining a fictional self—the devoted lover bridegroom—from which he cannot withdraw without withdrawing from life as well. "Impossible!" he cries out on hearing of Auranthe's secret trysts with Albert. "I cannot doubt—I will not—no—to doubt / Is to be ashes!—wither'd up to death!" (III, ii, 193–194).

Eyes in *Otho,* as in "The Eve of St. Agnes" and *Lamia,* represent the "theatrical" horizon of consciousness within which the image of the beloved, and thereby the lover's own reflected self-awareness, finds scope. "Auranthe!" cries Ludolph (III, ii, 5–10),

> Not all the gaze upon us can restrain
> My eyes, too long poor exiles from thy face,
> From adoration, and my foolish tongue
> From uttering soft responses to the love
> I see in thy mute beauty beaming forth!

Keats's hero is caught between the competing claims of the Beloved and of the crowd, between semi-private fantasy and, literally, "common" sense—what all agree to be true. Ludolph's subsequent insistence on Auranthe's innocence in the face of the evidence, and even of his own certainty of the truth, is an expression of his need to protect that exclusive boundary of awareness in which his chosen self-image can be realized. "Now I follow thee," he reflects on Auranthe, "a substance or a shadow, wheresoe'er / Thou leadest me" (IV, ii, 23–25).

Although Ludolph's purpose in going ahead with the mock wedding feast at the end of *Otho* is, evidently, to intensify the illusion of Auranthe's chastity so as better to set off the harsh truth, his motivations are hopelessly mixed. These are appearances he finds it hard to dismiss, appearances he has a high stake in maintaining, as his description of his bride suggests (V, v, 61–74):

> Deep blue eyes, semi-shaded in white lids,
> Finish'd with lashes fine for more soft shade,
> Completed by her twin-arch'd ebon-brows;
> White temples, of exactest elegance,
> Of even mould, felicitous and smooth;
> Cheeks fashion'd tenderly on either side,
> So perfect, so divine, that our poor eyes

Are dazzled with the sweet proportioning,
And wonder that 'tis so,—the magic chance!
Her nostrils, small, fragrant, fairy-delicate;
Her lips—I swear no human bones e'er wore
So taking a disguise;—you shall behold her!
She is the world's chief jewel, and, by heaven,
She's mine by right of marriage!—she is mine!

Even in the midst of his raptures, Ludolph knows Auranthe's face
is but a "disguise." And yet, that disguise is essential to defining his
own identity: "She is mine!" Ludolph's need to defend the truth of
his exalted vision outweighs his knowledge of Auranthe's perfidy. For
him, as for his creator in the encounter with "Charmian," faith in
the "theatrical" representation of the beloved struggles against the
knowledge that she must fade before objective, skeptical witnesses,
like the Reynolds sisters.

And yet, far from avoiding them, Ludolph cannot rest content
until he has enlisted the agreement of such witnesses to the reality of
his make-believe relationship. He invites a crowd of courtiers to the
wedding feast to vindicate his troubled faith in his dream. The
crowd's sense of unreality corresponds to the hero's own feelings of
self-estrangement: they know that their roles, like his, are false.
Among the "Lords, Ladies, Knights, Gentlemen" filling Otho's hall,
one comments (V, v, 1–4):

Grievously are we tantalised, one and all;
Sway'd here and there, commanded to and fro,
As though we were the shadows of a sleep,
And link'd to a dreaming fancy. What do we here?

Among these "Shadows in the shape of Man and women," this play
within the play, roles are determined by one paramount circumstance: the derangement of the Prince, whose every desire Otho has
directed to be indulged from fear of vexing his son to outright mad-
ness or death. But this circumstantial adaptation of social roles is
only a special case, in Keats's view, of the human condition. With
few exceptions, all of life is an adaptation of identity to the roles de-
manded by changed and changing social circumstances, "an acted
play" whose script is continually undergoing revision. By the last
scene of *Otho* the "script" is entirely at the mercy of Ludolph's obsession. If Otho would ignore the play he is in, Ludolph would re-

make it to suit himself. His is a love so intense and exclusive, so "infinite," in the Kierkegaardian sense, that he cannot exist outside it.

By making circumstances succumb to his role, rather than altering his role to conform to circumstances, Ludolph turns the world, if but for a moment, into his dream. Otho, however, forces nothing. He has no stake in making others suspend their disbelief in him or in his world. Thus it is appropriate that he should not appear at the feast until the very end, when Ludolph calls him to witness the announcement of a summary "verdict" on Auranthe (V, v, 140–151). Ludolph summons his father for the same reason that Lycius, in *Lamia*, dreads the entrance of the philosopher Apollonius: Otho, he knows, will not play along with these fantasies. He will help make Ludolph face the bitter reality: "She stings me through!" he tells his father, "Even as the worm doth feed upon the nut, / So she, a scorpion, preys upon my brain! / I feel her gnawing here!" (V, v, 157–160).

Auranthe, like Lamia, is finally destroyed by her lover's loss of faith: her death, presumably of terror at her pending humiliation before the wedding guests, might qualify as the only example in English literature of terminal stage fright. And Ludolph dies, not of self-inflicted wounds (while Keats lets him wave his dagger, that final melodramatic cliche is pointedly—excuse me—rejected), but because the mirror in which the Prince beheld himself has been shattered.

In *Otho the Great* we have our cake—rhetorical fireworks (much of it banal)—but we cannot eat. Just as a great deal of the characterization in the play is revealed to be posing, so a good many speeches turn out to be prosing. They perjure themselves. Ethelbert's dilatations and Conrad's "overacted" lines are examples, as is Ludolph's description of Auranthe's "taking disguise." But a particularly good instance of Keats's letting Pegasus out on a short leash is afforded by Ludolph's depiction of the palace he envisions to replace the more mundane scene of his banquet. The speech contains lines that are worthy of inclusion in "The Eve of St. Agnes" or *Lamia*. Yet each time we are encouraged to soar, Keats reminds us of where, and of what, we are (V, v, 31–48):

These draperies are fine, and, being a mortal,
I should desire no better; yet, in truth,
There must be some superior costliness,
Some wider-domed high magnificence!

I would have, as a mortal I may not,
Hangings of heaven's clouds, purple and gold,
Slung from the spheres; gauzes of silver mist,
Loop'd up with cords of twisted wreathed light,
And tassell'd round with weeping meteors!
These pendent lamps and chandeliers are bright
As earthly fires from dull dross can be cleans'd;
Yet could my eyes drink up intenser beams
Undazzled,—this is darkness,—when I close
These lids, I see far fiercer brilliances,—
Skies full of splendid moons, and shooting stars,
And spouting exhalations, diamond fires,
And panting fountains quivering with deep glows!
Yes—this is dark—is it not dark?

The phrases, "being a mortal" and "as a mortal I may not"; the vacillation from "these draperies" to "hangings of heaven's clouds" and back, from "weeping meteors" to "these pendent lamps," from "intenser beams" to "darkness," and then soaring again to "far fiercer brilliances" and finally sinking—"this is dark"—these sudden expansions and contractions of the soul not only recall the spiritual dislocations of a poem like "Ode to a Nightingale" but emphasize the illusory quality of a poetical tour de force. We are left, with Ludolph, in the comparative dark of the quotidian: the house lights go up in the theater of the imagination.

Lycius, the hero of *Lamia*, gets to live for a few brief days in the palace that Ludolph could only envision behind his closed eyelids. Indeed, throughout *Otho* we have the feeling we are already half in the magic realm of Keats's contemporary and more famous work. Just after his marriage, for instance, Ludolph is so frantic with joy that Otho is constrained to comment: "This is a little painful; just too much. / Conrad, if he flames longer in this wise, / I shall believe in wizard-woven loves / And old romances" (III, ii, 45–48).[39]

In *Lamia*, as in Keats's play, living under the spell of the waking dream depends crucially on who watches whom, who takes their cues from whom, whose eyes and presence are acknowledged by the dreamers and whose are ignored. "Ah, Goddess," Lycius tells the serpent-woman who has beguiled him on the road to Corinth, "see / Whether my eyes can ever turn from thee! / For pity do not this sad heart belie— / Even as thou vanishest so shall I die" (I, 257–260). At one point the young student, "bending to her open eyes," finds himself "mirror'd small in paradise" (II, 46–47). Here the image of the lover and of the entire world in which he conceives himself is indeed "comprized" in the Beloved's gaze. As in "The Eve of St. Agnes" and *Otho,* eyes reflect and make real the poet-lover's chosen self-image in its entirety. Lycius and Lamia keep each other alive by keeping each other constantly, and exclusively, in sight, reposing "where use had made it sweet, with eyelids closed, / Saving a tythe which love still open kept, / That they might see each other while they almost slept" (II, 22–25). When, at the end of the poem, Lamia "withers" at Apollonius's "demon eyes" (II, 289–290), and Lycius suddenly finds "no recognition in those orbs" (260) that mirrored him before, he, like Ludolph, dies of disillusionment.

Lycius' and Lamia's palatial fantasy is "smoked," as Keats might say, by their uninvited and skeptical guest, but the divine reality and endurance of Hermes' shared "dream" of love in the opening lines of the poem provide an instructive contrast to such mortal, makeshift paradises. "Bent warm on amorous theft" (I, 8), Hermes descends from Olympus to Crete, in search of a beautiful nymph whom Lamia, presently in serpent form, has made invisible to protect her from rapacious satyrs and other unwanted suitors: "And by my power is her beauty veil'd," Lamia tells the disappointed god, "To keep it unaffronted, unassail'd / By the love-glances of unlovely eyes . . . Pale grew her immortality, for woe / Of all these lovers, and she grieved so / I took compassion on her" (I, 100–106). In return for Hermes' transforming Lamia back into woman's shape, however, she will reverse her spell and let the god see the nymph. "Thou shalt behold her, Hermes, thou *alone*" (110; italics added), she promises him.

The nymph, in her affronted beauty, recalls the retiring Madeline, Hermes her Porphyro, to whose presence alone she responds; and Lamia herself, in this particular scene, seems to be recreating the role of Madeline's old nurse, Angela (a character patterned in turn on Juliet's nurse), who aids Porphyro in his "stratagem" by helping him sneak into Madeline's bedchamber undetected. The miracle that Hermes and the nymph achieve, moreover, also depends on complete retirement, though not on any narrative sleight of hand. "It was no dream," writes Keats of Hermes' vision, "or say a dream it was, / Real are the dreams of Gods, and smoothly pass / Their pleasures in a long, immortal dream" (I, 126–128). What, then, makes this dream real? And what prolongs it so? Keats continues (I, 134–145),

. . . upon the nymph his eyes he bent
Full of adoring tears and blandishment,

And towards her stept: she, like a moon in wane,
Faded before him, cower'd, nor could restrain
Her fearful sobs, self-folding like a flower
That faints into itself at evening hour.
But the God fostering her chilled hand,
She felt the warmth, her eyelids open'd bland,
And, like new flowers at morning song of bees,
Bloom'd, and gave up her honey to the lees.
Into the green-recessed woods they flew;
Nor grew they pale, as mortal lovers do.

Hermes' dream becomes real as that upon which his eyes are "bent"
acknowledges him, accepts his presence and his alone. The moment
that the nymph felt the warmth of the god's hand, "her eyelids
open'd bland," and the "new flowers" of her eyes "bloom'd" and
gave up their sweets. No longer fearful, the nymph ardently returns
Hermes' "adoring" gaze, and surrenders her blossoming self to it.

Because they keep their love to themselves, Hermes and the
nymph, like Porphyro and Madeline, do not die: the nymph's "immortality" will not "grow pale" at the gaze of profane adorers or
cynical lovers. Lamia, on the other hand, does grow "pale," "icy,"
"cold," a "deadly white," when exposed to Apollonius' unsympathetic scrutiny (II, 245–260):

... The bald-head philosopher
Had fix'd his eye, without a twinkle or stir
Full on the alarmed beauty of the bride,
Brow-beating her fair form, and troubling her sweet pride.
Lycius then press'd her hand, with devout touch,
As pale it lay upon the rosy couch:
'Twas icy, and the cold ran through his veins;
Then sudden it grew hot, and all the pains
Of an unnatural heat shot to his heart.
"Lamia, what means this? Wherefore dost thou start?
Knows't thou that man?" Poor Lamia answer'd not.
He gaz'd into her eyes, and not a jot
Own'd they the lovelorn piteous appeal:
More, more he gaz'd: his human senses reel:
Some hungry spell that loveliness absorbs;
There was no recognition in those orbs.

At the moment Lamia confronts another who does not admit the reality of her existence, she becomes a frozen, inhuman image, like

"smooth-sculptur'd" Porphyro, "pallid, chill, and drear," in the just-awakened eyes of Madeline.

If "The Eve of St. Agnes" demonstrates how lifeless icons of the self, wrought with consummate skill, can be brought to life by a proper "greeting of the Spirit," *Otho* and *Lamia* demonstrate the perils of such sorcery. In *Lamia,* particularly, we begin to feel that the closeted theater of a mutual waking dream is, finally, mere solipsism compounded. Here, as in *Otho,* Keats concedes that objective truth transcends what individuals, however so many and however willing to suspend disbelief, may agree to call "truth." At the end of part I, with Lycius and Lamia safely sequestered in their luxurious apartments, he writes that "none knew where" the lovers or their servants "could inhabit" (392–397):

> . . . the most curious
> Were foil'd, who watch'd to trace them to their house:
> And but the flitter-winged verse must tell,
> For truth's sake, what woe afterwards befel,
> 'Twould humour many a heart to leave them thus,
> Shut from the busy world of more incredulous.

Indeed, had *Lamia* ended here, Keats could have made essentially the point he made at the end of "The Eve of St. Agnes," where the lovers fade phantomlike into the elfin storm of legend and romance. Such lovers can achieve a "semireal" level of existence that appears, momentarily, to be "real" but turns out, on reflection, to be "a nothing." Similarly, to allow oneself to be so absorbed by the waking dream of "richer entanglements, / Enthralments far more self-destroying" that one mistakes a make-believe feast of love for true nourishment is to slowly starve the true self to death (II, 1–6):

> Love in a hut, with water and a crust,
> Is—Love, forgive us!—cinders, ashes, dust;
> Love in a palace is perhaps at last
> More grievous torment that a hermit's fast:—
> That is a doubtful tale from faery land,
> Hard for the non-elect to understand.

Real are the dreams of gods, certainly. But we are not gods. We are, ultimately, creatures that crave the affirmation of desire, and of the self that desires, in a world beyond dreams. This is not what we want to hear "from faery land," of course. We, the "non-elect" barred from paradise, savor our fantasies of paradisal love. But sooner or later, mortal circumstances impinge on our immortally aspiring imaginations. As we dream of "elfin storms," real storms flood our basement, and our home "over the southern moors" turns out to be a worthless deed to a Florida swamp.

Against such realizations, Lycius opposes the infinite expansion of his dream. It need not be destroyed, if only he can enlist the faith of the "busy world of more incredulous." As he and Lamia recline on their couch, reposing, like Porphyro and Madeline, halfway between private fantasy and shared reality, a still wider arena for self-display suddenly announces itself: Lycius hears a blast of trumpets from outside the palace (II, 28–39):

> . . . Lycius started—the sounds fled,
> But left a thought, a buzzing in his head.
> For the first time, since first he harbour'd in
> That purple-lined palace of sweet sin,
> His spirit pass'd beyond its golden bourn
> Into the noisy world almost forsworn.
> The lady, ever watchful, penetrant,
> Saw this with pain, so arguing a want
> Of something more, more than her empery
> Of joys; and she began to moan and sigh
> Because he mused beyond her, knowing well
> That but a moment's thought is passion's passing bell.

Instead of shrinking, like Porphyro, from the intrusive noise of the world outside, Lycius throws open the door, and from the moment his attention turns to the "noisy world," Lamia begins to despair. "You have deserted me," she tells Lycius, "where am I now? / Not in your heart" (42–43). Lamia herself is as "comprized" in Lycius, so now it seems, as he in her. Lycius answers (II, 48–54),

> "My silver planet, both of eve and morn!
> Why will you plead yourself so sad forlorn,
> While I am striving how to fill my heart
> With deeper crimson, and a double smart?
> How to entangle, trammel up and snare
> Your soul in mine, and labyrinth you there
> Like the hid scent in an unbudded rose?"

Though Lycius protests he would "snare" Lamia's very being in his own (words like "entangle" and "trammel up" remind us of "richer entanglements," "enthralments"), his pride, his thirst for a wider, worldly fame and "triumph" (II, 60), will have the opposite effect.

Lycius' desire to show Lamia, to let her "pace abroad majestical, / And triumph . . . Amid the hoarse alarm of Corinth's voice" (II, 59–61) stems from a fatal impulse to extend his precariously achieved "paradise" into society at large and thus to make that waking dream, and the self it comprises, live in the credulous eyes of others, of "the herd . . . with busy brain" (II, 150), "maz'd, curious and keen" (II, 156). Like his counterpart Ludolph, who defiantly seeks a public forum in which to defend the truth of his exalted vision, the better to suppress his nagging doubts, Lycius on some level suspects that Lamia is unreal, or he would not care so much to avoid the notice of Apollonius, his "trusty guide / And good instructor" (I, 375–376) while escorting Lamia through the city streets. Nor would he have left Apollonius "uninvited" to his lavish banquet, something for which the old philosopher, suspecting the reason, chides his pupil on arriving there (II, 157–169).

As in *Otho*, dream becomes theater.[40] And theatergoers, it seems, are not nearly as critical as philosophers. Perhaps nowhere else in his work does Keats's contempt for the cheap tastes and infantile raptures of his literary public appear more pronounced (II, 146–152):

> The day appear'd, and all the gossip rout.
> O senseless Lycius! Madman! wherefore flout
> The silent-blessing fate, warm cloister'd hours,
> And show to common eyes these secret bowers?
> The herd approach'd; each guest, with busy brain,
> Arriving at the portal, gaz'd amain,
> And enter'd marveling . . .

This "herd" becomes especially keen on the charade as "merry wine, sweet wine" (211), "the happy vintage" (203) touches their brains. "The gorgeous dyes, / The space, the splendour of the draperies, / The roof of awful richness, nectarous cheer, / Beautiful slaves, and Lamia's self, appear . . . No more so strange" (205–211). Love-blindness is not unlike being blind drunk. "Soon was God Bacchus at meridian height; / Flush'd were their cheeks, and bright eyes double bright" (II, 213–214).

Just as the courtiers in Otho's hall tailor their behavior to the whims of Ludolph, so the wondering herd entering Lamia's dream palace takes its cue from Lycius, the dreamer, questioning and challenging nothing. They are now themselves as much a part of this dream of life as the crowds of Corinth through which Lycius first accompanied his newfound love: "As men talk in a dream, so Corinth all, / Throughout her palaces imperial, / And all her populous streets and temples lewd, / Mutter'd" (I, 350–352). It is not, after all, such ephemeral shadows that threaten Lycius' happiness with their pliable attention, but that "uninvited guest" who enters with them, "with eye severe." Apollonius personifies that critical, detached, "philosophical" awareness of the self in a world not its own, which cannot be divorced from an awareness of others (he enters with them, invited or not), but which is not limited to what others may, in fact, think.

Apollonius, like Otho, is an audience that will not be manipulated. He bears witness to the reality, the facts of the matter. He intrudes like a country boor at Covent Garden, denouncing an illusion that all conspire to make true, forcing the actors to revert to their real characters. But since Lamia, apparently, has no real self, and since Lycius' identity is wholly wrapped up in what Lamia, something unreal, makes of him, the lovers cannot escape destruction when Apollonius declares the waking truth, in front of all (II, 295–308):

> "Fool! Fool!" repeated he, while his eyes still
> Relented not, nor mov'd . . .
> .   .   .   .   .
> Then Lamia breath'd death breath; the sophist's eye,
> Like a sharp spear, went through her utterly,
> Keen, cruel, perceant, stinging: she, as well
> As her weak hand could any meaning tell,
> Motion'd him to be silent; vainly so,
> He look'd and look'd again a level—No!
> "A Serpent!" echoed he; no sooner said,
> Than with a frightful scream she vanished:
> And Lycius' arms were empty of delight,
> As were his limbs of life, from that same night.

Watching and Witnessing: The Fall of Hyperion

If in "The Eve of St. Agnes" Keats compromises the "miraculous" quality of Porphyro's "stratagem" by enlisting our skepticism even as he enforces our willing suspension of disbelief, then in *Lamia* he may be said to be doing the opposite—qualifying our final skepticism, as expressed in Apollonius' verdict ("Fool! Fool!"), by his earlier reflections on "cold philosophy" (II, 229–238):[41]

... Do not all charms fly
At the mere touch of cold philosophy?
There was an awful rainbow once in heaven:
We know her woof, her texture; she is given
In the dull catalogue of common things.
Philosophy will clip an Angel's wings,
Conquer all mysteries by rule and line,
Empty the haunted air, and gnomed mine—
Unweave a rainbow, as it erewhile made
The tender-person'd Lamia melt into a shade.

But are Keats's sympathies, or antipathies, so clear even in this passage? Although the poet characteristically condemns philosophical or, as he calls it in his famous letter to Bailey, "consequitive reasoning" (I, 185) and implicitly condones credulousness, we should not lose sight of the extended metaphor implied by the image of the woven rainbow: "woof," "texture," "unweave." The rainbow, as an object of aesthetic appreciation, is like an arras or tapestry, a work of (in this case divine) craftsmanship, the cumulative "effect" of a transcendent design. In order to understand the principles involved in its construction, we must look at it philosophically, not as passive admirers. But the desire to understand those principles of an object's design that contribute to its aesthetic effect is the desire of the artist, not just the philosopher or critic of taste. It is the aim of the artist, not only as passive aesthete or enjoyer of beauty, but as its painstaking creator, to understand and to see through the *work* of his art.

The artist, when he leaves off contemplation and begins to create, must himself, at times, "murder to dissect." We might remind ourselves, if we still feel inclined to interpret Keats's passage on philosophy and the rainbow as a strict condemnation, that the poet was not above considering himself "an old Stager in the picturesque" (*Letters*, II, 135) or a "Stage Manager" of life (*Letters*, II, 169). Poetry was often, to his mind, a "stratagem," at times a "mere Jack a lanthern" (*Letters*, I, 242) and at other times, especially in his periods of most enthusiastic involvement, a *gradus ad parnassum*. The "old Stager" shows his hand in the gorgeous descriptions of "costly magnificence" in *Otho* and *Lamia*, of course, but also *sotto voce*, as in stanza 22 of "The Eve of St. Agnes," where, in an almost choric moment, the narrator suddenly addresses Porphyro, one of his own creations, in anticipation of Madeline's entrance: "Now prepare, / Young Porphyro, for gazing on that bed; / She comes, she comes again, like ring-dove fray'd and fled" (196–198).

The instrusive effect of these lines is slightly different from that of the conclusion, where we are pointedly reminded of the ephemeral, legendary quality of this tale.[42] The lines in stanza 22 begin like an address to the reader, a command, "Now prepare," but they end as an address to a character. The command reminds us that the poet is in control of these events, and the unanticipated change in address-ees suggests that we are, after all, very like "young Porphyro," fascinated like him by the spectacle, the texture, "the coloring of St. Agnes eve" (*Letters*, II, 234). We too are hidden watchers manipulated, led on, tantalized by a poetical "stratagem" we conspire to make "miracle."

As spectators, our minds float free. We are no longer "here," in this room, at this desk, in this chair, but neither are we in any recognizable "there." Watching from the unlocalized "present" of the poet's speech, we can hardly characterize our sense of dislocation in any other way than negatively, by distinguishing it from the sense of being embodied in any particular place at all.[43] The nearest analogy to the experience of reading the last lines of stanza 22 is that of watching events unfold in a theater, with the narrator standing by as Impressario, just this side of the proscenium, or as the playwright himself, quietly murmuring at our elbow. In "The Eve of St. Agnes" that darkened theater, similar to Porphyro's closet, is the reader's own mind, which for the moment submits to the directions of a "Stager" quite near at hand.

To call the act of reading a "theatrical" experience is, of course, to speak metaphorically, and specifically to invoke the notion of theater current in Keats's own day, with its emphasis on a voyeuristic verisimilitude, in contrast to the less finicky practices of the previous century. But in many ways the experience of attending the theater in the early nineteenth century was coming to resemble the experience of reading, particularly with its sense of a radical disembodiment of the perceiving self with respect to the world it perceived. E. J. Burton has suggested that, as a result of a "new emphasis on visual effect" and spectacle during the Regency period, the impression of a complete discontinuity between the world of the audience and that of the stage became more pronounced, a "separation, with, across the footlights, fuller and fuller presentation of the outward appearances and behavior of actual life." "The audience 'look in' on the lives of others; the old demand that the audience, as it were, play the action through with the people on stage, using imagination and constructive participation (i.e. accepting [proscenium] doors as various entrances in various houses and quick changes of locality without demur), has largely been abandoned. Instead, the audience are required to accept the stage picture and events as 'reality.' Every effort is made to suggest that the scene is as in 'real' life."[44] Burton adds that the introduction of gas lighting, first at Drury Lane in 1817, then at Covent Garden, "completed the process of concentrating attention on the stage picture, and, at the same time, broke the eighteenth-century 'entre-nous-ship' (as Charles Lamb phrased it) between audience and actors." "It was now possible to darken the auditorium during the performance. In their own world of blackness the audience looked away into the 'other world,'—a world of light, colour, and costume beyond the barrier of footlights."[45]

These changes in stage practice, occurring at the time Keats wrote, reflect the curious fact that the theater, since ancient times an arena for communal catharsis, was coming more and more to resemble a private dream of life. The playhouse conformed increasingly to Enlightenment notions of the mind, and the spectator to Enlightenment notions of the "self" that is really no self at all, but the Lockean *ego* sitting in its "dark room" or "closet" watching ghostly images of a physical world it cannot inhabit. While Locke obviously drew his metaphor from Restoration theatrical techniques that originated in the Stuart court masque, with its emphasis on perspectival illusion and *trompe l'oeil* and its use of the proscenium arch, it was not until the nineteenth century that the separation between spectacle and spectator became complete. During the Regency period the theater assumes the shape of the individual mind: a dark box enclosing a "self" without concrete definition or existence, in a darkness discontinuous with the world being watched. If, in *Otho* and *Lamia,* we find dream becoming theater, in the stage conventions of Keats's day we find theater becoming dream. The reader, Keats suggests in "The Eve of St. Agnes," inhabits just such a voyeuristic nonspace, a spot as unlocalized as Lamia's dream palace.

Keats's lavishness of description and realistic detail reinforce this spectacular, or "theatrical," effect, as critics have noted, and as Keats himself was aware. In a letter to John Taylor, dated November 17, 1819, he explains, "The little dramatic skill I may as yet have however badly it might show in a Drama would I think be sufficient for a Poem—I wish to diffuse the coloring of St. Agnes eve throughout a Poem in which Character and Sentiment would be the figures to such drapery" (II, 234). The "Poem" was *Lamia.* Note that what Keats attributes to his limited "dramatic skill" in "The Eve of St.

Agnes" are its "coloring" and "drapery," its staging and scenic effects. In *Lamia* such effects are conjured up more for the purpose of ultimate disillusionment than immediate gratification. Like *Otho the Great, Lamia* is directed at revealing the limits of "theatrical" verisimilitude, not simply at achieving it.

In this respect *Lamia* and *Otho*, both finished in August of 1819, reveal the extent of Keats's deepening skepticism following "The Eve of St. Agnes," which was written some six months earlier. There, the poet tactfully ignores us until the last lines: even in stanza 22, we are not directly addressed, and thus the spell of his words is not snapped by our being made suddenly aware of our proper selves, as so often happens in *Lamia,* where the narrator does not hesitate to pose rhetorical questions—"Whither fled Lamia, now a lady bright?" (I, 171)—or to anticipate his story quite deliberately—"Why this fair creature chose so fairly / By the wayside to linger, we shall see; / But first 'tis fit to tell . . ." (I, 200–202)—or to moralize on faery love and cold philosophy—"Do not all charms fly?" (II, 229)—or even to ask his readers for judgment on these proceedings—"What wreath for Lamia? What for Lycius? / What for the sage, old Apollonius?" (II, 221–222). In *Lamia,* quite in line with its Augustan style, we feel the presence of the narrator intruding more blatantly than in "St. Agnes," calling attention to the power that makes these absent things present, that makes beauty true, and that can, like Apollonius himself, unmake them. We can see the beginnings of this philosophical detachment and artistic self-consciousness in "The Eve of St. Agnes," but there it does not, until the last stanza, interfere with our ability to lose ourselves, like theatrical spectators, in what we see.

What we find happening to Keats, then, between the writing of "St. Agnes" and of *Lamia* is a growth in critical or "philosophical" detachment from his own theatrical representations. In the earlier poem he is content to comment, almost parenthetically, without disturbing our self-absorption; in the later poem, he openly challenges the verisimilitude of his own cunning "dramatic skill." We could say that in "St. Agnes" Keats is still identifying closely with his poet-lover protagonist, a "theatrical" self-image, and finessing in the last stanzas the question of that image's relationship to reality, whereas in *Lamia* he repudiates the "theatrical" alter ego more firmly, inasmuch as he obtrudes himself *in propria persona* as the creator of this fairy tale. Keats's "etherial" self, in other words, comes to be expressed more in the act of creation, the very *writing* of the poem, than in the acting of a part *in* his creation.

This more overt assertion of the writing self seems a natural out-growth of Keats's psychological development during the first half of 1819, when his ambivalent contempt for the patronizing public had deepened. By summer, that contempt had led Keats to take a more self-regarding attitude toward his work. In a letter to Taylor, dated August 23, 1819, he expressed his confidence in a new source of crea-tivity, something far different from chameleon speculation: "You will observe at the end of this if you put down the Letter 'How a sol-itarry [*sic*] life engenders pride and egotism!' True: I know it does but this Pride and egotism will enable me to write finer things than any thing else could—so I will indulge it" (II, 144).

In a letter to J. H. Reynolds a day later, he described similar feel-ings:

> You would not find me at all unhappy in [Winchester]; as all my thoughts and feelings which are of the selfish nature, home specula-tions every day continue to make me more Iron—I am convinced more and more day by day that fine writing is next to fine doing the top thing in the world; the Paradise Lost becomes a greater won-der—The more I know what my diligence may in time probably ef-fect; the more does my heart distend with Pride and Obstinacy—I feel it in my power to become a popular writer—I feel it in my strength to refuse the poisonous suffrage of a public ... I have nothing to speak of but myself—and what can I say but what I feel? If you should have any reason to regret this state of excitement in me, I will turn the tide of your feelings in the right channel by mentioning that it is the only state for the best sort of Poetry—that is all I care for, all I live for.   (II, 146–147)

"Egotism," "Pride," "Obstinacy": these, the predominating quali-ties of Milton's Satan, will drive Keats diligently to the production of "fine writing." Note how far he has come from equating "the best sort of Poetry" with spontaneous expression and chameleon faculties of mind: "fine writing" is now near cousin to "fine doing," less an unpremeditated outburst of verbal foliage than a deliberate activity that has consequences in the world. Furthermore, it commands praise and admiration without depending on its author's widespread popularity. Keats feels he has both the "power" to become popular and the "strength" to resist compromising himself for the sake of that popularity.

By the time he finished *Otho* and *Lamia,* Keats had come to see the public notion of "poet" as a sham, but not without its uses. In the same letter to Taylor on his pride and egotism, Keats writes, "I feel every confidence that if I choose I may be a popular writer; that I will never be; but for all that I will get a livelihood" (II, 144). Refusng popularity, he will, nevertheless, in a purely mercenary spirit, get sustenance: " 'There are so many verses,' I would have said to them, 'give me so much means to buy pleasure with as a relief to my hours of labour.' " Keats has managed to separate what he calls "my own being" from his need for love and admiration as a poet, a giant step toward maturity, and toward philosophical detachment. He has reached the point where he feels himself to be his own man. On the one hand, this means a heightened cynicism toward his poetic role—the mask can be manipulated for ulterior purposes, for example, for gain—but on the other hand, it means the freedom to set his own goals as an artist.

Given Keats's evolving philosophical seriousness during the spring and summer of 1819, his increasing "Egotism" and artistic self-consciousness, and his more pronounced skepticism toward the "dream of truth" and "theatrical" representations of any kind, we should not be surprised to find these emerging tendencies in his most intellectually ambitious allegory on the human condition, *The Fall of Hyperion*. *The Fall* was undertaken in September 1819, as a revision of an earlier, unfinished attempt at an epic allegory on the fall of the Titans, *Hyperion*, which Keats had abandoned the previous December. There is little difference between the two poems in the substance of the epic narrative itself, but *The Fall* provides an elaborate narrative introduction to the epic material of the earlier poem, an introduction in which Keats attempts to prove himself worthy of his vision. The poet dreams he has been admitted to Saturn's long-ruined temple as one of the elect among the ranks of the great poets, those "to whom the miseries of the world / Are misery, and will not let them rest" (I, 148–149). Only when his presence in the temple has been accepted by Moneta, the high priestess and guardian of these mysteries, is Keats granted an epic vision of the events originally narrated in *Hyperion*, repeated almost word for word. The tale seems to represent, through various personifications, the rise of self-consciousness, empathy, and the highest art of the epic philosopher-poet out of the experience of suffering and the heartfelt realization of our common mortality.

By placing the poet himself at center stage from the start, *The Fall of Hyperion* carries to its logical conclusion the movement toward authorial self-assertion that had appeared tentatively in "Eve of St.

Agnes" and had later become so pronounced in *Lamia:* the entire epic spectacle of the first *Hyperion,* which pre-dates "St. Agnes" by a month or two, now takes place before the gaze of the embodied poet, who has intruded on his own dream to the extent of becoming a character in it. *The Fall* confirms *Lamia's* evidence of a movement toward critical reflection and self-consciousness, the poet's affirmation not only of a privileged power to envision the imaginative events unfolding in the poem, to represent them convincingly, and to understand their precarious relation to "reality," but also of personal responsibility, as the poet who must write, for that power to envision, to represent, and to understand. It is he who must return to tell his dream of the Titans' sorrow, he who is its only witness.

Between *Hyperion* and *The Fall of Hyperion,* then, Keats's focus shifts to the question of the visionary's responsibility for his vision, a question which requires that the visionary step forth in his own proper person rather than remain "in character." Once Keats has done so, however, in the first part of canto I, his epic vision unfolds as the most literal kind of dream theater, a "high tragedy" enacted in *Moneta's* own "globed brain," with Moneta herself—the goddess of memory—as Impressario and Keats as her audience. It is an awkward adaptation of theatrical structure to the demands of epic—so awkward indeed that Keats cannot sustain it beyond canto II. But this epic-theatrical hybrid relieves Keats of the one duty as an epic visionary that he was not anxious to assume—the duty to explain what his vision means, to impose a single interpretation on these events—while at the same time allowing him to assume responsibility for this dream as his and his alone. Keats would become the embodied, and embodying, scribe of vision, its faithful witness and scrupulous artificer, but not its high philosopher.

To understand Keat's decision to frame his epic material in this theatrical manner, it is essential to distinguish witnessing from two similar activities: watching and explaining. The watcher, or mere spectator, loses himself in what he sees; the witness must remain in possession of himself in order to *bear witness,* to stand by what he has seen. But the witness is not called upon to explain what he has seen—only to give an accurate account of it to the best of his ability. The lyrical chameleon poet is a watcher; the philosophical poet, at least in the Western epic tradition of Dante and Milton, is an explainer. Keats wishes to bear witness. To understand what such witnessing entails on an epic level, and how it affects the poet's sense of his identity as a poet, one must trace the development of Keats's emerging awareness of his destiny as a philosophical, rather than "camelion" poet, and particularly his changing attitudes toward Wordsworth and Milton, the two great English exemplars of the philosophical epic tradition.

Keats's desire to "philosophize" on the human condition had been articulated as early as March 1818, in a verse-letter to J. H. Reynolds. The poet reports having suffered from "horrid moods, / Moods of one's mind!" that led him to see "too distinct into the core / Of an eternal fierce destruction"—the pain of life. He is unsure how to make sense of such unavoidable misery (*Letters*, I, 261–262):

> ... but my flag is not unfurl'd
> On the Admiral staff—and to philosophize
> I dare not yet!—Oh never will the prize,
> High reason, and the lore of good and ill
> Be my award.

It is to the attaining of that prize, the winning of "high reason" and a philosophical understanding of human "good and ill," that Keats bends his efforts in the course of the following months, in preparation for the first *Hyperion,* which he began that fall.

Not surprisingly, it is during this period, the summer of 1818, that Keats begins to place Milton as a poetic model in the same rank as Wordsworth, whom he had long admired as a profound and suggestive student of the human condition. In an oft-cited passage from a letter to Reynolds, dated May 3, 1818, where Keats compares human life to a "Mansion of Many Apartments" (I, 280–281) that he intends to explore, he praises Wordsworth's intrepid investigations of its "dark passages"—his undertaking to relieve the "burden of the Mystery" of human existence in poems like "Tintern Abbey"—and favorably contrasts the older poet's openness to experience with Milton's dogmatic Puritanism: Milton "did not think into the human heart, as Wordsworth has done." And yet, Keats goes on, "Milton as a Philosopher, had sure as great powers as Wordsworth" (I, 282). Keats has "nothing but surmises" at this point about the comparative philosophical value of each poet's work, "from an uncertainty whether Milton's apparently less anxiety for Humanity proceeds from his seeing further or no than Wordsworth: And whether Wordsworth has in truth epic passion, and martyrs himself to the human heart, the main region of his song" (I, 278–279).

The emphasis in the phrase, "epic passion," should fall on "pas-

sion." Of epic pride, Wordsworth seemed to have acquired an un-
healthy overabundance. As early as the previous February, after
having read *The Excursion,* Keats had expressed to Reynolds serious
doubts concerning the older poet. In what was to have been the middle section of his long philosophical poem on man, mind, and Nature, Wordsworth had taken it upon himself to lighten the burden of
the mystery a bit too imperiously for the younger poet's taste:

> It may be said that we ought to read our Contemporaries. that
> Wordsworth &c should have their due from us. but for the sake of a
> few fine imaginative or domestic passages, are we to be bullied into
> a certain Philosophy engendered in the whims of an Egotist—Every
> man has his speculations, but every man does not brood and pea-
> cock over them till he makes a false coinage and deceives himself—
> Many a man can travel to the very bourne of Heaven, and yet want
> confidence to put down his halfseeing . . . We hate poetry that has a
> palpable design upon us—and if we do not agree, seems to put its
> hand in its breeches pocket. (I, 223–224)

Keats felt that Wordsworth's egotism had led him to make, in *The
Excursion,* an *ex cathedra* statement about the human condition.
Wordsworth now seemed dissatisfied with the "half-knowledge" he
had glimpsed in "Tintern Abbey." He was unable to achieve what
Keats called "Negative Capability," a quality Keats much admired
in Shakespeare, who possessed it to an uncommon degree: the ability
to remain "in uncertainties, Mysteries, doubts, without any irritable
reaching after fact & reason" (I, 193). Keats was much happier with
the earlier Wordsworth, a passionate sojourner in experience, an ex-
plorer in "strange seas of thought," but not their cartographer.

The Wordsworth of *The Excursion* had lost touch with the passion
of human experience because he was too busy theorizing about it.
"Axioms in philosophy are not axioms until they are proved on our
pulses," Keats writes in his "Mansion of many Apartments" letter,
implying that the poet who undertakes to philosophize runs some
danger of anesthetizing himself—Milton's "apparently less anxiety
for Humanity" *may* proceed from "his seeing further" than a poet of
the heart, like the Wordsworth of "Tintern Abbey." If that is so, then
the price of philosophical insight and equanimity is too high. The
philosopher-poet must stay in touch with life in all its pain, all the
"weariness, the fever, and the fret" that go with the possession of the
"sole self."

That is what Tom's death was to teach Keats even more forcefully in December of 1818, causing him to lay *Hyperion* aside, and that is the conclusion he came to the following May, in the "Ode to a Nightingale." A poetry of pure "sensations" in which the self is annihilated, let alone a poetry of "richer entanglements" and "enthralments far more self-destroying," cannot maintain contact with disagreeables *as* disagreeables—it constantly flees them, or transmutes them into things of beauty, "intensity," "gusto." But a poetry that philosophizes *about* experience, that presents the poet's "half seeing" as absolute truth, or offers up as a vision what are merely, in Keats's own words on *Paradise Lost,* "Dogmas and superstitions" (I, 282), is just as insular and out of touch with real life. What bothers Keats about the change in Wordsworth between "Tintern Abbey" and *The Excursion* (Wordsworth, who had, in the latter, taken Milton as his own model) is what bothers the younger poet about Milton from early on: "From the Paradise Lost and the other Works of Milton," he writes Reynolds in his "Mansions" letter, "I hope it is not too presuming, even between ourselves to say, his Philosophy, human and divine, may be tolerably understood by one not much advanced in years" (I, 281).

It is remarkable, then, given his doubts about philosophy's fidelity to the painful contradictions of lived experience, and its inevitable restrictions on the poet's range of speculative empathy, that Keats should have undertaken *Hyperion,* and the rigors of its highly wrought Miltonic style, at all. He was ready to move beyond the self-indulgent and self-annihilating luxury of erotic fantasies and intense sensations, yet anxious to avoid the pitfalls of Wordsworth's philosophical egotism and "palpable design." There was a middle ground, though, what Keats later called, in his letter to George and Georgiana of March 1819, those "erroneous reasonings" which are the stuff of poetry as opposed to conventional philosophy, and which impress us even in the commonest bickering of everyday life: "Though a quarrel in the streets is a thing to be hated, the energies displayed in it are fine; the commonest Man shows a grace in his quarrel—By a superior being our reasoning[s] may take the same tone—though erroneous they may be fine" (II, 80).

If poetry cannot allow itself to take a philosophical position and remain poetry, it can at least represent that conflict of passions and opinions, that dramatic exchange of painful questionings, intense illuminations, and sorrowful resignations, those "instinctive attitudes" by which mortals guess at and, by degrees, approach such a position.

Hyperion is Keats's first attempt as a true philosopher-poet, which is to say, neither entirely one nor the other: neither a skeptic nor an illusionist, but a "superior being" who can get his readers both to enter into the fine "energies displayed" in the Titan's quarrels and to take them seriously as bearing on our own humanity, without imposing his personal opinions. Here, the poet seeks not so much to represent *the* truth about human existence (though he has his opinions and they are aired through surrogates) but to represent that process by which the truth is approached. It is a process that is to be "proved on our pulses" (I, 229), an education that is to be undergone without force-fed conclusions, but "fine" in its progression, nonetheless. *Hyperion* is epic theater.

The poem's theatrical qualities, however, are "statuesque" rather than dramatic, as critics have often noted: even allowing for its truncated length, the poem appears as an almost static series of tableaux, with very little authorial comment or direction and a great deal of emotive speech making on the model of the debates among the fallen angels in Milton's Pandemonium. *Hyperion,* as it stands, is a drama of ideas, not actions. If this is the work of a philosopher-poet, then Keats seems to be telling us that it is not up to the poet to do the philosopher's work, to tell his readers what to believe or how to respond to the pain and confusion of life, but to reveal to them—and thus to make them undergo vicariously—the full range of possible responses to adversity, with as little moralizing, and apparently as little action to distract us from the debate, as possible.

In *Hyperion* Keats sets out to depict not the ephemeral "truth" of imagined beauty, as in the romances, but the enduring facts of human experience and existence. He leaves off trying to equate "truth" with a closet dream that offers an alternative "reality" to that found in society or the world at large, and instead begins to equate truth with myth, those stories on which we model our lives and which show, allegorically, the relationship of consciousness to its object: specifically, the process of growth in identity, the acquiring of an individual soul. "Do you not see how necessary a World of Pains and troubles is to school an Intelligence and make it a soul? A Place where the heart must feel and suffer in a thousand diverse ways! Not merely is the Heart a Hornbook, It is the Minds bible, it is the Minds experience, it is the teat from which the Mind or intelligence sucks its identity—As various as the Lives of Men are—so various become their souls, and thus does God make individual beings, Souls, Identical Souls of the sparks of his own essence" (II, 102–103).

Kenneth Muir, in his seminal essay "The Meaning of *Hyperion*," first cited this passage from the journal-letter of April 1819 as "in a sense an interpretation" of *Hyperion:* "Here Keats was trying to find a purpose in human suffering, and setting up as an ideal the disinterested and sympathetic sharing of the sorrows of others."[46] But as Stuart Sperry observes, the "supreme concern" of *Hyperion,* as of "To Autumn," is its "involvement with process," not "purpose."[47] Unlike Milton or the Wordsworth of *The Excursion,* Keats does not preach in his epic, despite the tendency of critics to identify his views with those of Oceanus in book II: "My voice is not a bellows unto ire," the fallen lord of the sea warns the resentful Titans in their misery. "Yet listen, ye who will, whilst I bring proof / How ye, perforce, must be content to stoop: / And in the proof much comfort will I give, / If ye will take that comfort in its truth" (II, 176–180). But of course, such proof brings no comfort. "We fall by course of Nature's law, not force / Of thunder, or of Jove," Oceanus declares (181–182), and later "for 'tis the eternal law / That first in beauty should be first in might" (228–229). However much Keats may agree with such stoic arguments, he does not pretend that they can assuage the Titans' pain or rage. "Knowledge is Sorrow," he writes in his "Mansions" letter, reversing the famous phrase of Byron's Manfred: it is not comfort.

Had *Hyperion* been finished, events would probably have borne out Oceanus' predictions: as "sophist and sage" (168), he is the Apollonius of the piece, here to burst the Titans' last delusive bubble. But the point of putting this speech into the mouth of Oceanus is precisely to save Keats from having to make this point as epic narrator. Keats lets other Titans have their say as well—Saturn and Enceladus in opposition to Oceanus, Clymene in support—and we are encouraged to share in their fury, defiance, confusion, sorrow, and despair. The reader is not allowed to forego the experience, first, of the giants' dismay, next, of their newfound anger, and last, of their resurrected hopes, inspired by the appearance of the yet unfallen Hyperion at the end of book II.

The true philosopher-poet is the sage as showman, making us go "the same steps" as the characters he creates while they grope their way through life's dark passages, perhaps to no end. The poet thus becomes half-Daedelus, half-Impressario, drawing us into labyrinths of the mind and soaring dreams that can transform our self-understanding. In the portrait of Apollo "dying into life" under the gaze of Mnemosyne at the conclusion of the *Hyperion* fragment, Keats offers us an image of what such dreams comprise: an awareness of the pageant of human myth and history. "Knowledge enormous makes a God of me," cries Apollo (III, 113–120):

Names, deeds, gray legends, dire events, rebellions,
Majesties, sovran voices, agonies,
Creations and destroyings, all at once
Pour into the wide hollows of my brain,
And deify me, as if some blithe wine
Or bright elixir peerless I had drunk,
And so become immortal . . .

Keats implies that Apollo will redeem all the agonies that the Titans have suffered and will suffer, in their coming wars with the Olympians, by making from their pain the poetry and myth that will enlighten and inspire generations yet unborn.

But the philosopher-poet must do more than simply tell his dreams: he must also stand by them and show that he is qualified to do so. In *The Fall of Hyperion* Keats takes the place of Apollo and, using Dante's *Purgatorio* as his model,[48] proves himself a poet by undergoing his own purgatorial trial before the eyes of the goddess of memory, now no longer Mnemosyne, a beneficent Greek deity, but Moneta, a sterner Roman. The process of Apollo's deification in the earlier poem turns out to have been an allegory of the process of Keats's own awakening to the significance of the Titan's story, an awakening depicted in *The Fall* without the use of a surrogate. Once admitted among the poetical elect, Keats is himself enabled to see, and to relate, the tragic story of the Titans.

See, relate, but not explain. The emphasis on showing in *Hyperion* is even more pronounced in *The Fall,* where epic literally becomes visionary theater. We find frames within frames, a vision within a dream "now purposed to rehearse" (I, 16): to retell, certainly, but the word also suggests a dramatization conjured up for the mind's eye with the "fine spell of words" (I, 9). The way in which this vision is depicted—as something *in* Moneta's mind that can nevertheless be directly witnessed by the poet—reflects the "theatrical" assumptions implicit in Keats's notions of poetic narration in general. It further reflects the way in which the Lockean view of the mind as a theater or camera obscura—which eventually helped to shape the Romantic theater's strict adaptation to an empirical model of the mind—permeates Keats's concept of narrative. More clearly than in *Hyperion* it shows to what extent Keats has modified his Miltonic vision with a strong admixture of Shakespeare, the quintessential poet of Negative Capability.[49]

In Keats's descriptions of Moneta's secret knowledge, mental space is translated into a physical, theatrical space. The poet seems to conceive of the goddess's vision as something that literally fills the area enclosed by her skull. Moneta tells the poet: "The scenes / Still swooning vivid through my globed brain / With an electral changing misery / Thou shalt with those dull mortal eyes behold" (I, 244–247). Miriam Allott observes that "globed" probably refers to the "lobes of the brain," an assocation surviving from Keats's days as a medical student.[50] Certainly, "electral," meaning "electrical," has a contemporary physiological meaning as well. But Keats's vocabulary is also cameral. "At the view of sad Moneta's brow," he writes, "I ached to see what things the *hollow brain* / Behind enwombed: what *high tragedy* / In the *dark secret chambers of her skull* / Was *acting*" (I, 275–279; italics added). The poet seeks to be admitted to the theater of Moneta's mind. "Hollow brain" echoes the "wide hollows" of Apollo's brain in book III of *Hyperion,* into which is "poured" a godlike knowledge. "Let me *behold*," not "hear," entreats the new Apollo, "what *in thy brain* so ferments to and fro" (I, 289–290).

This theater of a godlike mind is at first "curtained . . . in mysteries" by Moneta's veils. But once the "curtains" are parted, the position of the poet—and of Moneta herself, in relation to the "high tragedy" of Keats's former epic, now unfolding in the goddess' skull—is exactly parallel to that of an audience in a theater with relation to the play on stage. All the action of the Titans' epic takes place as though in a charmed space that is immediately present, ostensibly one with that occupied by its "audience," the poet and the goddess, but in practice discontinuous. The novice and the Mother of Memory are not present, not "there" for the Titans at all. They may speak, but cannot be heard; they may gaze, but cannot be seen. Like the poet in stanza 22 of "St. Agnes," who obliquely addresses the reader at his side as he calls on "young Porphyro" to "prepare," so Moneta speaks in the ear of the newborn visionary (I, 300–310):

> . . . Then Moneta's voice
> Came brief upon mine ear,—"So Saturn sat
> When he had lost his realms."—Whereon there grew
> A power within me of enormous ken,
> To see as a god sees, and take the depth

Of things as nimbly as the outward eye
Can size and shape pervade. The lofty theme
At those few words hung vast before my mind,
With half unravel'd web. I set myself
Upon an eagle's watch, that I might see,
And seeing ne'er forget . . .[51]

There is an apparent contradiction between the way the poet characterizes his newfound power and the way he represents it. We would
naturally expect that seeing "as a god sees" *should* mean seeing into
"the depth / Of things," into their meaning, their hidden causes and
necessity, and thus relieving "the burden of the Mystery." Yet Keats
here represents seeing "in depth" as seeing *solely* with "the outward
eye," as though "upon an eagle's watch," the way an avid spectator
in a theater "might see, / And seeing ne'er forget" a memorable performance. I suggest that to "*take* the depth / Of things" is not necessarily to *pierce* them, just as taking the depth of the ocean is not the
same as diving into it. Keats is saying that his reach exceeds his
grasp, and that the real task at hand is, in any case, not to explain
but to remember, and thence to re-create. The notion of copying or
showing *over again* is reinforced by the image of the "lofty theme"
hanging vast before the poet's mind "with half-unravelled web." It
is up to the visionary poet to reweave the loosened threads of this
epic tapestry so that all may see it; he is not to augment it with his
own embroidered gloss on what it all means. He is its witness, not its
interpreter.

In *The Fall* epic theater defeats the impulse toward epic philosophy. When we see life as a "high tragedy," "as a god sees," or as "superior beings," we do not see it as an argument but as the
profoundest species of "amusement," speculation, suggestion. It will
not appear as a congeries of objects and others ordered in relation to
a finite point of view that admits certain conclusions only to deny
others. To a god, as *opposed* to a philosopher, all choices must remain
open, all conclusions possible, all experiences valid.

But for the poet, at least, the choice of entering into these experiences must be stoically declined. To witness is not simply to watch.
Though the *reader* is, apparently, supposed to identify with the various Titans in their distress, epic theater does not result in "camelion"
self-annihilation for the poet himself. Epic theater defeats not only
epic philosophy, but the impulse toward lyrical empathy as well. A
phrase like "half-unravel'd web" recalls the rainbow unwoven by

"cold philosophy" in *Lamia:* reweaving the fabric of Keats's epic theme will require the most painstaking attention to each thread and to the pattern of the whole. Apollo's "dying into life" in *Hyperion,* so suggestive of an intense, empathic imaginative experience, is transformed into a much more laborious, wearisome, and taxing imposition in *The Fall,* as Keats assumes Apollo's role. The poet remains, throughout, in full possession of himself, reflexive, acutely aware of his task. To "see, / And seeing ne'er forget" turns out to be an ordeal of self-consciousness for mere mortals such as he, not an ecstasy of self-oblivion. Keats describes the experience of watching Thea at the feet of motionless Saturn as an eternal agony of anticipation (I, 382–399):

Long, long, those two were postured motionless,
Like sculpture builded up upon the grave
Of their own power. A long awful time
I look'd upon them; still they were the same;
The frozen God still bending to the earth,
And the sad Goddess weeping at his feet;
Moneta silent. Without stay or prop
But my own weak mortality, I bore
The load of this eternal quietude,
The unchanging gloom, and the three fixed shapes
Ponderous upon my senses a whole moon.
For by my burning brain I measured sure
Her silver seasons shedded on the night,
And every day by day methought I grew
More gaunt and ghostly. Oftentimes I pray'd
Intense, that death would take me from the vale
And all its burthens. Gasping with despair
Of change, hour after hour I curs'd myself.

This is what it is really like for a mortal to experience the "moments big as years" (*Hyperion,* I, 64) that pass in the "dreams of gods"—and still remain himself. In *The Fall,* watching, the former avenue to self-annihilation, becomes literally both a *bearing* of witness, as of a heavy load "ponderous upon [the] senses," and a *standing by* what is watched. Unlike the chameleon poet, the philosopher-poet must bear the experience of such eternal gloom with no "stay or prop" but his own "weak mortality," his sole self. Keats remains aware of his separateness from the events he witnesses, and he makes us aware of that separateness as well.[52] He is there to offer us this vision, but not to partake of it. He is there to witness *these* disagreeables as disagreeable, but not to make them—or himself—evaporate.

It is a precarious balance that Keats maintains in *The Fall.* He will not bully us into accepting his interpretation of this tale, whatever that may be. But he will not allow himself to disappear either. He is before us throughout the first half of canto I, not hidden by darkness, not at our side, not "in the wings," and not disguised in the costume of a Porphyro or a Ludolph or a Lycius. If he is not comfortable with the burden he must bear, he is at last comfortable with the bearer. Here lies Keats's principal motivation for inserting himself into the recast version of *Hyperion,* contradictory as it may sound (and Keats was probably aware of the contradiction): his need to convince his audience that, as a poet, he did not need their approval. In Moneta's acceptance of him, her belief in him, lies the salvation of the poet's "etherial" self, the self that relies on no others to sustain it, the self he "knows to be."[53] And in his audience's silent, unacknowledged acquiescence in this ritual of election lies the vindication of that newly confirmed, and now embodied, self-image before the world.

Moneta, as I suggested in Chapter 3, represents in one sense an absolute and unqualified source of self-awareness, an internalized and accepting parental presence enabling Keats to assume an independent adult personality that can do without unqualified love and adoration in the eyes of others, withstand their condescension and disapproval.[54] What is represented in *The Fall* is the poet's election by this authoritative figure to the class of immortal poets, as opposed to the "Pet-lambs" or "little poets" or indolent dreamers of the literary crowd. It is a class distinguished not by its members' appearance, but by their ability to create things of lasting significance for passing generations: to *tell* what they dream, and to stand by what they tell. In this way they make their dreams a part of human history (I, 1–18):

> Fanatics have their dreams, wherewith they weave
> A paradise for a sect; the savage too
> From forth the loftiest fashion of his sleep
> Guesses at heaven: pity these have not
> Trac'd upon vellum or wild Indian leaf
> The shadows of melodious utterance.
> But bare of laurel they live, dream, and die;
> For Poesy alone can tell her dreams,

With the fine spell of words alone can save
Imagination from the sable charm
And dumb enchantment. Who alive can say
"Thou art no poet; may'st not tell thy dreams"?
Since every man whose soul is not a clod
Hath visions, and would speak, if he had lov'd
And been well nurtured in his mother tongue.
Whether the dream now purposed to rehearse
Be poet's or fanatic's will be known
When this warm scribe my hand is in the grave.

Thus does Keats offer us not a portrait of the poet as a lover in
search of love but himself in the synecdoche of a transcribing hand,
the token of his witness. Telling his dream will take the form of an
action, writing, the poet will take the form of its agent, the writer;
and the truth of both will appear in the continuum of history, where
action and agent will persist only as long as the artifact they leave
behind remains a friend to man. "Art thou not of the dreamer
tribe?" asks Moneta, puzzled by Keats's defense of the poet as "a
sage; / A humanist, physician to all men" (I, 189–190). "The poet
and the dreamer are distinct," she agrees, "Diverse, sheer opposite,
antipodes. / The one pours out a balm upon the world, / The other
vexes it" (I, 198-202). Debate continues over what passages of Moneta's discourse were meant by Keats to be included in the final version of *The Fall,* and over the logic or illogic of the shade's murky
distinctions among poets, dreamers, visionaries, and philanthropists.[55] It is not my purpose to dwell on these problems. Clearly, however Moneta's argument is taken apart, the poet has been granted
admission to and recognized as a member of an elite priesthood of
witnesses, devoted not simply to imagining and admiring but to
recording and preserving the sacred memory of past heroes and heroic events.

The need to demonstrate his election and to assert his independence from his audience's expectations of him as a solipsistic dreamer
or a fanatic is what motivates Keats's most extreme example of authorial intrusion. Once the poet has been admitted into the presence
of Moneta, it only remains for the veils to be parted and for her own
face to be revealed to him in order for his election to be confirmed.
And yet, when the veils are withdrawn, they reveal not an answering
glance, but an inward preoccupation that draws the poet into its
vortex (I, 264-271; italics added):

But for her eyes I should have fled away.
They held me back, with a benignant light,
Soft mitigated by divinest lids
Half closed, *and visionless entire they seem'd*
Of all external things—they saw me not,
But in blank splendor beam'd like the mild moon,
Who comforts those she sees not, who knows not
What eyes are upward cast . . .

While some kind of recognition has been granted, it is significant that Moneta's gaze should turn out to be "visionless entire . . . of all *external* things." The poet's conscious *presence* is accepted, but the merely embodied self, the self as a passive object of others' perceptions, is not recognized. The reason for this curious and unexpected turn is obvious, once we think about it: the poet seeks recognition but not of his ordinarily embodied self—such attention has, as we know, always made him uncomfortably self-conscious. And yet, Keats refuses to envision a more flattering stand-in here. He wants to be accepted into a community of visionaries, literally, "seers," not would-be celebrities. At the moment of truth the poet receives confirmation not of his physical resemblance to the conventional image of a poet (a resemblance quite tenuous in any case for a "little poet," whose preoccupation with that resemblance can turn him into a "Pet-lamb") but of his credentials, his power to see and to bear witness, in the act of writing, to what he sees. Thus, rather than dwelling on his outward form, Moneta, with her "blank" eyes, draws the poet into a fellowship of witnesses (I, 282–284):

. . . "Shade of Memory!"
Cried I, with act adorant at her feet,
"By all the gloom hung round thy fallen house,
By this last temple, by the golden age,
By great Apollo, thy dear foster child,
And by thy self, forlorn Divinity,
The pale Omega of a wither'd race,
Let me behold, according as thou said'st,
What in thy brain so ferments to and fro."—
No sooner had this conjuration pass'd
My devout lips, than side by side we stood,
(Like a stunt bramble by a solemn pine)
Deep in the shady sadness of vale . . .

Here Keats's earlier epic, *Hyperion* proper, begins.

"Like a stunt bramble"—Keats's humorous, self-deprecating reference to his embodied self signals a new confidence on the part of the "little poet" that what there is *in* him stands far taller than "five feet hight," and that it will prove itself so in the poems he writes in future years. Keats has finally overcome his need for recognition in the stereotypical and popular romantic role of poet and lover, content in the knowledge that he will achieve higher and more lasting fame for what he is privileged to have seen, and to have told, than for how others may have seen him, or for the tales they told about him.

This Living Hand

Why was *The Fall* left unfinished? The answers are many. "There were too many Miltonic inversions in it," Keats wrote to Reynolds on September 21, 1819: "Miltonic verse cannot be written but in an artful or rather artist's humour. I wish to give myself up to other sensations" (II, 167). The poet was tiring of his "eagle's watch," longing again for the luxurious self-oblivion of intense sensations. This is one explanation. But most Keatsians, while admitting that Keats had wearied of laborious Miltonic composition, cite additional causes for the abandonment of *The Fall.*

One was structural. As Muir points out, Keats "had already used up the climax of the first poem [Apollo's deification] in the first canto of the second version [the scene of Keats's election]."[56] Another reason was the inappropriateness of the allegorical mode as a medium for the poet's new, open-ended vision. Sperry argues, for instance, that *The Fall's* insurmountable allegorical rigidity could not accommodate Negative Capability, Keats's need to remain open to "the full complexity of man's experience."[57] Morris Dickstein believes that Keats's new humanism simply could not be conveyed by means of the inhuman allegorical figures of the Titans.[58] In addition, as Vendler points out, there was the problem of mixing theatrical, lyrical, and epic genres.[59]

To all of these, yet another reason must be added: Keats's dramatically insistent illustration of his freedom from what the world may think of him is, paradoxically, still another admission that he cares what it thinks of him. If one of the main points of transforming *Hyperion* was to offer, to his public, visionary evidence of his election to the class of true poets, not dreamers or pet-lambs, then the very need to offer evidence, Keats seems to have realized, was itself a sign of insecurity. Like Wordsworth writing of Simon Lee or the discharged soldier, Keats was seeking an audience for his demonstration of acknowledgment by an independent Other. Once this point had been made, once his election had been acted out, there was little reason for Keats to continue in a style, genre, and mode of figuration so unsuited to his new vision of life, mortal process, and evolving consciousness.

In the last of the odes, "To Autumn," which he wrote only days before he declared to Reynolds his abandonment of *Hyperion*, Keats's literary persona disappears entirely. Commentators on the two *Hyperions*, with the notable exception of Dickstein, see "To Autumn" as bearing the first fruits of Keats's new understanding of himself as a poet.[60] In the context of the odes that preceded it, Vendler argues, the poem represents "the moral admission of ineluctable sacrificial process"; and the poet's "resolve to enter the open fields of the reaped furrow" shows the Keats of past embowered bliss generously adopting "the whole world—not a sequestered portion of it—as the territory of growth and art."[61] Most striking, in line with Keats's new determination to take his place in the world as the author and not the embodied object of vision, "To Autumn" makes its profoundly philosophical point without the least vestige of authorial self-intrusion (in the first person), self-address (in the second), or self-reference (in the third).

"To Autumn" demonstrates *that* the poet is a patient watcher but does not show us the poet watching. He is like the figure of Autumn herself, who, in the second stanza, "by a cyder-press, with patient look . . . watchest the last oozings hours by hours." The personification is an emblem of Keats's own renewed dedication to the "eagle's watch" of a poetry that tries to relieve the burden of the mystery but without the preoccupation with election, or the agony of mortal impatience for immortal revelations that is so prominent a part of *The Fall*—without even the need to offer speculative interpretations of the processes observed. Keats's authorial self-consciousness appears not in the form of the self embodied as a character or persona in his verse but in the form of that invisible but active eye which alights on a symbol of the poet's own artificial, even premeditated, devices: the press transmutes nature into a product of human skill and ingenuity that nourishes the body as Keats would have his poetry nourish the soul.

In "To Autumn" Keats is not an actor on his own stage, nor a passive audience, but the patient witness and most unobtrusive

"Stager" of these representations. I can think of no more poignant epitaph for the poet than the fragment of verse he left on the recto of the manuscript of *The Jealousies,* one of his most meretricious works. Allott suggests that the fragment was to have been included as part of a speech in Keats's unfinished play, *King Stephen:*

> This living hand, now warm and capable
> Of earnest grasping, would, if it were cold
> And in the icy silence of the tomb,
> So haunt thy days and chill thy dreaming nights
> That thou would wish thine own heart dry of blood,
> So in my veins red life might stream again,
> And thou be conscience-calm'd. See, here it is—
> I hold it towards you.

I like to think that Keats never meant to include these lines, written at the end of 1819, in any longer work. Standing alone, they reveal the poet as neither chameleon nor philanthropist, neither pet-lamb nor philosopher, but as mortal scribe and signatory, a responsible witness to the visionary seriousness of his otherwise ephemeral imaginings. We detect the note of resentment toward us, the living, the suggestion that surviving this dead hand, we somehow incur a debt to be repaid—to make these bones live, this blood flow again, with the "red life" of our own embodied beings. Now dead indeed, this hand, "warm and capable," haunts us with its "earnest grasping"—with what it wrought by the pen it held—and the writer extends it as if to seek our own living warmth to rejuvenate it. Whether it recorded the sublime or the mundane, the good or the bad, the true or the false, poet's dream or fanatic's, the hand that wrote these words, though now "cold / And in the icy silence of the tomb," left its lasting mark on other minds, and it belonged to John Keats.

5 On Strange Seas of Thought: Reflections on the Post-Romantic Self as Mind

I walk through the long schoolroom questioning;
A kind old nun in a white hood replies;
The children learn to cipher and to sing,
To study reading—books and histories,
To cut and sew, be neat in everything
In the best modern way—the children's eyes
In momentary wonder stare upon
A sixty-year-old smiling public man.

I dream of a Ledaen body . . .

In the brief gap between the first and second stanzas of "Among School Children," the man who called himself "the last romantic" moves from finite self-awareness to mythopoeic vision with swift and breathtaking effortlessness. In an instant this "sixty-year-old smiling public man," this "paltry thing, / A tattered coat upon a stick," as he refers to himself in "Sailing to Byzantium," turns the young audience staring at him (and later, their kind old nun) into the stuff of his own soul's song:

And thinking of that fit of grief or rage
I look upon one child or t'other there
And wonder if she stood so at that age—
For even daughters of the swan can share
Something of every paddler's heritage—
And had that colour upon cheek or hair,
And thereupon my heart is driven wild:
She stands before me as a living child.

The inhabitants of the world surrounding William Butler Yeats, an Irish senator on an official school visit, suddenly become part of his dream, with barely a flicker of effort and not a second thought. Little more than a century after Keats's death, Yeats exhibits a supreme confidence in his gifts, keeping his visionary sense intact and independent of his embodied image, even giving a heightened impression of his imaginative integrity by reason of the striking discontinuity we observe between the "public man" he appears to be and the visionary poet we know he is.

The impression of discontinuity, however, is as important as it was for Gray's elegist. Yeats's double image reinforces his reader's sense of being a privileged intimate, not an outsider. Like his Romantic predecessors, Yeats convinces us that the true self cannot be adequately embodied, that physical self-representation borders on misrepresentation and distortion of the person within. For Yeats, as for Wordsworth, Coleridge, and Keats before him, what his audience sees is not the seer. The nun and her class are Yeats's "hoary-headed Swain," mundane empiricists of identity unable to penetrate to his visionary soul. They are our antitypes, counterexamples for our own kindred spirits. They show us how *not* to behold, as we pass from sight to insight, from the confrontations of social intercourse to the intimacies of interior monologue.

Yeats never doubts that such an audience of intimates exists, or can be created, among his readers, but Wordsworth, Coleridge, and Keats never seemed completely certain that it does, or can. Ever suspicious of their public, the early Romantics could not quite put it out of their thoughts. They understood the importance of maintaining a sure sense of self over the long run, and understood, too, where it was to be found. "Scanty the hour and few the steps beyond the Bourn of Care," writes Keats in a verse-letter to Benjamin Bailey (*Letters*, I, 345):

> Scanty the hour and few the steps because a longer stay
> Would bar return and make a Man forget his mortal way.
> O horrible! to lose the sight of well-remember'd face,
> Of Brother's eyes, Of Sister's Brow, constant to every place.

"One hour half ideot he stands by mossy waterfall," Keats continues, "But in the very next he reads his Soul's memorial" (I, 345).

At the bottom of the visionary well lie self-diffusion, extinction, insanity, death. Keats, like Wordsworth and Coleridge, understood why, when "at the Cable's length / Man feels the gentle Anchor" of familiar eyes and faces pulling him back, he "gladdens in its strength" (I, 345). Oppressive anxieties about the interior abyss on the one hand, and about self-finitude on the other, could be obviated by achieving the proper kind of recognition, whether from family—a sister, a wife—or from a devoted, though perhaps small, audience of sympathetic souls. Thus Wordsworth's distinction between "the Public" and "the People"; thus Coleridge's ingratiating "conversational tone"; thus Keats's ambivalent contempt for the readership whose notice he craves.

Later poetic manifestations of the solipsistic temptations and horrors that beset the Romantics are not hard to find in the ensuing century. Keats's dream palaces presage Tennyson's claustrophobic "Palace of Art"; Wordsworth's solitaries and Coleridge's grimly robotic mariners anticipate the "hollow men" of Eliot; and who is Arnold's "Scholar Gypsy," that imaginary and invisible peripatetic voyeur, if not a reincarnation of Wordsworth's sanguine Wanderer, a *spectator ab extra* even more immaculately uninvolved in the spectacle of life than his predecessor?

Rather than pursue the evolution of nineteenth-century English poetry, however, I would like to offer some parting thoughts on the novel. If poets remained fixed on the self as mind, novelists turned to the more vexing question of the self as a mind making its way in a society that belongs to others. In fiction the Romantic concern to make the true self real without compromising its integrity led to the rise of a literature preoccupied with the drama of reputations, rather than of deliberate actions, and with the ironies generated by the overlapping of various otherwise isolated, and not always compatible, "theaters" of self-representation and acknowledgment. It was not until the twentieth century, with the appearance of Joyce and Woolf, that the novel was to follow poetry down into the labyrinths of consciousness, to the presumed seat of true identity, which in *Finnegan's Wake*, at least, turned out to be the soul of "Everybody," as the Romantics had foreseen.

One finds, of course, in the novels of the Regency and Victorian periods, the assumption of a radical split between the psychological self and the social self, giving rise to endless opportunities for the sifting of motivation, the probing of hypocrisy and self-deception. And yet the great issues of the Victorian novel are not, as is so often asserted, the psychology and motivation of character, though these are important and arresting issues. Rather, they concern the ways in which qualities of character appear in the eyes of different persons and in different situations, and the problem of demarcating, and protecting from violation or betrayal, a most-intimate-circle of self-revelation in which "true" character can be expressed, acknowledged, and appreciated, that is, made "real."

In this respect Jane Austen's novels more accurately forecast the winds of change that will blow through the fiction of the century to follow than do more conventional weather vanes of prose narrative such as *Pamela* or *Tristram Shandy. Pamela* is revolutionary in its psychological emphasis and in Richardson's exploitation of first-person point of view, certainly, but it lacks the Victorian novel's fascination with secret knowledge of other people, and with the making or breaking of reputations. In Richardson's book everything hinges on the performance of a public and ritualized action: "Will Mr. B marry Pamela?" While there is a great distance between the "Mr. B" the world knows and the "Mr. B" Pamela portrays in her letters home, there is no tension generated by this difference. What the world thinks of Mr. B is of little moment.

In contrast, although Elizabeth Bennett's eventual marriage to Darcy is of considerable interest and importance to the plot of *Pride and Prejudice,* the reader's main interest is held throughout by the tensions that arise from misunderstandings concerning self-representation in different social contexts. The Darcy Eliza meets at the provincial dance turns out to be quite different from the Darcy his friends know and whom she meets later, on his own estate. The role of Wickham, who soils Darcy's reputation by false innuendo and insinuation, is of the utmost importance in advancing the plot. His presence makes clearer the fearful jeopardy reputations are placed in when strangers meet in contexts incompatible with one or the other's identity. As a stranger, Darcy is made singularly vulnerable to such gossip, and while we are given insights throughout the novel into what Elizabeth is thinking, we are given no hints as to what thoughts are going through the head of Darcy: who he truly is appears eventually through Elizabeth's contacts with him in situations that tend to increase in their degree of intimacy, that is, exclusiveness.

Marriage, in Austen's work as in George Eliot's, represents the ultimate circle of intimacy, and this may explain why marriage is of such importance in the novels of these two authors. Only to a spouse could the real personality within, as opposed to the public self, emerge fully, and not so much in direct professions of love as in indirect, often unconscious or inadvertent revelations of character. Living in wedlock, we let down our guard, become absentminded, less self-conscious. Dorothea's marriage to Causaubon in *Middlemarch* reveals him as he "truly" is, not because he feels it safe to confess his uncertainties and doubts concerning his scholarly competence but because these anxieties become more and more manifest in his observed behavior. His personality is revealed without his even suspecting it.

Family life in general assumes an exaggerated importance, compared to its role in earlier prose fiction, as a charmed circle for the moral and emotional support of the true self. A wholly new figure arises—Mr. Wemmick, the Janus-faced clerk whose personality depends entirely on his domestic or business environment. And another fascinating figure arises at this time, the Outsider, or Stranger, who seems to haunt Victorian fiction. This is a usually disreputable character possessed of secret knowledge that can affect the reputation and fortunes of a prominent character. Magwitch and Orlick are prime examples in Dickens's *Great Expectations*, a book, like *Middlemarch*, that takes as its theme the harrowing tensions generated by false self-representations. In Eliot's greatest novel a similar figure intrudes. The horror we feel at Raffles' appearance in the town of Middlemarch arises in no small measure from our awareness of his familiarity with a Bulstrode that even the banker's wife does not know. The charmed circle of marriage, the most intimate circle for the representation and acknowledgment of personal identity, has been violated.

The novel of the nineteenth century is concerned primarily, like the Romantics themselves, with the drama of the "true" self becoming "real" in the eyes of its proper audience. The tragedy of heroines like Isabel Archer or Tess Durberville is the same tragedy that faced many contemporary women: that to become real, they had to sacrifice their true selves. Isabel Archer's decision, in *The Portrait of a Lady*, to stay with the cold and brutal Osmond reduces itself, finally, to her need to remain whole and consistent in her commitment to the life choices that define her. Far more heroic a character than Keats's Ludolph, she does not take the coward's way out, but lives her lie.

Isabel's situation is complicated, like so many others in James's fiction, by the crossing of class lines and the incompatibility of cultural values, themes common in later Victorian literature. *Tess of the d'Urbervilles* is Hardy's bitter comment on the limitations to identity imposed by class, but also on those imposed by one's past. To have fallen once is, in both Angel Clare's and Alec d'Urberville's eyes, to have become a "fallen woman," and Tess cannot escape this imposed identity no matter where she hides. It is not the deed but its being found out that has destroyed her by book's end. It is what others—

Angel and Alec, and finally society itself—make of the deed as it reflects upon her "character." To the extent that this interpretation is accepted by Tess, she acquiesces in her own destruction, and therein, perhaps, lies the essential tragedy of her story: that Tess cannot discover and maintain a sense of herself unencumbered by the poison of others' points of view. She cannot see herself except as others see her. Murdering Alec, removing the most intimate mirror of a self she loathes, is her only recourse.

After Romanticism, heroism in the novel is expressed in the struggle to overcome the self-defining strictures of others' opinions, tragedy in the succumbing to such opinions, to the point of death, or death-in-life. The hero's most powerful adversary is the secret stranger, the inimical intimate—Lord Jim's "Gentleman" Brown, Tess's Alec, Isabel's Madame Merle—and his or her most powerful weapon against the enemy is the Beloved, the sympathetic Other, the "kindred Spirit"—Dorothea's Will Ladislaw, Huck's Jim, Catherine's Heathcliff. Clearly, those who wrote in the watershed of Romanticism, novelists as well as poets, could not put away the problem of the divided self, its precariously achieved integrity, its vulnerability to history, its often bewildering metamorphoses in the social crucible. The self was now adrift on a wide, wide ocean, "paved with innumerable faces," as De Quincey describes them in one of the dream sequences from *Confessions of an English Opium Eater:* "faces imploring, wrathful, despairing, surg[ing] upwards by thousands, by myriads, by generations," upon which "the mind tossed and surged," helpless to defend itself.

The Romantics "were the first that ever burst" into that sea. Coming to terms with the breakdown of long-standing traditions of decorum, class, profession—all the reassuring determinants of one's "place" in the world—they lived to see the identity of the person lose its anchorage in the wider society. Some of them, like John Clare, simply drifted away; some, like Southey, foundered close to shore. But the great poets took a bearing on the horizons of the known world, returning from "strange seas of thought" with "cloth of woven crimson, gold, and jet," or with tales of "a sunless sea" and "a Presence which is not to be put by," news never won without cost.

Notes
Index

Notes

1. The Idea of the Self as Mind

1. Northrop Frye, "Towards Defining an Age of Sensibility," in *Fables of Identity: Studies in Poetic Mythology* (New York: Harcourt Brace Jovanovich, 1963), pp. 130–137.

2. Amy Louise Reed, *The Background of Gray's "Elegy"* (New York: Columbia University Press, 1924), p. 216: "For the reader of 1751," she writes, "it was a marvelous synthesis of the thoughts and feelings of the melancholy poetry produced in the past fifty years, which had been so widely read and admired." "There is little that is either remarkable or new in Gray's poetry," writes D. S. Bland in "Gray and the Spirit of Romanticism," *Cambridge Journal*, 2 (1948):169–180, attacking the notion that Gray's " 'leukocholy' and egoism" anticipate in some way the flowering of Romanticism. John Draper, in *Funeral Elegy and the Rise of English Romanticism* (New York: New York University Press, 1929), goes so far as to admit that the "Elegy" does foreshadow "the reminiscent pensiveness of Wordsworth and of Keats," but cautions that such anticipations are rather fortuitous than prophetic.

3. Eleanor M. Sickels, *The Gloomy Egoist: Moods and Themes of Melancholy from Gray to Keats* (New York: Columbia University Press, 1932), p. 93.

4. Gray's poems are cited, by line number, from *The Complete Poems of Thomas Gray, English, Latin and Greek,* ed. H. W. Starr and J. R. Hendrickson (London: Oxford University Press, 1966).

5. Fredric Bogel, "Structure and Substantiality in Later Eighteenth-Century Literature," *Studies in Burke and His Time,* 15 (Winter 1973–74):143. Bogel expands his approach in the recently published *Literature and Insubstantiality in Later Eighteenth-Century England* (Princeton: Princeton University Press, 1984).

6. Keats's poems are cited, by line number, from *The Poems of John Keats,* ed. Jack Stillinger (Cambridge, Mass.: Harvard University Press, 1978).

7. Coleridge's poems are cited, by line number, from *Coleridge: Poetical Works,* ed. Ernest Hartley Coleridge (1912; rpt. London: Oxford University Press, 1967).

8. Unless otherwise indicated, the 1850 edition of *The Prelude* is cited throughout. Both the 1850 and the 1805 editions are cited, by book and line numbers, from *The Prelude: 1799, 1805, 1850,* ed. Jonathan Wordsworth, M.

H. Abrams, and Stephen Gill (New York: Norton, 1979). All other poems by Wordsworth are cited, by line number, from *The Poetical Works of William Wordsworth*, ed. Ernest de Selincourt and Helen Darbyshire, 5 vols. (London: Oxford University Press, 1940).

9. The sense in which I use the word "Other" has a long history in existential and phenomenological thought going back to Hegel. I accept Jacques Lacan's description of the Other in *The Language of the Self: The Function of Language in Psychoanalysis*, trans. Anthony Wilden (Baltimore: Johns Hopkins University Press, 1968), p. 31, as that entity through which one's "desire finds its meaning . . . not so much because the other holds the key to the object desired, as because the first object of desire is to be recognized by the 'other.' " The first object of desire is, by this definition, defeated in the "Elegy."

10. *The Letters of John Keats, 1814–1821*, ed. Hyder Edward Rollins, 2nd ed., 2 vols (Cambridge, Mass.: Harvard University Press, 1965), I, 387. All quotations of Keats's letters are from this edition.

11. A great deal of controversy has surrounded this crux, but I base my interpretation of "thee" on Cleanth Brooks's persuasive argument in *The Well-Wrought Urn* (London: Dennis Dobson, 1947), p. 95: "The meditation has gone on so fervently, that in talking to himself, the speaker has lost his identity as an ego." In fact, it is here that the "Elegy" most clearly shows its Romantic affinities, as the poet assumes the typical lyrical pose of one who talks to himself. Like Shelley's nightingale, he "sits in darkness and sings to cheer [his] own solitude with sweet sounds" ("A Defence of Poetry," in *Shelley's Literary and Philosophical Criticism*, ed. John Shawcross, London: Henry Frowde, 1909, p. 129).

Brooks's reading is seconded and ably defended by J. H. Sutherland, "The Stonecutter in Gray's *Elegy*," *Modern Philology*, 55 (1957):11–13, and Frank Brady, "Structure and Meaning in Gray's *Elegy*," in *From Sensibility to Romanticism: Essays Presented to Frederick A. Pottle*, ed. Frederick W. Hilles and Harold Bloom (New York: Oxford University Press, 1965), pp. 178–181. Brady provides an excellent summary of the controversy over "thee."

Other candidates for the poet's confidante include his friend, Richard West (Odell Shepherd, " 'A Youth to Fortune and to Fame Unknown,' " *Modern Philology*, 20 [1923]:347–373); some "young rustic versifier" (Herbert W. Starr, " 'A Youth to Fortune and to Fame Unknown': A Re-estimation," *Journal of English and German Philology*, 48 [1949]:97–107); and the anonymous Stonecutter who etched the epitaphs in the graveyard (Frank H. Ellis, "Gray's *Elegy*: The Biographical Problem in Literary Criticism," *PMLA*, 66 [1951]: 971–1008).

12. Bertrand H. Bronson makes this point about the young man's "wayward fancies" in "On a Special Decorum in Gray's Elegy," in *From Sensibility to Romanticism: Essays Presented to Frederick A. Pottle*, ed. Frederick W. Hilles and Harold Bloom (New York: Oxford University Press, 1965), p. 175.

13. Samuel Taylor Coleridge, *Biographia Literaria*, ed. James Engell and Walter Jackson Bate, 2 vols. (Princeton: Princeton University Press, 1983), I, 279.

14. Bogel, "Structure and Substantiality," p. 144. See also John E Sitter, "Mother, Memory, Muse, and Poetry after Pope," *ELH*, 44 (1978):312–336;

and D. V. Boyd, "Vanity and Vacuity: A Reading of Johnson's Verse Sat-
ires," *ELH*, 39 (1973):387–403. Two other excellent books on this topic have
appeared recently: Stephen D. Cox, *"The Stranger within Thee": Concepts of the
Self in Late 18th-Century Literature* (Pittsburgh: University of Pittsburgh Press,
1980) and John O. Lyons, *The Invention of the Self* (Carbondale: Southern Illinois University Press, 1978).

15. A distinction made by Lyons, who argues that the soul, which had
previously belonged to God, was replaced by the self, which belongs to the individual, and thus has no basis outside itself for assuming its own existence
(*Invention of the Self*, p. 4).

16. Two classic treatments of that history remain Basil Wiley's "Postscript:
On Wordsworth and the Locke Tradition," in *The Seventeenth Century Back-
ground: Studies in the Thought of the Age in Relation to Poetry and Religion* (New York:
Columbia University Press, 1952) and Ernest Tuveson's *The Imagination as a
Means of Grace* (Berkeley: University of California Press, 1960).

17. *The Prose Works of William Wordsworth*, ed. W. J. B. Owen and Jane
Worthington Smyser, 3 vols. (Oxford: Clarendon Press, 1974), I, 124.

18. F. G. Steiner, "Contributions to a Dictionary of Critical Terms: 'Egoism' and 'Egotism,' " *Essays in Criticism*, 2 (1952):444–452.

19. Coleridge, *Biographia Literaria*, I, 304.

20. David Hume, *Philosophical Works*, ed. T. H. Green and T. H. Grose, 4
vols. (London: Longmans, Green & Co., 1874), I, 534. Interestingly, the *Enquiry*, with its philosophical scrutiny of the insubstantial self within, appeared
in 1748, only three years before the publication of Gray's "Elegy."

21. This point is substantiated at length by Stephen D. Cox's readings of
eighteenth-century fiction in *"The Stranger within Thee."* See, e.g., p. 7.

22. Leibnitz, in the *Monadology* of 1714, had attempted to establish a universal principle of experiential harmony arising out of the interplay of the infinite plurality of individual human consciousnesses, each remaining a world
of perception unto itself. The result was metaphysically cumbersome and led
to irreconcilable contradictions. Kant, by comparison, is the soul of elegance,
and yet, like Leibnitz, he is unconcerned about the objective, embodied reality of the self. In the *Critique of Pure Reason*, he distinguishes between a "transcendental ego" or pure subject (consciousness per se) and an "empirical ego"
or subject-as-object (consciousness as embodied for itself in its contents or picture of the world). Though the first can become aware of the second, neither
can assume embodiment as something *in* the world. See *The Critique of Pure
Reason*, trans. Norman Kemp Smith (New York: St. Martin's Press, 1965), pp.
141–142, 154.

23. Robert Langbaum, *The Poetry of Experience* (London: Chatto & Windus,
1957), pp. 25–26. To the works of the so-called consciousness school of criticism we are all, I need hardly add, heavily indebted, and I especially to
Langbaum's ground-breaking early book and to Albert Gerard's *English Romantic Poetry: Ethos, Structure, and Symbol in Coleridge, Wordsworth, Shelley, and
Keats* (Berkeley: University of California Press, 1968), which defines "the main
structural principle of romantic poetry" as "the process of expansion and
contraction" of the soul: "To the romantic imagination there is no un-

bridgeable gap between self and non-self, between the soul of man and the world of matter" (p. 118).

24. With respect to the poets treated in this book, and in contrast to Langbaum's interest in the poem as a process of self-liberation and discovery, Frances Ferguson, in *Wordsworth: Language as Counter-Spirit* (New Haven: Yale University Press, 1977), notes how, for Wordsworth, language becomes a process of self-objectification and alienation. David Simpson, in *Wordsworth and the Figurings of the Real* (Atlantic Highlands, N.J.: Humanities Press, 1982), p. 11, observes that, for both Coleridge and Wordsworth, "figuration" by the imagination, while heightening the poet's sense of power over the perceived world, also radically isolated him from a community of perception. As for Keats, Christopher Ricks, in *Keats and Embarrassment* (Oxford: Oxford University Press, 1974), offers an intelligent and good-humored analysis of the difficulties and opportunities raised by the poet's precocious self-consciousness.

One of the latest and most impressive contributions to a general reassessment of the Romantic self is Frederick Garber's *The Autonomy of the Self from Richardson to Huysmans* (Princeton: Princeton University Press, 1982). See, for instance, his Preface, p. x, on "the dialectic of aloofness and association." Langbaum himself in a recent book, *The Mysteries of Identity: A Theme in Modern Literature* (New York: Oxford University Press, 1977), has come to recognize that "solipsism was the condition dreaded by the romanticists—the danger incurred by their individualism" (p. 7).

25. "What is a Poet? To whom does he address himself? And what language is to be expected from him?—He is a man speaking to men" (*Prose Works of Wordsworth*, I, 138).

26. René Descartes, *Philosophical Works*, trans. Elizabeth S. Haldane and G. R. T. Ross, 2 vols. (Cambridge: Cambridge University Press, 1911), I, 192. Descartes goes on to admit that there is a problem with using this dualistic image, since he feels "so to speak so intermingled with" his body that he *seems* "to compose with it one whole." But he rejects this sense of embodiment as illusory! "For all these sensations of hunger, thirst pain, etc. are in truth none other than certain confused modes of thought which are produced by the union and *apparent* intermingling of mind and body" (emphasis mine).

27. John Locke, *Works*, 9 vols. (London, 1824), I, 142–143. By "person," Locke understands "a thinking, intelligent being that has reason and reflection, and can consider itself as itself, the same thinking thing in different times and places." Similarly, "personal identity" consists in "the sameness of a rational being" or "consciousness," "one individual, immaterial substance" (I, 333, 334).

28. Ibid., I, 98.

29. Descartes, *Philosophical Works*, I, 155–156. For a later, phenomenological attempt to buttress the Cartesian argument for the existence of other minds, attended with many of the same difficulties, see Edmund Husserl, *Cartesian Meditations: An Introduction to Phenomenology*, trans. Dorion Cairns (The Hague: Martinus Nijhoff, 1960), pp. 108–120.

30. For a view that challenges the traditional interpretation of La Mettrie's work as purely "materialistic," see the introduction to *La Mettrie's*

"l'Homme Machine": A Study in the Origins of an Idea, ed. Abram Vartanian (Princeton: Princeton University Press, 1960).

31. *The Poetry and Prose of William Blake,* ed. David Erdman, commentary by Harold Bloom (Garden City, N.Y.: Doubleday, 1970), p. 141.

32. Ibid.

33. Jean-Paul Sartre, *The Transcendence of the Ego,* trans. Forrest Williams and Robert Kirkpatrick (New York: Noonday Press, 1957), p. 97.

34. Emil Harth, in *Windows on the Mind: Reflections on the Physical Basis for Consciousness* (New York: William Morrow & Co., 1982), insists that not even consciousness is possible without the assumption of embodiment, and that thinking and reflection may be said to occur as much in the so-called peripheral mechanisms of the nervous system—that is, throughout the body—as in the brain's highest center of thought, the neocortex (p. 101).

35. Henry James, *The Portrait of a Lady,* 2 vols. (New York: Scribner's, 1908), I, x-xi.

36. Hume, *Philosophical Works,* I, 544–545.

37. Ibid., I, 548–549.

38. The role of society and its signs in the formation of the self is stressed in William Kirkpatrick's *Selfhood and Civilization* (New York: Macmillan, 1941); in D. G. Cooper and R. D. Laing, *Reason and Violence: A Decade of Sartre's Philosophy, 1950–1960* (New York: Pantheon, 1964, see esp. p. 167); and, from an anthropological point of view, in Clifford Geertz, *The Interpretation of Cultures* (New York: Basic Books, 1973).

Two classics in the socio-psychological origins of self-consciousness remain Erving Goffman's *The Presentation of the Self in Everyday Life* (Garden City, N.Y.: Doubleday, 1959) and George Herbert Meade's *Mind, Self, and Society,* ed. Charles W. Morris (Chicago: University of Chicago Press, 1934). Both writers stress the importance of embodiment in maintaining a clear sense of identity, but Goffman often seems to reduce the self to its body, and social situations to "theater," pushing his thesis too far. Meade, however, clearly distinguishes between the idea of the self and the idea of the body as a merely physiological organism. He asserts that the self is not essential to the operations of the body, but that "the physiological organism is essential to [the self]" (pp. 136–139), above all as the means whereby consciousness becomes reflexive. The body is not the self, but the essential mediator in that relationship between consciousness and the Other through which a self is realized and becomes known to itself.

39. Maurice Merleau-Ponty, "The Child's Relations with Others," trans. W. Cobb, in *The Primacy of Perception,* ed. J. M. Edie (Evanston: Northwestern University Press, 1964), p. 127.

40. Ibid., p. 152.

41. Ibid.

42. Ibid., p. 153.

43. See R. D. Laing, *The Divided Self* (Baltimore: Penguin Books, 1965), pp. 35–36.

44. Paul Ricoeur, *The Conflict of Interpretations,* ed. Don Ihde (Evanston: Northwestern University Press, 1974), p. 112.

45. Ibid., pp. 106–107.

46. Lacan, *Language of the Self*, p. 67. Not only theorists of phenomenology and psychoanalysis, but philosophers in the positivist tradition as well have come to accept embodiment as necessary to the concept of personal identity. Thus, A. J. Ayer, in his essay, "The Concept of a Person," reprinted in *The Concept of a Person and Other Essays* (New York: St. Martin's Press, 1963), believes "that personal identity depends upon the identity of the body, and that a person's ownership of states of consciousness consists in their standing in a special relation to *the body by which he is identified*" (p. 116; emphasis mine). P. F. Strawson, in *Individuals* (London: Methuen, 1959), maintains that "the concept of the pure individual consciousness—the pure ego—is a concept that cannot exist" (p. 102).

47. Erik Erikson, *Identity, Youth and Crisis* (New York: Norton, 1968), p. 217.

48. Ibid., p. 211.

49. See particularly Erikson, *Identity*, p. 159, where he divides the process of adolescent individuation into three stages corresponding to childhood stages of self-identification: "introjection" or incorporation of another's self-image; "identification," or interaction with trustworthy representatives of a meaningful hierarchy of roles; and "identity formation," or the choice, repudiation, and assimilation of identifications first made in childhood.

50. *Prose Works of Wordsworth*, III, 481.

51 J. H. van den Berg, *The Changing Nature of Man: Introduction to a Historical Psychology: Metabletica*, trans. H. F. Crols (1961; rpt. New York: Dell, 1975), p. 170.

52. Ibid., p. 169.

53. For the literary effects of these developments in the concept of self and others, see Wylie Sypher, *The Loss of the Self in Modern Literature and Art* (New York: Vantage Books, 1964); Henri Peyre, *Literature and Sincerity* (New Haven: Yale University Press, 1963); and Lionel Trilling, *Sincerity and Authenticity* (Cambridge, Mass.: Harvard University Press, 1972). Trilling particularly notes that the "new consciousness" emerging during the Romantic period was characterized by "the negotiation of the self through role-playing" (p. 76). Two articles of central importance to the question of the Romantic poet's relation to his audience are Randy Stanford, "The Romantic Hero and that Fatal Selfhood," *Centennial Review*, 12 (1968):430–452 and Frederick Garber, "Self, Society, Value, and the Romantic Hero," *Comparative Literature*, 19 (1967):321–333. Aside from van den Berg, by far the finest sociological analysis of the changing concepts of self and identity during the late eighteenth and early nineteenth centuries is Richard Sennett's *The Fall of Public Man* (Cambridge, Mass.: Harvard University Press, 1974).

54. This is not to say that the Romantics themselves were at all sympathetic to Descartes. Thomas McFarland, in his "Coleridge and Descartes," from *Coleridge and the Pantheist Tradition* (Oxford: Clarendon Press, 1969), pp. 320–323, emphasizes the extent of disagreement and misunderstanding between a pantheistic idealist like Coleridge and a skeptic like Descartes, but also provides an accurate guide to the extent of Coleridge's, and his contemporaries', indebtedness to the Cartesian principle of the *cogito*.

55. *Compact Edition of the Oxford English Dictionary* (Oxford: Oxford University Press, 1971), p. 3642.

56. One of Langbaum's major premises in *The Poetry of Experience*.

57. A view first expressed by Edward Bostetter in *The Romantic Ventriloquists* (Seattle: University of Washington Press, 1963), pp. 66-81.

58. *The Notebooks of Samuel Taylor Coleridge*, ed. Kathleen Coburn, 3 vols. (New York: Pantheon, 1961), I, #1592.

59. Geoffrey Hartman, "Romanticism and 'Anti-Selfconsciousness,'" *Centennial Review*, 6 (1962):553–565.

60. Hegel was the first among philosophers of the early nineteenth century to perceive the necessary link between self-consciousness and other-consciousness, a view that departs radically from the post-Renaissance assumptions of his predecessors: "Self-consciousness exists in itself and for itself, in that, and by the fact that it exists for another self-consciousness; that is to say, it *is* only by being acknowledged or 'recognized'" (*The Phenomenology of Mind*, trans. J. B. Baillie, 1910; rpt. New York: Harper & Row, 1967, p. 229). In the Hegelian universe of Absolute Mind, the self's "outwardness" or physical expression is incorporated into the phenomenological dialectic as a moment in Spirit's long historical evolution toward complete self-consciousness of expression in a culture's or society's laws, religion, and art.

61. See J. Hillis Miller, *The Disappearance of God: Five Nineteenth-Century Writers* (Cambridge, Mass.: Harvard University Press, 1963), pp. 8–9.

2. Wordsworth

1. Unless otherwise indicated, the 1850 edition of *The Prelude* is cited throughout. Both the 1850 and the 1805 editions are cited, by book and line numbers, from *The Prelude: 1799, 1805, 1850*, ed. Jonathan Wordsworth, M. H. Abrams, and Stephen Gill (New York: Norton, 1979). All other poems by Wordsworth are cited, by line number, from *The Poetical Works of William Wordsworth*, ed. Ernest de Selincourt and Helen Darbyshire, 5 vols. (London: Oxford University Press, 1940).

2. See *The Prelude: 1799, 1805, 1850*, p. 493, for the original draft written in the first person.

3. David Ferry, *The Limits of Mortality: An Essay on Wordsworth's Major Poems* (Middletown, Conn.: Wesleyan University Press, 1959), p. 88.

4. Ibid.

5. Ibid., p. 53.

6. Edward Bostetter, too, detects in Wordsworth a profound, if unacknowledged, antipathy to humanity and an inability to enter fully into the sufferings of others. See his chapter on Wordsworth in *The Romantic Ventriloquists* (Seattle: University of Washington Press, 1963), pp. 52–66; Willard Sperry, in *Wordsworth's Anti-Climax* (Cambridge, Mass.: Harvard University Press, 1935), traces the later development of this aspect of Wordsworth's personality: "He does not see other human beings for what they are in themselves. This is . . .

surely nothing but the perpetuation of a temper which had been essential to the inspired years" (p. 225).

7. David Perkins, in his chapter on Wordsworth in *The Quest for Permanence* (Cambridge, Mass.: Harvard University Press, 1965), pp. 32–62, considers these moments representative of the most intense of Wordsworth's imaginative experiences, "of the sort to which we are tempted to apply the vague word, mystic" (p. 58). In them, "Wordsworth had a profounder [than ordinary] sense of oneness with the external universe," and his "feelings are so completely embodied in what he sees that the imagery of nature is also the imagery or expression of his own mood" (pp. 59–60). In a note on page 58 Perkins cites, and agrees with, R. D. Havens's use of the word "mystic" to describe such experiences in *The Mind of a Poet* (Baltimore: Johns Hopkins University Press, 1941), pp. 155–178.

Mary Moorman, in *William Wordsworth: A Biography*, vol. 1, *The Early Years, 1770–1803* (Oxford: Clarendon Press, 1957), cites the 1805 version of *The Prelude* (II, 429–430) for the earliest evidence of Wordsworth's awareness, at 17, of Nature's "one life," but traces such feelings further back, to the poet's earliest childhood, and his ability, even then, to receive into his "mind a landscape in such a manner that it was invested with the intensity of a dream" (p. 83). Havens, too, feels that these mystical experiences "had no definite beginning but were a development from the trance-like states of boyhood" (*Mind of a Poet*, p. 174).

Philosophically considered, the argument against interpreting such experience as mystical or "idealistic" was first put forth by Arthur Beatty, in *William Wordsworth: His Doctrine and Art in Their Historical Relations* (Madison: University of Wisconsin Press, 1960). Beatty's argument for an empirical relationship obtaining between mind and nature in Wordsworth's poetry is tempered by C. C. Clarke, in *Romantic Paradox: An Essay on the Poetry of Wordsworth* (London: Routledge & Kegan Paul, 1962), where he argues that Wordsworth attempted, "paradoxically," to reconcile the idealism of the landscape as shapes *in* the mind with the sense of things as real and *outside* the mind (p. 65). Melvin Rader, in *Wordsworth: A Philosophical Approach* (Oxford: Clarendon Press, 1967), pp. 81–118, details five stages in Wordsworth's intellectual development, culminating in "The Stage of Imagination and Synthetic Reason," with Beatty's empirical stage occurring in early manhood.

Certainly one of the most penetrating, sweeping, and influential studies of Wordsworth's visionary or numinous moments is still Geoffrey Hartman's *Wordsworth's Poetry, 1787–1814* (New Haven: Yale University Press, 1971), in which he argues that "the supervening consciousness" which overcomes Wordsworth at such times "is *consciousness of self raised to apocalyptic pitch*" (p. 17). This particular reading of Wordsworth, and the school of "idealism" out of which it grows, is strongly rejected by Alan Grob in *The Philosophic Mind: A Study of Wordsworth's Poetry and Thought, 1797–1805* (Columbus: Ohio State University Press, 1973). Grob specifically dismisses Hartman (p. 43) and the "pantheistic" treatment of Wordsworth in general, and reaffirms Beatty's original empirical reading of the poet on philosophical and other grounds, not always, to my mind, very convincingly.

The latest comprehensive study of Wordsworth's visionary states, their solipsistic structure, and their place in his poetry is Jonathan Wordsworth's *William Wordsworth: The Borders of Vision* (Oxford: Clarendon Press, 1982), a work which draws much of its inspiration from Hartman.

8. *Poetical Works of Wordsworth,* IV, 463.

9. A. D. Nuttall, *A Common Sky: Philosophy and the Literary Imagination* (London: Chatto & Windus, 1974), p. 252. Clarke makes much the same point (*Romantic Paradox,* p. 22). However, Michael H. Friedman, *The Making of a Tory Humanist: William Wordsworth and the Idea of Community* (New York: Columbia University Press, 1979), interprets the passage in the Fenwick note as a self-deluding revision of the original experience (pp. 20–22).

10. Interestingly, Étienne Bonnot de Condillac, a writer much admired by Wordsworth, argued in his *Treatise on the Sensations* that the external, objective reality of the world could be proved based solely on the sense of touch. See Ernst Cassirer's comments in *The Philosophy of the Enlightenment,* trans. Fritz C. A. Koeller and James P. Pettegrove (Boston: Beacon Press, 1955), p. 117.

11. Richard J. Onorato, *The Character of the Poet: Wordsworth in "The Prelude"* (Princeton: Princeton University Press, 1971). See particularly "In the Presence of a Poetic Obsession" (pp. 69–87) and "Some Versions of Child and Mother" (pp. 182–205). F. W. Bateson put the matter more simply in *Wordsworth: A Reinterpretation* (London: Longman's, Green, & Co. 1954), p. 42: "With nobody left to love him, or to be loved by him, Wordsworth fell in love with nature." See also Wallace Douglas, *Wordsworth: The Construction of a Personality* (Youngstown: Kent State University Press, 1968) for a more strictly psychological (at times, reductive) argument.

12. Albert O. Wlecke, *Wordsworth and the Sublime* (Berkeley: University of California Press, 1973), pp. 56, 64. John Jones, *The Egotistical Sublime: A History of Wordsworth's Imagination* (London: Chatto & Windus, 1954), observes that "the condition of insight" is "a kind of alert day-dream, an inclusive state" (p. 89).

13. Frederick Garber, *Wordsworth and the Poetry of Encounter* (Urbana: University of Illinois Press, 1971), pp. 18–19.

14. Mary Moorman has noted that the incident described in this poem is probably fictionalized, lifted from Thomas Wilkinson's manuscript account of his trip to Scotland. See Moorman, *William Wordsworth,* p. 519.

15. This is one of the central theses of Friedman's book. Wordsworth, he argues, "sought to confirm himself in, through, and by participation in a social community larger than himself [where] he could obtain a firmness, a per-durability, that his painfully changeable sense of self could not obtain in solitude" (*A Tory Humanist,* p. 59).

16. Frances Ferguson, *Wordsworth: Language as Counter-Spirit* (New Haven: Yale University Press, 1977), also finds a dreamlike derealization occurring in this passage (p. 140). R. F. Storch, however, in "Wordsworth and the City: 'Social Reason's Inner Sense,' " *Wordsworth Circle,* 1 (1970):114–122, finds nothing sinister in such experiences, and considers Wordsworth's horror of city life a positive, not a negative, virtue.

17. Ferguson, *Language as Counter-Spirit,* p. 143: "For if the poet has been

seeing himself as a poor pensioner on outward forms, the blind beggar is the very embodiment of that state. Not merely his perception of the world, his pleasure or displeasure in it, but existence itself is derived and passive for this blind man." Ferguson also notes the parallel between the beggar's "label" and Wordsworth's own "story" in *The Prelude* (pp. 144–145). David Simpson, *Wordsworth and the Figurings of the Real* (Atlantic Highlands, N.J.: Humanities Press, 1982), agrees with this interpretation, adding that the blind beggar passage "describes a man who cannot see the message he holds up to others; he is divorced from his own social 'identity' " (pp. 52–53).

18. Nuttall, *A Common Sky,* p. 133. Rader, too, comments that Wordsworth's solitaries "seem made all of a piece with the world around them" (*A Philosophical Approach,* p. 191). David Perkins, *Wordsworth and the Poetry of Sincerity* (Cambridge, Mass.: Harvard University Press, 1964) observes the "striking difference between [Wordsworth's] presentation of natural objects, so vivid, concrete, and detailed, and the presentation of human beings, so often mere stark abstractions" (p. 116). The Cumberland beggar is one of those solitaries whom Geoffrey Hartman terms "border figures," "at once natural and human," animate and inanimate (*Wordsworth's Poetry,* p. 202). It is these figures, and the peculiar imaginative state in which they are apprehended, upon which Jonathan Wordsworth focuses in *The Borders of Vision.*

19. There is certainly something of Lear on the heath in this image—the blood that must struggle with the cold, the grey locks beaten against the old man's face by the wind. "Is man no more than this?" we might wonder, "no more but such a poor, bare forked animal?" One comes away with the impression that Wordsworth is more excited by the dramatic potential of such an image than cast down by its harsh reality. "The reaction," notes Bostetter, comparing the effect to that of the "still, sad music of humanity" in "Tintern Abbey," "is that of one who, withdrawn, watches a tragic drama or listens to an andante by Mozart: humanity is important as a remote stimulus to make him feel more intensely, but not to disturb or torment him. Similarly, in *The Old Cumberland Beggar* the old man['s] . . . presence does not distress, but rather gives a sense of well-being" (*Romantic Ventriloquists,* p. 55).

20. James H. Averill, *Wordsworth and the Poetry of Human Suffering* (Ithaca: Cornell University Press, 1980), also observes that "the analogy between the old, nearly blind man and a parish registry of charitable deeds tends to turn the Beggar into a piece of writing" (p. 127).

21. He would, in effect, argue to preserve destitution for the sake of allowing the better-off of the world the "after-joy" and "pleasure unpursued" (103) of a cheaply bought glow of charitable feeling. The poet's opposition to casting the Beggar into a workhouse depends on his assumption that vagrancy and poverty are themselves positive goods because of the charitable impulses they inspire, not that the poor laws are no solution to the problems of vagrancy and poverty. "There is no suggestion . . . that this is simply the lesser of two evils: the question of why there should be beggary at all never comes up," writes Bostetter, who takes the poet's rationalization of mendicancy as evidence of "an important stage in the process of Wordsworth's social and intellectual retreat" from his earlier revolutionary fervor, "the deliberate limiting

of the range of his perceptions about human nature" (*Romantic Ventriloquists* pp. 55–56).

22. Samuel Taylor Coleridge, *Biographia Literaria,* ed. James Engell and Walter Jackson Bate, 2 vols. (Princeton: Princeton University Press, 1983), II, 150. See also *Specimens of the Table Talk of the Late Samuel Taylor Coleridge,* ed. H. N. Coleridge, 2 vols. (1835), the entry for July 21, 1832: "It seems to me that [Wordsworth] ought never to have abandoned the contemplative position which is peculiarly—perhaps I might say exclusively—fitted for him. His proper title is *Spectator ab extra.*"

23. In a letter to Wordsworth, dated January 30, 1801, Charles Lamb captured the effect with characteristic penetration—"Here the mind knowingly passes a fiction upon herself, first substituting her own feelings for the Beggar's, and, in the same breath detecting the fallacy, will not part with the wish." See *The Letters of Charles and Mary Anne Lamb,* ed. Edwin W. Marrs, Jr., 3 vols. (Ithaca: Cornell University Press, 1975), I, 265.

24. Ferry, *Limits of Mortality,* p. 7.

25. But Wordsworth did fear, at times, that she had betrayed him—betrayed him into a careless enthusiasm for the "natural" goodness of humankind, with disastrous results. See Paul Sheats, *The Making of Wordsworth's Poetry* (Cambridge, Mass.: Harvard University Press, 1973), pp. 70–79, for a fine account of how Wordsworth's faith in the natural man led him into the bewildering thickets of the French Revolution and, finally, a painful sense of betrayal by Nature herself. See also Onorato, *The Character of the Poet,* pp. 32–36 and 353–355.

26. Wordsworth's essays are cited, by volume and page number, from *The Prose Works of William Wordsworth,* ed. W. J. B. Owen and Jane Worthington Smyser, 3 vols. (Oxford: Clarendon Press, 1974). Unless otherwise indicated, all quotations of the "Preface" to *Lyrical Ballads* are from the 1800 version.

27. Moorman, *William Wordsworth,* p. 65n. refers to a poem of Wordsworth's schooldays, "Idyllium" (*Poetical Works of Wordsworth,* I, 264), in which he recounts the joy of these walks and mourns the death of his dog:

If, while I gazed to nature blind,
In the calm Ocean of my mind
Some new-created image rose
In full-grown beauty at its birth,
Lovely as venus from the sea
Then, while my glad hand sprung to thee,
We were the happiest pair on earth.

28. A similarity first observed, to my knowledge, by David Perkins, in *Quest for Permanence,* pp. 16–17.

29. Nuttall observes: "In either poem the phrase ['in the eye of'] conceals a metaphysical fusion: the old beggar . . . is held in a kind of perceptual field of force; he is there, the focus of the landscape, because nature herself is watch-

ing him. In the episode of the solitary soldier the subjective reference has narrowed; the soldier owes his visionary identity to the watching eyes of Wordsworth, the everlasting passer-by, *spectator haud particeps"* (*A Common Sky*, p. 135).

30. Ferry, *Limits of Mortality*, p. 4.

31. Bostetter, *Romantic Ventriloquists*, pp. 57–58.

32. Patrick Crutwell, "Wordsworth, the Public, and the People," *Sewanee Review*, 64 (1956):73, 75. Anecdotes describing Wordsworth's impatience with even the slightest hint of misunderstanding or disapproval from his audience are numerous. One of the best known is contained in a letter from Charles Lamb to Thomas Manning, dated February 15, 1801, where Wordsworth is described as jumping to the conclusion that Lamb's choice of favorites from among the *Lyrical Ballads* impugned the excellence of the rest: "The Post did not sleep a moment. I received almost instantaneously a long letter of four sweating pages from my reluctant Letterwriter, the purport of which was, that he was sorry his 2d. vol. had not given me more pleasure (Devil a hint did I give that it had *not pleased me*) and 'was compelled to wish that my range of Sensibility was more extended, being obliged to believe that I should receive large influxes of happiness & happy Thoughts' (I suppose from the L. B.—)" (*Letters of Charles and Mary Anne Lamb*, I, 272). In the same letter, Lamb reports Coleridge's equally frantic defense of his friend (p. 273).

33. The lines were later published as part of the preface to *The Excursion;* they were originally meant to conclude the first book of the projected *Recluse,* the long philosophical poem for which *The Prelude* was to have served as introduction.

34. Coleridge, particularly, objected to the perversity of this ideal, noting that in any case the language adopted by Wordsworth's rustics, and by the poet himself, was anything but peculiar to "low and rustic life," since Wordsworth had so qualified his general rule that it was in practice useless as a way of distinguishing "rustic" language from that of "common-sense." See *Biographia Literaria*, I, 52.

35. Coleridge, *Biographia Literaria*, I, 49–52: "I dare assert, that the parts [of "The Thorn"] . . . which might as well or still better have proceeded from the poet's own imagination, and have been spoken in his own character, are those which have given, and which will continue to give universal delight; and that the passages exclusively appropriate to the supposed narrator . . . are felt by many unprejudiced and unsophisticated hearts, as sudden and unpleasant sinkings." John Shawcross, in his edition of the *Biographia* (1909; rpt. London: Oxford University Press, 1962) comments in his notes to this passage, "Coleridge here fails to take into consideration (what a careful perusal of Wordsworth's introductory note to *The Thorn* must have made clear to him) Wordsworth's real object in the poem. This was to represent the facts as they actually appeared to the mariner . . . and as he would have actually portrayed them" (II, 274). For further commentary on Wordsworth's real intentions in "The Thorn," see Stephen M. Parrish, " 'The Thorn': Wordworth's Dramatic Monologue," *ELH*, 24 (1957):153–163. For Parrish's comments on the *Lyrical Ballads* as a whole, see his later book, *The Art of the "Lyrical Ballads"* (Cam-

bridge, Mass.: Harvard University Press, 1973), where he observes that Coleridge's particular objects of dislike are Wordsworth's dramatic passages, where the poet speaks in a voice not his own (p. 136).

36. *Poetical Works of Wordsworth*, II, 512.

37. Ibid., my emphasis.

38. Moorman, *William Wordworth*, p. 114.

39. Ibid., pp. 193–194.

40. Hartman, *Wordsworth's Poetry*, p. 116n, points out that it was France that declared war on England.

41. As Paul Sheats notes, Wordsworth had to mask "his true feelings and his true identity in silence. The ironic price of loyalty to nature, love, and truth is loss of candor and integrity" (*The Making of Wordsworth's Poetry*, p. 77).

42. Ibid., p. 115. See also Sheats's fine analysis of "Guilt and Sorrow," pp. 113–114.

43. This is a point emphasized by M. H. Abrams in *Natural Supernaturalism: Tradition and Revolution in Romantic Literature* (New York: Norton, 1971), pp. 78, 116–117.

44. Perkins, *Quest for Permanence*, p. 25.

45. Harold Bloom's reading of "Tintern Abbey" in *The Visionary Company: A Reading of English Romantic Poetry* (Garden City, N.Y.: Doubleday, 1961), pp. 139–149, remains, to my mind, the finest and most succinct summary of this approach. The poem, he writes, captures "a moment of renewed covenant with a remembered and beloved landscape" (p. 142), made possible by a "personal myth of memory as salvation" (p. 148).

Onorato summarizes the attempt at temporal and mental reintegration as follows: "In 'Tintern Abbey' Wordsworth is adjusting his disturbed feelings about past and present to each other. The artist, composing the elements of his personal experience to present a continuous sense of himself in time, seems to achieve the feeling of composure" (*The Character of the Poet*, p. 87).

46. Clarke comments on "these beauteous forms": "The scene contemplated is at once substantial and insubstantial, present and past . . . rigid distinctions between outer and inner—that is, between sense-image and feeling—fall into abeyance" (*Romantic Paradox*, pp. 40–41).

47. Bateson argues that Wordsworth is fleeing "the contrariness of human affairs" (*A Reinterpretation*, p. 113).

48. A point made by Grob: "There is . . . continuity of mental content . . . but there is little else, except perhaps memory, upon which to base the identity and continuity of the receptive self" (*Philosophic Mind*, p. 59).

49. See, for instance, Onorato, *The Character of the Poet*, pp. 82ff.

50. Ibid, p. 82.

51. *The Letters of William and Dorothy Wordsworth*, ed. Ernest de Selincourt, 2nd ed. rev. Chester L. Shaver, 3 vols. (Oxford: Clarendon Press, 1967), I, 366. This is in response to Sara's expression of boredom with the poem's predecessor, "The Leech-gatherer." Wordsworth, in a characteristically testy mood over Sara's incomprehension, writes much in the manner of the 1800 "Preface": "You speak of his speech as tedious: everything is tedious when one does

not read with the feelings of the Author." Dorothy was no less sensitive than her brother to any imputations of insipidity. "When you feel any poem of his to be tedious," she writes Sara, "ask yourself in what spirit it was written— whether merely to tell the tale and be through with it, or to illustrate a particular character or truth etc, etc." (I, 367).

52. David Simpson sees Wordsworth's use of extreme figuration like this as a form of both liberation and self-imprisonment. He observes, of the description of the Leech-gatherer, "that the use of metaphor is in fact double-edged, and that there is a high degree of ambiguity about whether it serves to vivify the inanimate . . . or deanimate the human" (*Figurings of the Real*, p. 110).

53. Garber, *The Poetry of Encounter*, p. 141. Garber argues against the assumption that Wordsworth's imagination tends to "depersonalize" his solitaries (pp. 140–141).

54. *The Letters of John Keats, 1814–1821*, ed. Hyder Edward Rollins, 2nd ed. 2 vols. (Cambridge, Mass.: Harvard University Press, 1965), I, 185.

55. Moorman conjectures that Wordsworth's sudden despondency in the poem stemmed from his increasingly severe headaches and other bodily indispositions when composing (*William Wordsworth*, p. 539).

56. Jonathan Wordsworth disagrees with this judgment. See pp. 159–160 of *The Borders of Vision*, where he argues that worry over Coleridge would be a more likely reason for Wordsworth's dismay.

57. John Jones notes that Wordsworth's indirect reporting of the Leech-gatherer's other replies reinforces the old man's visionary aura (*Egotistical Sublime*, p. 62). I suggest that this reinforcement is due in large measure to the fact that the Leech-gatherer's indirect speech strengthens our impression that the poet is preoccupied with the visual *appearance* rather than the aural *presence* of the man.

58. Anthony E. M. Conran, "The Dialectic of Experience: A Study of Wordsworth's *Resolution and Independence*," *PMLA*, 75 (1960):74.

59. Moorman places Wordsworth's first extended loss of "celestial light" as early as his return from France in 1793, but feels that he regained it during his stays with Dorothy at Racedown and Alfoxden (*William Wordsworth*, pp. 531–532). Ferry, *Limits of Mortality*, pp. 172–173, sets the date of decline at about 1805. Rader observes that, by 1800 or so, Wordsworth's "trance-like moments seemed to have ceased" (*A Philosophical Approach*, p. 113), and refers to the poet's own statement in *The Prelude* (1805), XI, 335–338: "the hiding-places of my power / Seem open, I approach, and then they close; / I see by glimpses now, when age comes on / May scarcely see at all."

60. Among these were renewed grief at having abandoned Annette, his physical infirmities (particularly those associated with composition), his Tory leanings, and the harsh criticism of Francis Jeffrey.

3. Coleridge

1. Coleridge's poems are cited, by line number, from *Coleridge: Poetical Works*, ed. Ernest Hartley Coleridge (1912; rpt. London: Oxford University

Press, 1967).

2. *The Notebooks of Samuel Taylor Coleridge,* ed. Kathleen Coburn, 3 vols. (New York: Pantheon, 1961), I, #1554.

3. Ibid., II, #2109.

4. Ibid., II, #2091.

5. Kelvin Everest, *Coleridge's Secret Ministry: The Context of the Conversation Poems, 1795–98* (New York: Barnes and Noble, 1979), p. 10.

6. See, for instance, Lawrence Hanson's comments in *The Life of Samuel Taylor Coleridge* (New York: Russell & Russell, 1962), p. 128. Norman Fruman, *Coleridge, the Damaged Archangel* (New York: Braziller, 1971), attributes this "anxiety to please" to Coleridge's "ceaselessly gnawing self-doubts and fear of rejection. Insincerity, flattery, even sycophancy in the presence of those whose approval he desired, heavily punctuate the records of his life . . . Adverse criticism in any form was neurotically painful to him" (p. 118).

7. *Notebooks of Coleridge,* II, #2389.

8. See Stephen Potter, *Coleridge and S. T. C.* (London: Jonathan Cape, 1935), pp. 11–21.

9. Notebook 23, fols. 31v–32r, quoted by Kathleen Coburn in *The Self Conscious Imagination: A Study of the Coleridge Notebooks in Celebration of the Bicentenary of His Birth, 21 October 1772* (London: Oxford University Press, 1974). See also the more positively phrased notebook entry (*Notebooks of Coleridge,* I, #1679): "My nature requires another Nature for its support, & reposes only in another from the necessary Indigence of its Being . . . the same Soul diversely incarnate."

10. Walter Jackson Bate, *Coleridge* (New York: Macmillan, 1968), p. 1. One of the most sensitive and comprehensive studies of the childhood origins of Coleridge's insecurities is still Norman Fruman's *Coleridge, the Damaged Archangel,* particularly pp. 13–25, "The Parched Roots."

11. *Notebooks of Coleridge,* II, "Notes," #1991.

12. Letter to his brother, George Coleridge, May 11, 1808, in *Collected Letters of Samuel Taylor Coleridge,* ed. Earl Leslie Griggs, 5 vols. (Oxford: Clarendon Press, 1959), III, 103, 105.

13. Geoffrey Yarlott, *Coleridge and the Abyssinian Maid* (London: Methuen, 1967), pp. 3–4

14. Certainly the finest investigation of this philosophical background to date is Thomas McFarland's *Coleridge and the Pantheist Tradition* (Oxford: Clarendon Press, 1969), which elegantly reduces the conflict Coleridge felt between the sublime materialism of Spinoza and the transcendental idealism of Kant to the dichotomy between two contradictory philosophical attitudes that Coleridge was trying to reconcile: the "It is" and "I am" frames of mind. See also G. N. G. Orsini, *Coleridge and German Idealism* (Carbondale: University of Southern Illinois Press, 1969) and Owen Barfield, *What Coleridge Thought* (Middletown, Conn.: Wesleyan University Press, 1971).

15. Paul Magnuson, *Coleridge's Nightmare Poetry* (Charlottesville: University Press of Virginia, 1974), p. 4.

16. Letter to Sara Coleridge, November 13, 1802, in *Letters of Coleridge,* II, 881.

17. The critical verdict on the last section of the poem is mixed, and likely to remain so. Albert Gerard, for instance, in *English Romantic Poetry* (Berkeley: University of California Press, 1968) agrees that the conclusion is tame, but argues that it is consistent with the "double process of contraction and expansion" that structures the poem as a whole (pp. 28-29). Other critics are not so kind. Humphry House feels that the ending "killed the new-born life" of the ecstatic first part (*Coleridge: The Clark Lectures, 1951-52,* London: Rupert Hart-Davis, 1953, p. 78); Max Schulz argues that Coleridge's "abject assertion of faith in Christ denies [his] joyous vision of cosmic unity" (*The Poetic Voices of Coleridge,* Detroit: Wayne State University Press, 1963, p. 86); and Edward Bostetter maintains that the declamatory tone of the poet's recantation throws his sincerity into doubt (*The Romantic Ventriloquists,* Seattle: University of Washington Press, 1963, p. 92). More recently, Jean-Pierre Mileur, *Vision and Revision: Coleridge's Art of Imminence* (Berkeley: University of California Press, 1982) has observed that, in any case, "the self-description of the final lines reveals the anxiety, the lack of a sense of the self's legitimacy in the world" (p. 40).

18. See, e.g., Harold Bloom, *The Visionary Company* (Garden City, N.Y.: Doubleday, 1961), p. 230.

19. It was House, *Clark Lectures,* pp. 114-115, who first related the details of the poem's imagery, particularly of the pleasure dome, the caves of ice, and the fountain, to "the act of poetic creation" (p. 122).

20. Thus, S. K. Henninger, Jr. "A Jungian Reading of 'Kubla Khan' " *Journal of Aesthetics and Art Criticism,* 18 (1960): 358-367, has interpreted the poem as a description of the process of "individuation" apart from society, the psyche's attempts at independent self-integration.

21. The preoccupation with a distant strife recurs throughout Coleridge's work. In "Reflections on having Left a Place of Retirement," "Fears in Solitude," and "France: an Ode" the poet is situated much like the monarch of Xanadu: in the midst of domestic content, in "the Valley of Seclusion" ("Reflections," 9) or in "a green and silent spot, amid the hills, / A small and silent dell" ("Fears," 1-2), he hears "from far" the rumblings of public discord and civil and foreign strife. In these poems the poet stands, figuratively, on the boundary between domestic and social life, the arenas of self-confirmation in which the private and public self, respectively find a place.

22. Kathleen M. Wheeler, *The Creative Mind in Coleridge's Poetry* (Cambridge, Mass.: Harvard University Press, 1981), p. 26.

23. House, whom I follow here, argues strongly against a merely speculative reading of "could I" and "should" (*Clark Lectures,* p. 115). If the poet sings, his listeners *will* see.

24. Max Schulz, "Coleridge and the Enchantments of Earthly Paradise," in *Reading Coleridge,* ed. Walter B. Crawford (Ithaca: Cornell University Press, 1979), pp. 116-159, argues that "Kubla Khan" symbolically represents one pole of Coleridge's fretful oscillation "between expansive desire to encompass all and fearful recoil from 'Vacancy and formlessness,' between sallying forth in the loving comfort of 'a goodly company' ('Ancient Mariner,' 604) and enclosing himself within the secure walls of Xanadu" (p. 131).

25. Bostetter, *Romantic Ventriloquists,* p. 96, with reference to "Religious Musings."

26. Lane Cooper, *Late Harvest: Sketches, Philosophical Reviews, and Papers on Coleridge, Wordsworth, and Byron* (Ithaca: Cornell University Press, 1952), p. 77.

27. Robert Darnton, *Mesmerism and the End of the Enlightenment in France* (Cambridge, Mass.: Harvard University Press, 1968). In England mesmerism's influence, while more moderate and indirect, was only slightly less far-reaching than in France.

28. Fred Kaplan, *Dickens and Mesmerism: The Hidden Springs of Fiction* (Princeton: Princeton University Press, 1978), sees mesmerism as having arisen in response to "the problems of personal and public identity" just emerging at this time and soon to give rise to the neurological illnesses of Victorian society (p. 9). His argument is condensed in his earlier article, " 'The Mesmeric Maria': The Early Victorians and Animal Magnetism," *Journal of the History of Ideas,* 35 (1974): 690–702.

29. Too manifest for some tastes. Darnton points out that mesmerism broke down social barriers in group sessions and was therefore looked upon with suspicion by the defenders of the *ancien regime* (*Mesmerism,* pp. 82–105).

30. Kaplan, for instance, has linked the phenomenon with evangelical Methodism and its "emphasis on enthusiasm and public conversion" (*Dickens and Mesmerism,* p. 36); and Maria M. Tatar, *Spellbound: Studies on Mesmerism and Literature* (Princeton: Princeton University Press, 1978), notes that Mesmer's techniques "figure as the crude antecedents of the cathartic method and the 'talking cure' employed by Breuer and Freud to relieve the symptoms of hysteria" (p. 29).

31. Recent studies have shown that hypnotic behavior is in fact a form of role playing that is not unlike what happens on stage when an actor becomes caught up in his or her performance. See Theodore Sarbin, "Contributions to Role-Taking Theory: I, Hypnotic Behavior," *Psychological Review,* 57 (1951): 255–270; Robert W. White, "A Preface to the Theory of Hypnotism," *Journal of Abnormal and Social Psychology,* 36 (1941): 477–505; and M. B. Arnold, "On the Mechanism of Suggestion and Hypnosis," *Journal of Abnormal and Social Psychology,* 41 (1946):107–128.

32. *Coleridge: Poetical Works,* p. 296.

33. Wheeler, *The Creative Mind,* pp. 20, 168n2.

34. Ibid., pp. 22–23. In Wheeler's opinion the "Preface" shows us the visionary "I" of the last section of the poem, the "epilogue," so to speak, but in an ordinary state of unimaginative perception, a counter-example that shows the reader how *not* to read the poem (pp. 22–25).

35. See John Livingston Lowes, *The Road to Xanadu: A Study in the Ways of the Imagination,* 2nd ed. (Cambridge, Mass.: Harvard University Press, 1930), p. 358. Wheeler rightly claims credit, however, for noting the parallel between dreaming monarch and dreaming poet (*The Creative Mind,* pp. 22–25).

36. I have deliberately avoided the term "logocentric" so as not to raise the question of how Coleridge's poetic utterances might relate to deconstructive readings of the works as fictions of "Presence"—a question that would merit an entire book.

37. Samuel Taylor Coleridge, *Biographia Literaria,* ed. James Engell and Walter Jackson Bate, 2 vols. (Princeton: Princeton University Press, 1983), I, 304.

38. My concept of the *logos* is indebted principally to Ernst Cassirer, *Language and Myth,* trans. Susanne K. Langer (1946; rpt. New York: Dover Books, 1963), who argues that the categories of logic and the notions of "concept," "essential form," and "properties" are all presupposed by acts of speech (pp. 24ff). Objects of empirical thought and abstract manipulation can arise only in a world first appropriated by language and myth, which create "momentary deities" (p. 22) to give definition to a single moment and significance to a single place in the otherwise undifferentiated stream of sensations. Thus, concludes Cassirer, ultimately "the demand for the *Unity* of the Deity . . . takes its stand on the linguistic expression of Being, and finds its surest support in [the concept of] the Word" (p. 75).

39. *Notebooks of Coleridge,* II, #2274.

40. Ibid., II, #2086.

41. The generic phrase, "conversation poems," was coined by George Maclean Harper, "Coleridge's Conversation Poems," *Quarterly Review,* 244 (1925): 284–298. For my purposes, I do not include among them "Reflections on Having Left a Place of Retirement" and "Fears in Solitude" since, properly speaking, these are clearly "reflections" and not addressed to others or meant to be overheard by others. The subtitle of "The Nightingale" was originally "A Conversational Poem" in the first edition of the *Lyrical Ballads* and later changed.

42. Yarlott, *The Abyssinian Maid,* p. 93.

43. *Notebooks of Coleridge,* II, #2546.

44. Gerard, *English Romantic Poetry,* pp. 55–57, relates these developments to Coleridge's growing interest in the symbol and symbolic expression, an interest that, Gerard argues, profoundly influenced the poet's ideas of transcendental insight between 1796, the year he wrote "The Eolian Harp," and 1797, the year of "This Lime-Tree Bower."

45. A good source of information about Coleridge's later philosophy is Owen Barfield's *What Coleridge Thought.* Like Gerard, Barfield links Coleridge's specific use of the concept of *logos* to his interest in the creation of symbolic forms.

McFarland (*The Pantheist Tradition,* pp. 191–255) relates Coleridge's final concept of *logos* to Martin Buber's notion of the "I-Thou" relationship of the self with divinity, by which the real existence of the world and of others is established. Bate (*Coleridge,* pp. 214–219) provides a good capsule summary of Coleridge's later philosophical and theological speculations on the *logos* and its role in the poet's Trinitarian thought.

46. *Notebooks of Coleridge,* I, #1154.

47. The image of organic Harps trembling into harmonious thought is taken up again in "The Nightingale," where the poet imagines that (77–82)

. . . the moon
Emerging, hath awakened earth and sky

With one sensation, and those wakeful birds
Have all burst forth in choral minstrelsy,
As if some sudden gale had swept at once
A hundred airy harps!

See also Schulz, *Poetic Voices*, pp. 89–92.

48. The term used by Richard Haven in *Patterns of Consciousness: An Essay on Coleridge* (Amherst: University of Massachusetts Press, 1969).

49. Harper, "Conversation Poems," p. 291; Schulz, *Poetic Voices*, p. 84; Gerard, *English Romantic Poetry*, pp. 29–30; House, *Clark Lectures*, pp. 79–81.

50. Bate, *Coleridge*, p. 50.

51. House, for instance, *Clark Lectures*, p. 81, and Magnuson, *Nightmare Poetry*, pp. 17, 38.

52. Mileur makes much the same point when he says that the "strategy" of "bestowal"—similar to Bate's notion of "ushering"—which informs the poem "denies the necessity of choosing between the figurative and the real, the privileged and the shared experience," allowing the poet to assume that what *he* takes to be the content of other minds is in fact so (*Vision and Revision*, pp. 42–45).

53. See, for instance, Schulz, *Poetic Voices*, pp. 94–97, for an excellent metaphysical reading.

54. The similarities have been noted by Yarlott, *The Abyssinian Maid*, p. 116, and Schulz, *Poetic Voices*, p. 87, among others.

55. Haven, *Patterns of Consciousness*, p. 70.

56. Ibid., p. 72.

57. See, for example, Magnuson, *Nightmare Poetry*, pp. 17: "The best of the Conversation Poems begin with Coleridge's feelings of loss and isolation and move outwards to re-establish a viable connection with nature and with the community of other minds." He continues, "Only in 'This Lime-Tree Bower' is there *a complete unity of the actual sensations and Coleridge's imaginative re-creations of them*" (p. 18, italics added). But of course, the "actual sensations" in these "centers of perception distinct from Coleridge himself" are wholly a matter of speculation.

R. A. Durr, " 'This Lime-Tree Bower My Prison' and a Recurrent Action in Coleridge," *ELH* 26 (1959):514–530, is emphatic about keeping clear the distinction between the real and the imaginary, for only in this way can we understand that the poet's imaginative expansion of soul encompasses the world around him (see esp. pp. 526–527).

58. Durr anticipated this point with his observations on the bower as an emblem of the mind. With the poet's return to the bower, "we learn that it too has been aglow" ("Recurrent Action" p. 528) with the fire that infused the imagined landscape of the Quantock Hills.

59. Again, the presumptive nature of this visual communion is usually overlooked in commentary on the passage. Even Mileur, who seems otherwise quite aware of the illusory nature of Coleridge's presumptions of imaginative empathy, makes this assumption: "This is the actual revelation toward which the poem moves: that nature—its sights, sounds, and smells—is privileged be-

cause it provides that level of experience shared by all which serves as the basis for the conviction that there is among men a community of thought and feeling. It is this community of the subjective rather than the unity (elusive indeed) of the individual identity which provides . . . that faith that sustains a vision of an immanent Almighty Spirit" (*Vision and Revision,* pp. 43–44).

60. Lamb himself seems to have noticed the coercive thrust of Coleridge's apostrophes. "For God's sake (I was never more serious)," he writes on August 6, 1800, after having read the poem again in the second edition of *Lyrical Ballads,* "don't make me ridiculous any more by terming me gentle-hearted in print, or do it in better verses . . . I should be ashamed to think that you could think to gratify me by such praise, fit only to be a cordial to some green-sick sonneteer" (*The Letters of Charles and Mary Anne Lamb,* ed. Edwin W. Marrs, Jr., 3 vols., Ithaca: Cornell University Press, 1975, I, 217–218).

61. The phrase is taken from Leon Waldoff's "The Quest for Father and Identity in 'The Rime of the Ancient Mariner,' " *Psychoanalytic Review,* 58 (1971):439–453, where Waldoff concludes that the poem "raises serious doubts about the morality and wisdom of the Romantic faith in the self. It is a poem in which self-assertion seems to lead toward guilt, nightmarish experiences, and cosmic alienation" (p. 444).

62. Michael G. Cooke, *The Romantic Will* (New Haven: Yale University Press, 1976), p. 31. "It is the act of the anonymous man," writes Edward Bostetter in *Romantic Ventriloquists:* "Nowhere does the Mariner describe himself or leave clues to his character" (p. 110).

63. Yarlott, *The Abyssinian Maid,* p. 171; see also John Beer, *Coleridge the Visionary* (London: Chatto & Windus, 1970), p. 149, on the Mariner's lack of social ties.

64. Haven, *Patterns of Consciousness,* pp. 27–28.

65. Richard Harter Fogle, *The Permanent Pleasure: Essays on the Classics of Romanticism* (Athens: University of Georgia Press, 1974), pp. 30, 35–36.

66. Cooke, *The Romantic Will,* p. 231n49: "There is a sense that the ship's 'drop' out of the ordinary world is a drop into directionless space without 'shapes of men [or] beasts.' Certainly the kirk, the hill, and the lighthouse top cease to be points of reference, even to the memory."

67. Ibid.

68. John O. Lyons, *The Invention of the Self* (Carbondale: Southern Illinois University Press, 1978), p. 4. It has often been observed that the problem of alienation as it appears in Coleridge's work closely resembles the problem as set forth by the poet's contemporary, Kierkegaard. Alvin D. Alley, "Coleridge and Existentialism," *Southern Humanities Review,* 2 (1968): 451–461, has drawn attention to the similarities between Coleridge's and Kierkegaard's thought, pointing out that the poet's work reveals a "central existential theme of man's estrangement from normal society and of the despair that directly results from this isolation" (p. 451).

69. *Coleridge: Poetical Works,* p. 189.

70. Ibid., pp. 190–191. Cooke, *The Romantic Will,* p. 30, observes the sailors' superstitious desperation "for signs, for orientation."

71. Robert Penn Warren, "A Poem of Pure Imagination: An Experiment

in Reading," *Selected Essays* (New York: Random House, 1958), pp. 223–224.

72. Ibid., p. 242.

73. House, *Clark Lectures,* p. 103.

74. Abe Delson, "Symbolism of the Sun and Moon in 'The Rime of the Ancient Mariner,' " *Texas Studies in Language and Literature,* 15 (1973):720. For what I consider an overly fastidious reading, see Elliot B. Gose, "Coleridge and Luminous Gloom: An Analysis of the 'Symbolical Language' in 'The Rime of the Ancient Mariner,' " *PMLA,* 75 (1960):238–244, who argues that the Ancient Mariner's eventual change of heart is not very clearly connected with the moon's influence because it is *"within* the shadow of the ship" that the Mariner sees the sea-serpents' "flash of golden fire."

75. Beer, *Coleridge the Visionary,* p. 93.

76. Warren, "Pure Imagination," p. 257.

77. Ibid.

78. As Beer points out (*Coleridge the Visionary,* p. 112), Coleridge, in *Aids to Reflection,* 1825, note to pp. 251–252, identified "Intuitive Reason" or the "Nous" as "the Source of Ideas and ABSOLUTE Truths, and the Principle of the Necessary and the Universal in our Affirmations and Conclusions." The sun, in other words, can be seen as representing the power of the Primary Imagination that works through all minds in common to bring a common world to light. "The sun, in the poem as a whole, is a symbol not of wrath and retribution, but of God and the image of God in human reason" (*Coleridge the Visionary,* p. 161). I disagree, however, with Beer's view that the Mariner's vision and the true divine vision are essentially the same, and not in opposition to each other, for it seems clear to me that it is precisely his vision that sets the Mariner apart from the common reality of things established by the Nous working through all minds.

79. A good example of where Beer and I differ. He sees the resurrected attendant spirits singing around the mast as an indication that the "bad sun" of wrath and retribution, which the Mariner beholds with fallen eyes before his conversion experience, has been changed to the "good sun" of redemption and human reason. But I believe that the Mariner's remaining apart is an important indication that this shared perceptual faith is not one he can partake of—his vision is other, and can only be imposed, not shared.

80. Bostetter, *Romantic Ventriloquists,* p. 111.

81. *Lyrical Ballads, 1798 and 1800,* ed. R. L. Brett and A. R. Jones (London: Methuen & Co., 1965), p. 25.

82. *Coleridge: Poetical Works,* p. 199 and note.

83. Ibid., p. 198.

84. Beer, *Coleridge the Visionary,* p. 161.

85. *Coleridge: Poetical Works,* p. 197.

86. Ibid., p. 208.

87. James Gillman, *The Life of Samuel Taylor Coleridge* (London: William Pickering, 1838), p. 37n.

88. *Coleridge: Poetical Works,* p. 216.

89. See, for instance, Jonas Spatz, "The Mystery of Eros: Sexual Initiation in Coleridge's 'Christabel,' " *PMLA,* 90(1975):107–116; Edward Proffitt,

" 'Christabel' and Oedipal Conflict," *Research Studies*, 46(1974):249; Arthur Wormhoudt, *The Demon Lover: A Psychoanalytic Approach to Literature* (1949; rpt. Freeport, N.Y.: Books for Libraries Press, 1968), p. 19; and Richard Harter Fogle, *The Idea of Coleridge's Criticism* (Berkeley: University of California Press, (1962), p. 142: "In some occult sense the enchantress Geraldine and Christabel's mother . . . are one and the same."

90. Roy P. Basler, *Sex, Symbolism, and Psychology in Literature* (New Brunswick: Rutgers University Press, 1948), pp. 25–51, was the first to point out that the sinister theme of sexual perversion and repression which insinuates itself throughout the poem can be traced to Christabel's inability to accept her own sexual maturity, "her passionate though thwarted love for her absent 'betrothed knight' " (p. 29). Other "psychoanalytic" critics include Wormhoudt, Spatz, Proffitt, and David Beres, "A Dream, a Vision, and a Poem," *International Journal of Psychoanalysis*, 32(1951):97–116.

91. For a more detailed explanation of the mechanism of transference and its parental origins, see Sandor Ferenczi, *Sex in Psychoanalysis* (1909; rpt. New York: Dover, 1956), pp. 34–61.

92. See Chapter 1, note 49 on "introjection."

93. Edward Bostetter, *"Christabel:* The Vision of Fear," *Philological Quarterly*, 36(1957):183–194; Fruman, *Coleridge, the Damaged Archangel*, pp. 365–412, 548n26; Yarlott, *The Abyssinian Maid*, pp. 40–49. On Coleridge's hatred of his mother, see Beres, "A Dream," pp. 106–108.

94. See, e.g., Fruman, *Damaged Archangel*, pp. 370–373.

95. See, e.g., Bostetter, "Vision of Fear," and *Romantic Ventriloquists*, p. 132.

96. Yarlott, *The Abyssinian Maid*, p. 276. See also his chapter on "Dejection," pp. 244–279.

4. Keats

1. Keats's letters are cited, by volume and page number, from *The Letters of John Keats, 1814-1821,* ed. Hyder Edward Rollins, 2nd ed. 2 vols. (Cambridge, Mass.: Harvard University Press, 1965).

2. Bernice Slote, *Keats and the Dramatic Principle* (Lincoln: University of Nebraska Press, 1958) is still the best source of information on Keats's stage knowledge and "dramatic temper" of mind. For Keats's interest in the theater of his time, see especially pp. 120–125. A more recent, but less helpful, work on the subject is Pratyush Ranjan Purkayastha, *The Romantics' Third Voice: A Study of the Dramatic Works of the English Poets* (Salzburg: Institut für Englische Sprache und Literatur Universität Salzburg, 1978), esp. pp. 303–343.

3. Christopher Ricks, *Keats and Embarrassment* (Oxford: Oxford University Press, 1974), p. 9.

4. Marion Montgomery, in "Keats's Journey Homeward to Habitual Self," *Southern Review*, 8 (1975):273–289, notes how Keats is "habitually captivated by 'things'—by multiplicity itself," and unfavorably contrasts his "indiscriminate" imaginative attraction to the inhuman world with the "Shakespearean virtue which so attracted [him] . . . for entering into all states

and conditions of *man*" (p. 250). Keats is "a spiritual parasite upon this world" (p. 289).

John Jones, *John Keats's Dream of Truth* (London: Chatto & Windus, 1969), goes so far as to observe "a very crucial sense in which there are no human beings in Keats's poetry" (p. 20), but only bundles of sensations. With respect to Keats's phrase "filling some other Body," Jones writes, "Always the nub of the matter is end-stopped feeling operating with a catholicity grand enough to contain human beings, but to contain them on terms which we would not elsewhere think of as humanly tolerable," a "mindless introversion" (p. 21).

5. "He has confirmed that he can conceive of a billiard Ball that it may have a sense of delight from its own roundness, smoothness <& very> volubility. & the rapidity of its motion." From Woodhouse's notes on Keats's letter of October 27, 1818 on the "poetical Character," in *The Keats Circle: Letters and Papers, 1816–1878*, ed. Hyder Edward Rollins, 2nd ed., 2 vols. (Cambridge, Mass.: Harvard University Press, 1965), I, 59.

6. Keats's poems are cited, by line number (preceded by part number where appropriate), from *The Poems of John Keats*, ed. Jack Stillinger (Cambridge, Mass.: Harvard University Press, 1978).

7. Kenneth Muir, "The Meaning of the Odes," in *John Keats: A Reassessment*, ed. Kenneth Muir (Liverpool: Liverpool University Press, 1969), pp. 64–74, makes this point (p. 69), but without invoking Shelley's analogy.

8. Maurice Merleau-Ponty vividly describes, in phenomenological terms, such an experience of self-loss in darkness in *The Phenomenology of Perception*, trans. Colin Smith (London: Routledge & Kegan Paul, 1962), p. 283.

9. Richard P. Benton, "Keats and Zen," *Philosophy East and West*, 16 (1966):33–47, noting that as a poet "Keats uncovered his Self or Buddha nature in a manner closely resembling Zen Awakening, or *satori*" (p. 34), finds that in the "Ode to a Nightingale," "the nightingale itself appears to be a symbol of the larger Self that is universal and eternal in us" (p. 39).

10. There is some disagreement over whether or not Keats does achieve the union he longs for in this stanza. See Walter Jackson Bate, *John Keats* (Cambridge, Mass.: Harvard University Press, 1963), p. 505, for an affirmative verdict, Earl Wasserman, *The Finer Tone: Keats's Major Poems* (Baltimore: Johns Hopkins University Press, 1953), p. 198, for a negative. Morris Dickstein, *Keats and His Poetry: A Study in Development* (Chicago: University of Chicago Press, 1971) reserves judgment on the success of the poet's momentary flight, but points out that, in any case, "by the next line" ('haply') and thereafter ('But here there is no light') the poet is separate from the bird" (p. 209).

11. Helen Vendler, *The Odes of John Keats* (Cambridge, Mass.: Harvard University Press, 1983), pp. 103–104, suggests that Keats, having left behind the realm of Flora and old Pan in his earlier poetry, is here identifying closely with Ruth as an exile in a new, strange, and forbidding landscape, standing "amid the alien corn" of his own future poetic harvest.

12. The merging or submersion of identity, the "loss of ego" in the perception of a beautiful object, is a common theme in Keats studies. See, e.g., David Perkins's lucid analysis of this passage, and others like it, in *The Quest for Permanence* (Cambridge, Mass.: Harvard University Press, 1965) p. 209. See also

Clarence Thorpe, *The Mind of John Keats* (New York: Russell & Russell, 1964), pp. 50, 109; and Edward Bostetter, *The Romantic Ventriloquists* (Seattle: University of Washington Press, 1963), pp. 157ff. Merleau-Ponty observes that there is "thinking" in such an experience, "but the thinking starts from nowhere" (*Perception*, p. 283).

Newell F. Ford, however, in "Keats, Empathy, and the 'Poetical Character,'" *Studies in Philology*, 45 (1948):477-490, argues that Keats's "self" was by no means completely "annihilated" in experiences like these. See also his "The Meaning of 'Fellowship with Essence' in *Endymion*," *PMLA*, 62 (1947):1061-1076.

13. Dickstein, *Study in Development*, p. 219. John Jones, *John Keats's Dream of Truth* (London: Chatto & Windus, 1969), observes the tension between the endings of the Nightingale and the Urn odes: "The Nightingale closes on the hostility of Keatsian opposites. 'What the Imagination seizes as beauty must be truth—whether it existed before or not.' But also, 'The Fancy cannot cheat so well / As she is fam'd [?feign'd] to do.' The *Grecian Urn* attempts to decide. Therein its singular ambition" (p. 222).

14. Ricks, *Embarrassment*, p. 33.

15. Leigh Hunt reported, in his *Autobiography*, ed. Roger Ingpen, 2 vols. (New York: E. P. Dutton & Co., 1903), that "Keats, being a little too sensitive on the score of his origin, felt inclined to see in every man of birth a sort of natural enemy" (II, 41).

16. Robert Gittings, in *Letters of John Keats* (London: Oxford University Press, 1970), p. 402, notes the mistaken identification of the addressee of this letter in Rollins' edition of the letters and in others', and correctly identifies the correspondent.

17. Insofar as it can be distinguished from "camelion" self-annihilation, what Keats has in mind here seems closer to the disinterestedness of "Negative Capability," "when man is capable of being in uncertainties, Mysteries, doubts, without any irritable reaching after fact & reason" (*Letters*, I, 193). As Arthur Clayborough has noted, in " 'Negative Capability' and 'The Camelion Poet' in Keats's Letters: The Case for Differentiation," *English Studies*, 54 (1973):569-575, there is little of the "intensity" of the "camelion Poet" in Keats's definition of his famous "quality": "Clearly, to write in this fashion demands a certain egotism" (p. 574).

18. "Sarah Jeffrey" in Rollins's edition. See note 16.

19. Vendler, *Odes*, p. 34.

20. Ibid., p. 27.

21. Newell F. Ford, *The Prefigurative Imagination of John Keats* (Stanford: Stanford University Press, 1951), notes love's preeminence in this passage (p. 22). Harold Bloom, *The Visionary Company* (Garden City, N.Y.: Doubleday, 1961), reads the entire poem as an illustration of the "gradations of happiness" (*Letters*, I, 218) that Keats identified in this passage, suggesting that "friendship" is the theme of Book III, while "Book IV is devoted to richer entanglements, 'enthrallments far more self-destroying,' " i.e., Endymion's final union with Cynthia (p. 393).

22. This is a point that Ford emphasizes throughout *The Prefigurative Imagi-*

nation; see, e.g., p. 25. Stanley C. Russell, " 'Self-Destroying' Love in Keats," *Keats-Shelley Journal,* 16 (1967):79–91, writes of Keats's love of sensations and the sensuous, "He is speaking here of sensuous enjoyment" (p. 80). Miriam Allott, in " 'Isabella,' 'The Eve of St. Agnes,' and 'Lamia,' " in *John Keats: A Reassessment,* ed. Kenneth Muir (Liverpool: Liverpool University Press, 1969), pp. 40–63, objects to what she takes to be Ford's oversimplification, finding in the development of the longer narratives evidence of Keats's growing ability "to penetrate 'sensation' by 'thought' " (p. 52). Nevertheless, she too notes that in the "patterned sequence of images" by which Keats expressed his attitude toward "the relationship between the ideal and the actual" (p. 47), "erotic experience is always the supreme sensuous culmination" (p. 48).

23. See *Paradise Lost,* VIII, 449–451, where God tells Adam, "What next I bring shall please thee, be assured: / Thy likeness, thy fit help, thy other self, / Thy wish exactly to thy heart's desire." Rollins notes the relevant passage.

24. Robert Gittings, *Keats: The Living Year* (London: Heinemann, 1954), notes the recurrence of the pattern of the "feast and the Lady" in the romances of the "Great Year" and in *Otho the Great,* and connects it to Keats's dinner with Isabella Jones in October 1818, and his eventual falling-out with her (pp. 172–174).

25. Stillinger, *Poems of Keats,* p. 301n gives the stanza:

'Twas said her future lord would there appear
Offering, as sacrifice—all in the dream—
Delicious food, even to her lips brought near,
Viands, and wine, and fruit, and sugar'd cream,
To touch her palate with the fine extreme
Of relish: then soft music heard, and then
More pleasures follow'd in a dizzy stream
Palpable almost: then to wake again
Warm in the virgin morn, no weeping Magdalen.

26. An important resemblance first noted by Arthur Carr, "John Keats' Other 'Urn,' " *University of Kansas City Review,* 20 (1954):237–242. Carr anticipates in part my own approach; see, e.g., p 237. See also Stuart Sperry, *Keats the Poet* (Princeton: Princeton University Press, 1973), who points out that Keats uses "the imagery of sculpture to express the way feeling is arrested or repressed, then liberated and fulfilled in a new onrush of emotion" (p. 207). In Jones's view Madeline lives "the life of the pure object"—"desired and admired, but never known" (*Keats's Dream,* p. 234).

27. Carr writes, "Porphyro strives to create, by self-control and sympathetic insight, a reality to outrun [Madeline's] dreams . . . The perfection of his device is to capture, by imaginative artifice, a moment both sensual and innocent, to arrest it briefly, to live in Madeline's dream, and then to make the illusion merge successfully with reality" ("Other 'Urn,' " p. 240). See also Sperry, *Keats the Poet,* pp. 204-210, on the poem as "a drama of wish-fulfillment."

28. Gerald Enscoe, *Eros and the Romantics* (The Hague: Mouton, 1967), p. 138.

29. Jack Stillinger "The Hoodwinking of Madeline: Scepticism in *The Eve of St. Agnes,*" *Studies in Philology,* 58 (1961):538.

30. Earl Wasserman, *The Finer Tone: Keats' Major Poems* (Baltimore: John Hopkins University Press, 1953) p. 134: "Or we might equally well have depended upon the pleasure thermometer to supply the internal organizing principle of the romance. In general, the entrance into the castle and the experience in the thoughtless chamber correspond to the first two stages of the thermometer—penetration into essence by the senses and by the imagination."

31. Stillinger, "The Hoodwinking of Madeline," 555. See also p. 552: "In *Lamia,* the hoodwinked dreamer is of course Lycius," and p. 553: "In each [of the great odes] the speaker begins as a dreamer, hoodwinked."

32. Ibid., p. 543.

33. Søren Kierkegaard, *Fear and Trembling,* trans. Walter Lowrie (Princeton: Princeton University Press, 1954), pp. 52–53. Frederic Will, "A Confrontation of Kierkegaard and Keats," *Personalist,* 43 (1962):338–351, contends that, insofar as poet-lovers like Ludolph or Lycius or Porphyro can be taken as typical of the Keatsian aesthetic hero, Kierkegaard's work stands as an indictment of all Keats cherished: "The aesthetic man is self-indulgent, passive, follows the promptings of sense, and above all refuses to accept the real demands which the very existence of other selves constitutes for him" (p. 349). In the opposing camp Lucio P. Ruotolo, "Keats and Kierkegaard: The Tragedy of Two Worlds," *Renascence,* 16 (1964):175–190, contends that Keats appreciated the contradictions of life in a Kierkegaardian, "existentialist" manner, and that, like Ludolph, Lycius and Porphyro, he tried to hold on, "absurdly," to both the realm of the ideal and of the real.

34. Slote, *The Dramatic Principle,* pp. 104–113, while acknowledging *Otho's* drawbacks, treats it with considerable fairness, attributing its most glaring weaknesses to the difficulties of collaboration.

35. Joseph W. Donohue, Jr., *Dramatic Character in the English Romantic Age* (Princeton: Princeton University Press, 1970), p. 36.

36. Joseph W. Donohue, Jr., *Theatre in the Age of Kean* (Totowa, N.J.: Rowman & Littlefield, 1975), p. 59.

37. Rollins, *The Keats Circle,* II, 67.

38. *The Letters of Charles Armitage Brown,* ed. Jack Stillinger (Cambridge, Mass.: Harvard University Press, 1966), p. 48.

39. *The Poems of John Keats,* ed. Miriam Allott (London: Longman, 1970), p. 580n., also refers to the resemblance.

40. Richard H. Fogle, in fact, looks at Lamia the serpent-woman and *Lamia* the poem as excellent demonstrations of Coleridge's theory of the "willing suspension of disbelief," in "Keats's *Lamia* as Dramatic Illusion," *Nineteenth-Century Literary Perspectives: Essays in Honor of Lionel Stevenson,* ed. Claude de L. Ryals (Durham, N.C.: Duke University Press, 1974), pp. 65–75.

41. And also by his dazzling concentration on the more superficial, "pictorial" qualities of the tale, as Jones (*Keats's Dream,* p. 248) points out.

42. Stanza 22 is an excellent example of what Robert Adams identifies as

Keats's tendency to "overstep his frames" or "contexts." See *"Trompe l'oeil* in Shakespeare and Keats," *Sewanee Review,* 61 (1953):238-255.

43. In *The Round Table* William Hazlitt, whose theories of art, literature, and personal identity greatly influenced Keats, noted how the sense of a proper embodied self was lost in the experience of reading: "It is, indeed, the evident tendency of all literature to generalize and *dissipate* character . . . All men become alike mere readers—spectators, not actors in the scene, and lose all proper personal identity." See *Complete Works,* ed. P. P. Howe, 21 vols. (London: J. M. Dent & Sons, 1930), IV, 12.

44. E. J. Burton, *The British Theater: Its Repertory and Practice* (London: Herbert Jenkins, 1960), p. 189. See also George Rowell, *The Victorian Theater: A Survey* (London: Oxford University Press, 1956) p. 15.

45. Burton, *British Theater,* p. 188. See also Donohue, *Dramatic Character,* pp. 180-181. For a contrary view of the effects of the new gas lighting, i.e., that it "helped to make stage and pit a single performance," see Slote, *The Dramatic Principle,* p. 51.

46. Kenneth Muir, "The Meaning of Hyperion," in *John Keats: A Reassessment,* p. 111. The idea of reading *The Fall* as an epic about the evolution of consciousness, however, was first put forth by J. R. Caldwell, "The Meaning of *Hyperion,"PMLA,*51 (1936):1080-1097, where three stages of supernatural existence are identified corresponding to the Titans before The Fall, the Titans afterward, and Apollo, "the chameleon poet, who has no settled character" (p. 1093).

47. Sperry, *Keats the Poet,* p. 336. Sperry argues that, compared to "To Autumn," *"Hyperion* fails through the inability to evolve a framework for transcending process, for reconciling man to the knowledge of sorrow and loss." I disagree.

48. First observed by John Livingston Lowes, *"Hyperion* and the *Purgatorio,"* *TLS,* January 11, 1936. See also J. Saly, "Keats's Answer to Dante: 'The Fall of Hyperion,' " *Keats-Shelley Journal,* 14 (1965):65-78. Sperry, however (*Keats the Poet,* pp. 312-316), argues that Dante did not replace Milton as Keats's model but rather changed the way in which Keats understood the message of *Paradise Lost* and its relation to his own epic.

49. Vendler, *Odes,* p. 221, observes that "the model for art in Moneta's mind becomes . . . Shakespeare . . . the Shakespearean mind-in-creation."

50. Allott, *Poems of John Keats,* p. 672n. Others have remarked on this pronounced physicality. See for instance G. Wilson Knight, *The Starlit Dome* (New York: Barnes and Noble, 1960), p. 291.

51. Contrast in this respect the situation of Keats and Moneta with that of Dante and Virgil in Keats's prototype for *The Fall.* Keats and Moneta stand, watch, and listen as events unfold as in a diorama; Dante and Virgil take part in events, engage in conversations and quarrels with the inhabitants of Hell, Purgatory, and Heaven. Nothing else, perhaps, could so clearly and simply illustrate the differences between the Romantic concept of "visionary power" and that which had obtained in previous centuries. Keats and Moneta are voyeurs, an audience; Dante and Virgil are active participants.

52. And the style of the poem reflects this ascetic feeling of distance and separateness, as Paul Sheats has observed in "Stylistic Discipline in *The Fall of Hyperion,"* *Keats-Shelley Journal,* 17 (1968):75-88.

53. John Middleton Murry, *Keats and Shakespeare* (London: Oxford University Press, 1925), observing the parallels between the Apollo of *Hyperion* and the figure of Keats in *The Fall*, notes the significance, for Keats's confrontation with Moneta, of Apollo's earlier encounter with Mnemosyne, seeing each scenario as a maturational rite de passage (p. 92).

54. Geoffrey Hartman, "Spectral Symbolism and in Keats's 'Hyperion,' " in *The Fate of Reading*, ed. Geoffrey Hartman (Chicago: University of Chicago Press, 1975), pp. 57–73, is not alone in detecting Moneta's "spectral symbolism" as a mother figure—her stature and authority confirm such a reading. D. G. James, *The Romantic Comedy* (London: Oxford University Press, 1963), pp. 144–147, first called attention to Moneta / Mnemosyne's role as "the mother of the great poets" (p. 147). Vendler sees the statue of Saturn in the sanctuary of the temple as a corresponding, but ineffectual, father figure (*Odes*, p. 209), and agrees that Keats's introduction of these "fallen parental Titan-presences represents an attempt to see himself as an adult."

55. The best discussion of Moneta's speeches on this matter, distinguishing among poets, dreamers, and philanthropists, is still John Middleton Murry, "The Poet and the Dreamer," in his *Studies in Keats* (New York: Noonday Press, 1955), pp. 238–249. Murry argues, quite convincingly in light of Keats's apparent intentions, that lines I, 187–210 should be cancelled altogether. Morris Dickstein agrees (*Study in Development*, p. 248).

56. Muir, "The Meaning of 'Hyperion,' " p. 122.

57. Sperry, *Keats the Poet*, pp. 333–334.

58. Dickstein, *Study in Development*, pp. 261–262. Bostetter, in *The Romantic Ventriloquists*, p. 170, expresses a similar view.

59. Vendler, *Odes*, p. 284.

60. Thus Muir, "Meaning of 'Hyperion,' " p. 122: "The conflict apparent in 'The Fall of Hyperion' was not resolved: but it was allayed by being faced . . . [It] could be solved only in action, by an integration of theory and practice—in other words, by writing the kind of poetry of which Moneta would have approved," i.e., "To Autumn." Vendler, *Odes*, pp. 227–228, reads "To Autumn" as the culmination of Keats's extended reflections on art and life, symbol and reality, eternity and mortality in the odes and *The Fall*. Sperry argues that "To Autumn" adopts the theme of *The Fall*—"process"—but successfully reconciles us "to the knowledge of sorrow and loss" by "its acceptance of an order innate in our experience—the natural rhythm of the seasons" (*Keats the Poet*, p. 336).

Dickstein, on the other hand, argues that "the main story of Keats' literary life ends" with *The Fall*, characterizing "To Autumn" as "no more than a flawless and seemingly effortless footnote to the odes of April and May. It should not be used to prove that his poetic career culminates in impersonal serenity and naturalistic harmony" (*Study in Development*, p. 262).

61. Vendler, *Odes*, p. 14. It is, in this sense, antisolipsistic: "The poem does not go inward (to a shrine, to a bower, to the *penetralia*); it moves outward to engirdle the earth. It both stations the self in the center of the world, watching and listening, and dissolves the same self into music" (p. 287).

Index